Bret Harte's
TALES OF THE GOLD RUSH

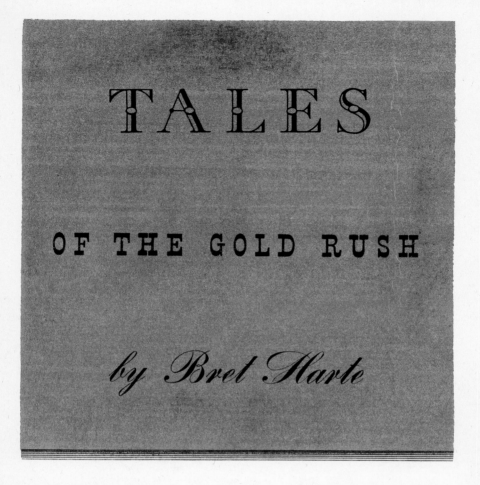

TALES

OF THE GOLD RUSH

by Bret Harte

ILLUSTRATED BY FLETCHER MARTIN

WITH AN INTRODUCTION BY OSCAR LEWIS

THE LIMITED EDITIONS CLUB, NEW YORK: 1944

INTRODUCTION

THE LUCK OF ROARING CAMP, the four thousand word short story that made its author famous, was published in 1868, and for the next thirty-four years Bret Harte's name was a household word throughout the English-speaking world. Both before and after his swift rise to prominence, his life was uncommonly interesting. Few writers have had careers so varied, so full of outer contrasts and inner contradictions.

He was born in 1836, son of a visionary, restless and never very successful schoolmaster, who was currently conducting a private academy at Albany, New York. The child was christened Francis Brett, which he gradually shortened, first to Fr. Brett, then to F. Bret; finally he abandoned the first name entirely. Brett was the family name of his maternal grandmother, whose forebears had long been prominent in the Hudson River valley. Frank, as he was always known to his family, was the third of four children, a sensitive, studious and never robust child. His first years were spent moving from town to town, for his father could never hold a teaching job more than a term or two. The nomadic schoolmaster died in 1845, when Frank was nine; a few years later his mother sailed for California and there remarried. Frank and his younger sister joined her there in 1854. He was seventeen when he first saw the land his pen was to make familiar to millions, and his formal education had ended three years earlier. His schooling, like his home life, had been curiously lacking in continuity; in eight years he attended eight different schools.

A persistent uncertainty obscures Harte's first years in California. He lived for a time at Oakland, of which growing village his stepfather presently became mayor. Then for a few months he followed in his father's footsteps and taught school, probably in one of the already half-deserted towns of the Southern Mines. When his school shut down (the families of most of his pupils having moved away), he tried his luck at the placers. No one knows in what creek-beds he gained his mining experience, but his stay at the diggings must have been brief, for he was back in Oakland by the beginning of 1856. Another interlude of teaching followed, and there is evidence too that he may have been for a few weeks a messenger on a Wells Fargo stage, riding beside the driver on the high seat, the company's strong-box in his keeping.

That about covers Harte's first-hand experience with the life he was to write about, with extraordinary industry and varying success, for close to half a century. He had early formed an ambition to be an author (his first published work was a poem, written when he was eleven and sent anonymously to a New York newspaper) and he presently began to make progress. By the spring of 1857 his contributions—poems and short prose pieces—were appearing in San Francisco weeklies. He spent a year at Union, on the Humboldt Bay, learning the typesetter's trade in the office of the town's newspaper and filling in as editor during the owner's absences. During one of the periods when he was temporarily in charge, a particularly revolting massacre took place in the vicinity: a gang of hoodlums raided an Indian settlement and murdered some sixty of the inhabitants: men, women and children. Harte's denunciation of this savagery was so blistering that citizens of Union threatened to wreck the newspaper plant; the editor hurried home and fired his crusading assistant.

Harte returned to San Francisco and went to work as a compositor on the *Golden Era,* a widely read literary weekly; in his spare time he wrote short pieces for its columns. His work was cast in the humorous or satirical vein then relished by the *Era's* readers; its quality was not remarkable, but it was a cut above the average, and after a few months he was given a column to fill with local happenings and random comment. This job he did to his own satisfaction and that of the paper's readers; within a year he was looked on as one of the town's rising young journalists. His progress continued. He became a protégé of Jessie Benton Fremont and by her influence was given a clerkship in the office of the Surveyor General, the first of a series of government jobs he was to hold. He presently found another patron, Thomas Starr King, the Unitarian clergyman whose eloquence whipped Northern sympathizers to a frenzy of patriotism in the months after Sumter. At King's great public meetings the preacher-orator sometimes read a war poem written for the occasion by the local poet, Fr. Bret Harte. Young Harte's friendship with King had another and more lasting outcome: he regularly attended the latter's Sunday morning services and so came to know Anna Griswold, who sang in the choir. They were married in 1862; two sons were born within the next three years.

To support his growing family, Harte wrote industriously: for the *Golden Era* and, after 1864, for the *Californian*, on which weekly he was presently associated with a notable group that included Charles Warren Stoddard, Ina Coolbrith, Joaquin Miller and Mark Twain. His efforts to place his work with editors in the East began to succeed and, in 1863, he left one government clerkship for another, this time in the Branch Mint, where the salary was larger and his duties pleasantly light. At thirty he was one of the ornaments of the city's literary and bohemian life. His first two books appeared in 1867: *Condensed Novels and Other Papers* and a volume of verse, *The Lost Galleon*. Both were compilations of material already published in magazines or newspapers; neither was particularly successful, but they were intimations of his growing local renown.

When his first two books appeared he was almost unknown outside California; twelve months later he was a national figure. In July, 1868, Anton Roman, San Francisco bookseller, published the first number of the *Overland Monthly*, a magazine designed to reflect the resources, progress and, particularly, the culture of the west coast, in much the same manner as the *Atlantic Monthly* was currently doing on the far seaboard. Roman chose Harte as editor and, to the magazine's second number, Harte contributed an unsigned, seven-page story about a group of miners who, by the death of a prostitute, found themselves with a new-born infant on their hands. The story had drama, sentiment and humor; it was tersely told and both its theme and background were new. It was not only a sharp departure from Harte's usual writings but it struck a new note in fiction; curiously, both these facts were immediately recognized. *The Luck of Roaring Camp* shocked a few and charmed thousands, but it was not until months later (the August *Overland* having been shipped East by steamer and news of its reception having made the long trip in reverse) that Harte learned the extent of his triumph. The publishers of the *Atlantic* wrote asking for similar stories; soon this letter was followed by a second proposing a book of Gold Rush tales; presently came word of the story's republication in England, and finally the greatest honor of all: a letter of praise from Charles Dickens and an invitation not only to contribute to Dickens' paper, *All the Year Round*, but to visit him when he came to England.

Harte could not at once hurry eastward to reap the rewards of his new fame. He had a wife to support, and two children, and he had never been prudent in money matters. He waited two years before he made the plunge. Meantime his first *Overland* story had been followed by others: *The Outcasts of Poker Flat, Miggles, Tennessee's Partner.* Before the year 1868 was out he had enough material for his first Gold Rush book. *The Luck of Roaring Camp and Other Stories* was published at Boston in 1870; it was twice reprinted that year, reissued in London, and received the unstinted praise of critics in both countries.

Meantime he had written, and laid away in his desk, a humorous poem about a euchre game and an artless Chinese who turned the tables on two miners bent on fleecing him; he called it *Plain Language from Truthful James.* Harte thought the poem too frivolous for the dignified pages of the *Overland;* not until months later, confronted by a shortage of copy, did he slip it unobtrusively into the magazine's back pages. It thus appeared in September, 1870—and made a sensation far greater even than *The Luck.* Under the title *The Heathen Chinee* it swept the country: it was reprinted countless times, in newspapers, on playing cards and broadsides; it was set to music, illustrated, pasted on shop windows, hawked in the streets and quoted from one end of the land to the other. It is said that no other poem in history achieved so wide a renown in so brief a time; today it remains a prime favorite among fanciers of humorous verse. Harte himself never liked it; in after years the one sure way to annoy him was to introduce him as the author of *The Heathen Chinee.*

But it was these verses more than *The Luck* that impressed Harte's name on the public consciousness, and, when he set off for the East in 1871, caused his progress across the country to take on the aspect of a triumphal march. For the next two or three years he rode high, easily the most widely popular author of his day. He met the literary lions of Boston and New York. He went on several long lecture tours. The *Atlantic Monthly* contracted to publish all he wrote for a period of a year and to pay him $10,000 for the privilege, an unprecedented sum in those days.

He was on top of the wave, but already the tide was turning. His lectures were comparative failures; they were badly managed, and his platform manner proved a disappointment; he gained little from them either financially or in added reputation. Nor was the *Atlantic* connection more successful: during the year his contract ran he produced little, and the quality of his work was inferior to what he had done on the west coast. He remained in the East, at Boston, New York, Newport and elsewhere, for seven years. It was a period of struggle to support himself and his growing family (a third child was born in '72 and a fourth in '75) on the extravagant scale his fancy dictated. Hoping for quick financial success, he slighted the mining camp tales on which his fame was based and tried a series of other ventures. In 1875 he published a novel, *Gabriel Conroy*. When this failed to sell widely he turned to the stage and, alone or in collaboration, wrote several plays, the first of a long series of like efforts. Most of his plays were produced and a few had moderately long runs; none brought him real financial or artistic success. By 1878, discouraged at the cool reception of his latest play, overworked and deeply in debt, he went to Washington and angled for a diplomatic appointment. He was offered a minor post, that of Commercial Agent at Crefeld, Germany, a manufacturing town on the Rhine. He accepted with relief.

Harte remained at Crefeld two years. In 1880 he was given a more lucrative post, that of consul at Glasgow. He spent five years there, resigning in 1885 when the administration changed at Washington, and moving to London where he remained the balance of his life.

During his long absence abroad Harte's reputation at home had declined, but in England he was a figure to be reckoned with, moving in the highest literary circles of late-Victorian London. His wife remained in America and gradually it became known that their separation was permanent and mutually agreeable. As long as he lived, he provided for his family as liberally as his earnings permitted. When his income as consul was cut off his pen again became his sole means of support. From 1885 on he wrote steadily, turning out scores of stories of the gold camps he had known but briefly more than twenty-five years earlier. Much of this was hack work, artificial in plot and sentimental in treatment; but Gold Rush stories were what was expected of him and he gave the editors (and the public) what they wanted. From time to time he returned to writing for the theatre, still hoping for the financial lightning that never struck, but after each failure he turned again to fiction laid in the Sierra towns and camps. He carried on courageously for seventeen years, little more than a drudge, his once world-wide fame gradually slipping away, still honored by loyal friends in England, still religiously sending monthly drafts to his family. At last, in 1902, after a long illness, he was stricken at his desk, laid down his pen and died. He was sixty-five.

What of his contribution, his—to use the pompous but convenient phrase—place in American literature? During the last period of his life and for many years afterwards his reputation was not high. Critics dismissed him as a sincere but mediocre writer who industriously exploited a slender talent by creating a California that never existed and peopling it with characters who bore little resemblance to the authentic Argonauts. He was called verbose, repetitious and incurably sentimental. His stock character types, his Yuba Bills and Colonel Starbottles and Jack Hamlins, were considered fair game for the satirists and writers of parody, and in a sense they were. Harte was of his period and in the main he followed the prevailing mode. He wrote far too much for his own ultimate good— a common failing in his day and ours among men who must support themselves and their dependents by their pens. But every author deserves to be remembered by his best work, and when one applies a selective process to the twenty volumes of Harte's collected works, what remains is found to be surprisingly good, entertaining, vigorous and informative, vastly superior to the general run of fiction of half a century ago.

For Harte had one important advantage over all but a few of his contemporaries: he knew how to write. Let the reader open this collection of his stories and begin reading at random. If he is at all discerning he will discover after only a few paragraphs that here is a man who has mastered the technique of his trade, who knows what effect he wants and how to go about getting it. At its best his style is simple, fluent and crystal clear. He knows how to construct a story and how to extract from it whatever dramatic and emotional values his material offers. He has humor, a lively sense of satire, a sort of benevolent tolerance for the follies of mankind, and an artful skill at sketching in the backgrounds against which his characters live and move. Writers on the evolution of the short story credit him with having pioneered a new type of fiction: the story of local color, and he remains today a master in this field. He has another title to lasting fame. The California Gold Rush is everywhere looked on as a singularly adventurous and romantic period, one of the most stirring episodes of human history. That it is so regarded is due, more than to any other factor, to the stories of Bret Harte, who lived in the gold towns for a few weeks or months during his youth, and who wrote about them all the rest of his life.

OSCAR LEWIS

NOTE: There have been three book-length biographies of Bret Harte, the best and most recent of which is *Bret Harte: Argonaut and Exile*, by George R. Stewart, Jr. (Houghton Mifflin Company, Boston, 1931); I have drawn on it liberally in preparing this sketch. *The Letters of Bret Harte*, edited by Geoffrey Bret Harte, were published in 1926 (also by Houghton Mifflin) and, in 1935, a comprehensive bibliography of Harte's writings was compiled by workers on a Federal SERA project and issued in mimeograph form as Monograph 10 of the California Literary Research series. Bret Harte's collected writings are published in twenty volumes by the Houghton Mifflin Company.

THE TALES

Bret Harte's

TALES OF THE GOLD RUSH

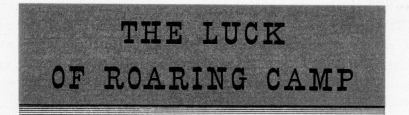

THE LUCK
OF ROARING CAMP

T HERE WAS COMMOTION in Roaring Camp. It could not have
been a fight, for in 1850 that was not novel enough to have
called together the entire settlement. The ditches and claims were
not only deserted, but "Tuttle's grocery" had contributed its gamblers, who, it will be remembered, calmly continued their game the
day that French Pete and Kanaka Joe shot each other to death over
the bar in the front room. The whole camp was collected before a
rude cabin on the outer edge of the clearing. Conversation was
carried on in a low tone, but the name of a woman was frequently
repeated. It was a name familiar enough in the camp, — "Cherokee
Sal."

Perhaps the less said of her the better. She was a coarse and, it is
to be feared, a very sinful woman. But at that time she was the only
woman in Roaring Camp, and was just then lying in sore extremity,
when she most needed the ministration of her own sex. Dissolute,
abandoned, and irreclaimable, she was yet suffering a martyrdom
hard enough to bear even when veiled by sympathizing womanhood, but now terrible in her loneliness. The primal curse had come
to her in that original isolation which must have made the punishment of the first transgression so dreadful. It was, perhaps, part
of the expiation of her sin that, at a moment when she most lacked
her sex's intuitive tenderness and care, she met only the half-
contemptuous faces of her masculine associates. Yet a few of the
spectators were, I think, touched by her sufferings. Sandy Tipton

1

thought it was "rough on Sal," and, in the contemplation of her condition, for a moment rose superior to the fact that he had an ace and two bowers in his sleeve.

It will be seen also that the situation was novel. Deaths were by no means uncommon in Roaring Camp, but a birth was a new thing. People had been dismissed the camp effectively, finally, and with no possibility of return; but this was the first time that anybody had been introduced *ab initio*. Hence the excitement.

"You go in there, Stumpy," said a prominent citizen known as "Kentuck," addressing one of the loungers. "Go in there, and see what you kin do. You've had experience in them things."

Perhaps there was a fitness in the selection. Stumpy, in other climes, had been the putative head of two families; in fact, it was owing to some legal informality in these proceedings that Roaring Camp — a city of refuge — was indebted to his company. The crowd approved the choice, and Stumpy was wise enough to bow to the majority. The door closed on the extempore surgeon and midwife, and Roaring Camp sat down outside, smoked its pipe, and awaited the issue.

The assemblage numbered about a hundred men. One or two of these were actual fugitives from justice, some were criminal, and all were reckless. Physically they exhibited no indication of their past lives and character. The greatest scamp had a Raphael face, with a profusion of blonde hair; Oakhurst, a gambler, had the melancholy air and intellectual abstraction of a Hamlet; the coolest and most courageous man was scarcely over five feet in height, with a soft voice and an embarrassed, timid manner. The term "roughs" applied to them was a distinction rather than a definition. Perhaps in the minor details of fingers, toes, ears, etc., the camp may have been deficient, but these slight omissions did not detract from their aggregate force. The strongest man had but three fingers on his right hand; the best shot had but one eye.

Such was the physical aspect of the men that were dispersed around the cabin. The camp lay in a triangular valley between two hills and a river. The only outlet was a steep trail over the summit of a hill that faced the cabin, now illuminated by the rising moon. The suffering woman might have seen it from the rude bunk whereon she lay, — seen it winding like a silver thread until it was lost in the stars above.

A fire of withered pine boughs added sociability to the gathering. By degrees the natural levity of Roaring Camp returned. Bets were freely offered and taken regarding the result. Three to five that "Sal would get through with it;" even that the child would survive;

side bets as to the sex and complexion of the coming stranger. In the midst of an excited discussion an exclamation came from those nearest the door, and the camp stopped to listen. Above the swaying and moaning of the pines, the swift rush of the river, and the crackling of the fire rose a sharp, querulous cry, — a cry unlike anything heard before in the camp. The pines stopped moaning, the river ceased to rush, and the fire to crackle. It seemed as if Nature had stopped to listen too.

The camp rose to its feet as one man! It was proposed to explode a barrel of gunpowder; but in consideration of the situation of the mother, better counsels prevailed, and only a few revolvers were discharged; for whether owing to the rude surgery of the camp, or some other reason, Cherokee Sal was sinking fast. Within an hour she had climbed, as it were, that rugged road that led to the stars,

and so passed out of Roaring Camp, its sin and shame, forever.
I do not think that the announcement disturbed them much, except
in speculation as to the fate of the child. "Can he live now?" was
asked of Stumpy. The answer was doubtful. The only other being of
Cherokee Sal's sex and maternal condition in the settlement was an
ass. There was some conjecture as to fitness, but the experiment
was tried. It was less problematical than the ancient treatment of
Romulus and Remus, and apparently as successful.

When these details were completed, which exhausted another
hour, the door was opened, and the anxious crowd of men, who
had already formed themselves into a queue, entered in single file.
Beside the low bunk or shelf, on which the figure of the mother
was starkly outlined below the blankets, stood a pine table. On this
a candle-box was placed, and within it, swathed in staring red
flannel, lay the last arrival at Roaring Camp. Beside the candle-
box was placed a hat. Its use was soon indicated, "Gentlemen," said
Stumpy, with a singular mixture of authority and *ex officio* com-
placency, — "gentlemen will please pass in at the front door, round
the table, and out at the back door. Them as wishes to contribute
anything toward the orphan will find a hat handy." The first man
entered with his hat on; he uncovered, however, as he looked about
him, and so unconsciously set an example to the next. In such communities good and bad actions are catching. As the procession filed
in comments were audible, — criticisms addressed perhaps rather
to Stumpy in the character of showman: "Is that him?" "Mighty
small specimen;" "Hasn't more'n got the color;" "Ain't bigger nor
a derringer." The contributions were as characteristic: A silver
tobacco box; a doubloon; a navy revolver, silver mounted; a gold
specimen; a very beautifully embroidered lady's handkerchief
(from Oakhurst the gambler); a diamond breastpin; a diamond
ring (suggested by the pin, with the remark from the giver that
he "saw that pin and went two diamonds better"); a slung-shot;
a Bible (contributor not detected); a golden spur; a silver teaspoon
(the initials, I regret to say, were not the giver's); a pair of surgeon's shears; a lancet; a Bank of England note for £5; and about
$200 in loose gold and silver coin. During these proceedings Stumpy
maintained a silence as impassive as the dead on his left, a gravity

as inscrutable as that of the newly born on his right. Only one incident occurred to break the monotony of the curious procession. As Kentuck bent over the candle-box half curiously, the child turned, and, in a spasm of pain, caught at his groping finger, and held it fast for a moment. Kentuck looked foolish and embarrassed. Something like a blush tried to assert itself in his weather-beaten cheek. "The d—d little cuss!" he said, as he extricated his finger, with perhaps more tenderness and care than he might have been deemed capable of showing. He held that finger a little apart from its fellows as he went out, and examined it curiously. The examination provoked the same original remark in regard to the child. In fact, he seemed to enjoy repeating it. "He rastled with my finger," he remarked to Tipton, holding up the member, "the d—d little cuss!"

It was four o'clock before the camp sought repose. A light burnt in the cabin where the watchers sat, for Stumpy did not go to bed that night. Nor did Kentuck. He drank quite freely, and related with gusto his experience, invariably ending with his characteristic condemnation of the newcomer. It seemed to relieve him of any unjust implication of sentiment, and Kentuck had the weaknesses of the nobler sex. When everybody else had gone to bed, he walked down to the river and whistled reflectingly. Then he walked up the gulch past the cabin, still whistling with demonstrative unconcern. At a large redwood-tree he paused and retraced his steps, and again passed the cabin. Halfway down to the river's bank he again paused, and then returned and knocked at the door. It was opened by Stumpy. "How goes it?" said Kentuck, looking past Stumpy toward the candle-box. "All serene!" replied Stumpy. "Anything up?" "Nothing." There was a pause—an embarrassing one—Stumpy still holding the door. Then Kentuck had recourse to his finger, which he held up to Stumpy. "Rastled with it,—the d—d little cuss," he said, and retired.

The next day Cherokee Sal had such rude sepulture as Roaring Camp afforded. After her body had been committed to the hillside, there was a formal meeting of the camp to discuss what should be done with her infant. A resolution to adopt it was unanimous and enthusiastic. But an animated discussion in regard to the manner and feasibility of providing for its wants at once sprang up. It was remarkable that the argument partook of none of those fierce personalities with which discussions were usually conducted at Roaring Camp. Tipton proposed that they should send the child to Red Dog, — a distance of forty miles, — where female attention could be procured. But the unlucky suggestion met with fierce and unanimous opposition. It was evident that no plan which entailed parting from their new acquisition would for a moment be entertained. "Besides," said Tom Ryder, "them fellows at Red Dog would swap it, and ring in somebody else on us." A disbelief in the honesty of other camps prevailed at Roaring Camp, as in other places.

The introduction of a female nurse in the camp also met with objection. It was argued that no decent woman could be prevailed to accept Roaring Camp as her home, and the speaker urged that "they didn't want any more of the other kind." This unkind allusion to the defunct mother, harsh as it may seem, was the first spasm of propriety, — the first symptom of the camp's regeneration. Stumpy advanced nothing. Perhaps he felt a certain delicacy in interfering with the selection of a possible successor in office. But when questioned, he averred stoutly that he and "Jinny" — the mammal before alluded to — could manage to rear the child. There was something original, independent, and heroic about the plan that pleased the camp. Stumpy was retained. Certain articles were sent for to Sacramento. "Mind," said the treasurer, as he pressed a bag of gold-dust into the expressman's hand, "the best that can be got, — lace, you know, and filigree-work and frills, — d—n the cost!"

Strange to say, the child thrived. Perhaps the invigorating climate of the mountain camp was compensation for material deficiencies. Nature took the foundling to her broader breast. In that rare atmosphere of the Sierra foothills, — that air pungent with balsamic odor, that ethereal cordial at once bracing and exhilarating, — he may have found food and nourishment, or a subtle chemistry that transmuted ass's milk to lime and phosphorus. Stumpy inclined to the belief that it was the latter and good nursing. "Me and that ass," he would say, "has been father and mother to him! Don't you," he would add, apostrophizing the helpless bundle before him, "never go back on us."

By the time he was a month old the necessity of giving him a

name became apparent. He had generally been known as "The Kid," "Stumpy's Boy," "The Coyote" (an allusion to his vocal powers), and even by Kentuck's endearing diminutive of "The d—d little cuss." But these were felt to be vague and unsatisfactory, and were at last dismissed under another influence. Gamblers and adventurers are generally superstitious, and Oakhurst one day declared that the baby had brought "the luck" to Roaring Camp. It was certain that of late they had been successful. "Luck" was the name agreed upon, with the prefix of Tommy for greater convenience. No allusion was made to the mother, and the father was unknown. "It's better," said the philosophical Oakhurst, "to take a fresh deal all round. Call him Luck, and start him fair." A day was accordingly set apart for the christening. What was meant by this ceremony the reader may imagine who has already gathered some idea of the reckless irreverence of Roaring Camp. The master of ceremonies was one "Boston," a noted wag, and the occasion seemed to promise the greatest facetiousness. This ingenious satirist had spent two days in preparing a burlesque of the Church service, with pointed local allusions. The choir was properly trained, and Sandy Tipton was to stand godfather. But after the procession had marched to the grove with music and banners, and the child had been deposited before a mock altar, Stumpy stepped before the expectant crowd. "It ain't my style to spoil fun, boys," said the little man, stoutly eying the faces around him, "but it strikes me that this thing ain't exactly on the squar. It's playing it pretty low down on this yer baby to ring in fun on him that he ain't goin' to understand. And ef there's goin' to be any godfathers round, I'd like to see who's got any better rights than me." A silence followed Stumpy's speech. To the credit of all humorists be it said that the first man to acknowledge its justice was the satirist thus stopped of his fun. "But," said Stumpy, quickly following up his advantage, "we're here for a christening, and we'll have it. I proclaim you Thomas Luck, according to the laws of the United States and the State of California, so help me God." It was the first time that the name of the Deity had been otherwise uttered than profanely in the camp. The form of christening was perhaps even more ludicrous than the satirist had conceived; but strangely enough, nobody saw it and nobody laughed. "Tommy" was christened as seriously as he would have been under a Christian roof, and cried and was comforted in as orthodox fashion.

And so the work of regeneration began in Roaring Camp. Almost imperceptibly a change came over the settlement. The cabin assigned to "Tommy Luck" — or "The Luck," as he was more frequently called — first showed signs of improvement. It was kept scrupulously clean and whitewashed. Then it was boarded, clothed, and papered. The rosewood cradle, packed eighty miles by mule, had, in Stumpy's way of putting it, "sorter killed the rest of the furniture." So the rehabilitation of the cabin became a necessity. The men who were in the habit of lounging in at Stumpy's to see "how 'The Luck' got on" seemed to appreciate the change, and in self-defense, the rival establishment of "Tuttle's grocery" bestirred itself and imported a carpet and mirrors. The reflections of the latter on the appearance of Roaring Camp tended to produce stricter habits of personal cleanliness. Again Stumpy imposed a kind of quarantine upon those who aspired to the honor and privilege of holding The Luck. It was a cruel mortification to Kentuck — who, in the carelessness of a large nature and the habits of frontier life, had begun to regard all garments as a second cuticle, which, like a snake's, only sloughed off through decay — to be debarred this privilege from certain prudential reasons. Yet such was the subtle influence of innovation that he thereafter appeared regularly every afternoon in a clean shirt and face still shining from his ablutions. Nor were moral and social sanitary laws neglected. "Tommy," who was supposed to spend his whole existence in a persistent attempt to repose, must not be disturbed by noise. The shouting and yelling, which had gained the camp its infelicitous title, were not permitted within hearing distance of Stumpy's. The men conversed in whispers or smoked with Indian gravity. Profanity was tacitly given up in these sacred precincts, and throughout the camp a popular form of expletive, known as "D—n the luck!" and "Curse the luck!" was abandoned, as having a new personal bearing. Vocal music was not interdicted, being supposed to have a soothing, tranquilizing quality; and one song, sung by "Man-o'-War Jack," an English sailor from her Majesty's Australian colonies, was quite popular as a lullaby. It was a lugubrious recital of the exploits of "the Arethusa, Seventy-four," in a muffled minor, ending with a prolonged dying fall at the burden of each verse, "On b-oo-o-ard of the Arethusa." It was a fine sight to see Jack holding The Luck, rocking from side to side as if with the motion of a ship, and crooning forth this naval ditty. Either through the peculiar rocking of Jack or the length of his song, — it contained ninety stanzas, and was continued with conscientious deliberation to the bitter end, — the lullaby generally had the desired effect. At such times the men would lie at full length under the trees in the soft summer twilight, smoking their pipes and drinking in the melodious utterances. An indistinct idea that this was pastoral happiness pervaded the camp. "This 'ere kind o' think," said the Cockney Simmons, meditatively reclining on his elbow, "is 'evingly." It reminded him of Greenwich.

On the long summer days The Luck was usually carried to the gulch from whence the golden store of Roaring Camp was taken. There, on a blanket spread over pine boughs, he would lie while the men were working in the ditches below. Latterly there was a rude attempt to decorate this bower with flowers and sweet-smelling shrubs, and generally some one would bring him a cluster of wild honeysuckles, azaleas, or the painted blossoms of Las Mariposas. The men had suddenly awakened to the fact that there were beauty and significance in these trifles, which they had so long trodden carelessly beneath their feet. A flake of glittering mica, a fragment of variegated quartz, a bright pebble from the bed of the creek, became beautiful to eyes thus cleared and strengthened, and were invariably put aside for The Luck. It was wonderful how many treasures the woods and hillsides yielded that "would do for Tommy." Surrounded by playthings such as never child out of fairyland had before, it is to be hoped that Tommy was content. He appeared to be serenely happy, albeit there was an infantine gravity about him, a contemplative light in his round gray eyes, that sometimes worried Stumpy. He was always tractable and quiet, and it is recorded that once, having crept beyond his "corral," — a hedge of tessellated pine boughs, which surrounded his bed, — he dropped over the bank on his head in the soft earth, and remained with his mottled legs in the air in that position for at least five minutes with unflinching gravity. He was extricated without a murmur. I hesitate to record the many other instances of his sagacity, which rest, unfortunately, upon the statements of prejudiced friends. Some of them were not without a tinge of superstition. "I crep' up the bank just now," said Kentuck one day, in a breathless state of excitement, "and dern my skin if he wasn't a-talking to a jaybird as was a-sittin' on his lap. There they was, just as free and sociable as anything you please, a-jawin' at each other just like two cherrybums." Howbeit, whether creeping over the pine boughs or lying lazily on his back blinking at the leaves above him, to him the birds sang, the squirrels chattered, and the flowers bloomed. Nature was his nurse and playfellow. For him she would let slip between the leaves golden shafts of sunlight that fell just within his grasp; she would send wandering breezes to visit him with the balm of bay and resinous gum; to him the tall redwoods nodded familiarly and sleepily, the bumblebees buzzed, and the rooks cawed a slumbrous accompaniment.

Such was the golden summer of Roaring Camp. They were "flush times," and the luck was with them. The claims had yielded enormously. The camp was jealous of its privileges and looked suspiciously on strangers. No encouragement was given to immigration, and, to make their seclusion more perfect, the land on either side of the mountain wall that surrounded the camp they duly preëmpted. This, and a reputation for singular proficiency with the revolver, kept the reserve of Roaring Camp inviolate. The expressman — their only connecting link with the surrounding world — sometimes told wonderful stories of the camp. He would say, "They've a street up there in 'Roaring' that would lay over any street in Red Dog. They've got vines and flowers round their houses, and they wash themselves twice a day. But they're mighty rough on strangers, and they worship an Ingin baby."

With the prosperity of the camp came a desire for further improvement. It was proposed to build a hotel in the following spring, and to invite one or two decent families to reside there for the sake of The Luck, who might perhaps profit by female companionship. The sacrifice that this concession to the sex cost these men, who

were fiercely skeptical in regard to its general virtue and useful-
ness, can only be accounted for by their affection for Tommy. A
few still held out. But the resolve could not be carried into effect
for three months, and the minority meekly yielded in the hope
that something might turn up to prevent it. And it did.

The winter of 1851 will long be remembered in the foothills.
The snow lay deep on the Sierras, and every mountain creek
became a river, and every river a lake. Each gorge and gulch was
transformed into a tumultuous watercourse that descended the
hillsides, tearing down giant trees and scattering its drift and débris
along the plain. Red Dog had been twice under water, and Roaring Camp had been forewarned. "Water put the gold into them
gulches," said Stumpy. "It's been here once and will be here
again!" And that night the North Fork suddenly leaped over its
banks and swept up the triangular valley of Roaring Camp.

In the confusion of rushing water, crashing trees, and crackling
timber, and the darkness which seemed to flow with the water
and blot out the fair valley, but little could be done to collect the
scattered camp. When the morning broke, the cabin of Stumpy,
nearest the river-bank, was gone. Higher up the gulch they found
the body of its unlucky owner; but the pride, the hope, the joy,
The Luck, of Roaring Camp had disappeared. They were returning
with sad hearts when a shout from the bank recalled them.

It was a relief-boat from down the river. They had picked up,
they said, a man and an infant, nearly exhausted, about two miles
below. Did anybody know them, and did they belong here?

It needed but a glance to show them Kentuck lying there, cruelly
crushed and bruised, but still holding The Luck of Roaring Camp
in his arms. As they bent over the strangely assorted pair, they
saw that the child was cold and pulseless. "He is dead," said one.
Kentuck opened his eyes. "Dead?" he repeated feebly. "Yes, my
man, and you are dying too." A smile lit the eyes of the expiring
Kentuck. "Dying!" he repeated; "he's a-taking me with him. Tell
the boys I've got The Luck with me now;" and the strong man,
clinging to the frail babe as a drowning man is said to cling to a
straw, drifted away into the shadowy river that flows forever to
the unknown sea.

THE OUTCASTS OF POKER FLAT

As Mr. John Oakhurst, gambler, stepped into the main street of Poker Flat on the morning of the 23d of November, 1850, he was conscious of a change in its moral atmosphere since the preceding night. Two or three men, conversing earnestly together, ceased as he approached, and exchanged significant glances. There was a Sabbath lull in the air, which, in a settlement unused to Sabbath influences, looked ominous.

Mr. Oakhurst's calm, handsome face betrayed small concern in these indications. Whether he was conscious of any predisposing cause was another question. "I reckon they're after somebody," he reflected; "likely it's me." He returned to his pocket the handkerchief with which he had been whipping away the red dust of Poker Flat from his neat boots, and quietly discharged his mind of any further conjecture.

In point of fact, Poker Flat was "after somebody." It had lately suffered the loss of several thousand dollars, two valuable horses, and a prominent citizen. It was experiencing a spasm of virtuous reaction, quite as lawless and ungovernable as any of the acts that had provoked it. A secret committee had determined to rid the town of all improper persons. This was done permanently in regard of two men who were then hanging from the boughs of a sycamore in the gulch, and temporarily in the banishment of certain other objectionable characters. I regret to say that some of these were ladies. It is but due to the sex, however, to state that their impropriety was professional, and it was only in such easily established standards of evil that Poker Flat ventured to sit in judgment.

Mr. Oakhurst was right in supposing that he was included in this category. A few of the committee had urged hanging him as a possible example and a sure method of reimbursing themselves from his pockets of the sums he had won from them. "It's agin justice," said Jim Wheeler, "to let this yer young man from Roaring Camp—an entire stranger—carry away our money." But a crude sentiment of equity residing in the breasts of those who had been fortunate enough to win from Mr. Oakhurst overruled this narrower local prejudice.

Mr. Oakhurst received his sentence with philosophic calmness, none the less coolly that he was aware of the hesitation of his judges. He was too much of a gambler not to accept fate. With him life was at best an uncertain game, and he recognized the usual percentage in favor of the dealer.

A body of armed men accompanied the deported wickedness of Poker Flat to the outskirts of the settlement. Besides Mr. Oakhurst, who was known to be a coolly desperate man, and for whose intimidation the armed escort was intended, the expatriated party consisted of a young woman familiarly known as "The Duchess;" another who had won the title of "Mother Shipton;" and "Uncle Billy," a suspected sluice-robber and confirmed drunkard. The cavalcade provoked no comments from the spectators, nor was any word uttered by the escort. Only when the gulch which marked the uttermost limit of Poker Flat was reached, the leader spoke briefly and to the point. The exiles were forbidden to return at the peril of their lives.

As the escort disappeared, their pent-up feelings found vent in a few hysterical tears from the Duchess, some bad language from Mother Shipton, and a Parthian volley of expletives from Uncle Billy. The philosophic Oakhurst alone remained silent. He listened calmly to Mother Shipton's desire to cut somebody's heart out, to the repeated statements of the Duchess that she would die in the road, and to the alarming oaths that seemed to be bumped out of Uncle Billy as he rode forward. With the easy good humor characteristic of his class, he insisted upon exchanging his own riding-horse, "Five-Spot," for the sorry mule which the Duchess rode. But even this act did not draw the party into any closer sympathy. The young woman readjusted her somewhat draggled plumes with a feeble, faded coquetry; Mother Shipton eyed the possessor of "Five-Spot" with malevolence, and Uncle Billy included the whole party in one sweeping anathema.

The road to Sandy Bar — a camp that, not having as yet experienced the regenerating influences of Poker Flat, consequently seemed to offer some invitation to the emigrants — lay over a steep mountain range. It was distant a day's severe travel. In that advanced season the party soon passed out of the moist, temperate regions of the foothills into the dry, cold, bracing air of the Sierras. The trail was narrow and difficult. At noon the Duchess, rolling out of her saddle upon the ground, declared her intention of going no farther, and the party halted.

The spot was singularly wild and impressive. A wooded amphitheatre, surrounded on three sides by precipitous cliffs of naked granite, sloped gently toward the crest of another precipice that overlooked the valley. It was, undoubtedly, the most suitable spot for a camp, had camping been advisable. But Mr. Oakhurst knew that scarcely half the journey to Sandy Bar was accomplished, and the party were not equipped or provisioned for delay. This fact he pointed out to his companions curtly, with a philosophic commentary on the folly of "throwing up their hand before the game was played out." But they were furnished with liquor, which in this emergency stood them in place of food, fuel, rest, and prescience. In spite of his remonstrances, it was not long before they were more or less under its influence. Uncle Billy passed rapidly from a bellicose state into one of stupor, the Duchess became maudlin, and Mother Shipton snored. Mr. Oakhurst alone remained erect, leaning against a rock, calmly surveying them.

Mr. Oakhurst did not drink. It interfered with a profession which required coolness, impassiveness, and presence of mind, and, in his own language, he "couldn't afford it." As he gazed at his recumbent fellow exiles, the loneliness begotten of his pariah trade, his habits of life, his very vices, for the first time seriously oppressed him. He bestirred himself in dusting his black clothes, washing his hands and face, and other acts characteristic of his studiously neat habits, and for a moment forgot his annoyance. The thought of deserting his weaker and more pitiable companions never perhaps occurred to him. Yet he could not help feeling the want of that excitement which, singularly enough, was most conducive to that calm equanimity for which he was notorious. He looked at the gloomy walls that rose a thousand feet sheer above the circling pines around him, at the sky ominously clouded, at the valley below, already deepening into shadow; and, doing so, suddenly he heard his own name called.

A horseman slowly ascended the trail. In the fresh, open face of the newcomer Mr. Oakhurst recognized Tom Simson, otherwise known as "The Innocent," of Sandy Bar. He had met him some months before over a "little game," and had, with perfect equanimity, won the entire fortune — amounting to some forty dollars — of that guileless youth. After the game was finished, Mr. Oakhurst drew the youthful speculator behind the door and thus addressed him: "Tommy, you're a good little man, but you can't gamble worth a cent. Don't try it over again." He then handed him his money back, pushed him gently from the room, and so made a devoted slave of Tom Simson.

There was a remembrance of this in his boyish and enthusiastic greeting of Mr. Oakhurst. He had started, he said, to go to Poker Flat to seek his fortune. "Alone?" No, not exactly alone; in fact (a giggle), he had run away with Piney Woods. Didn't Mr. Oakhurst remember Piney? She that used to wait on the table at the Temperance House? They had been engaged a long time, but old Jake Woods had objected, and so they had run away, and were going to Poker Flat to be married, and here they were. And they were tired out, and how lucky it was they had found a place to camp, and company. All this the Innocent delivered rapidly, while Piney, a stout, comely damsel of fifteen, emerged from behind the pine-tree, where she had been blushing unseen, and rode to the side of her lover.

Mr. Oakhurst seldom troubled himself with sentiment, still less with propriety; but he had a vague idea that the situation was not fortunate. He retained, however, his presence of mind sufficiently to kick Uncle Billy, who was about to say something, and Uncle Billy was sober enough to recognize in Mr. Oakhurst's kick a superior power that would not bear trifling. He then endeavored to dissuade Tom Simson from delaying further, but in vain. He even pointed out the fact that there was no provision, nor means of making a camp. But, unluckily, the Innocent met this objection by assuring the party that he was provided with an extra mule loaded with provisions, and by the discovery of a rude attempt at a log house near the trail. "Piney can stay with Mrs. Oakhurst," said the Innocent, pointing to the Duchess, "and I can shift for myself."

Nothing but Mr. Oakhurst's admonishing foot saved Uncle Billy from bursting into a roar of laughter. As it was, he felt compelled to retire up the cañon until he could recover his gravity. There he confided the joke to the tall pine-trees, with many slaps of his leg, contortions of his face, and the usual profanity. But when he returned to the party, he found them seated by a fire — for the air had grown strangely chill and the sky overcast — in apparently amicable conversation. Piney was actually talking in an impulsive girlish fashion to the Duchess, who was listening with an interest and animation she had not shown for many days. The Innocent was holding forth, apparently with equal effect, to Mr. Oakhurst and Mother Shipton, who was actually relaxing into amiability. "Is this yer a d—d picnic?" said Uncle Billy, with inward scorn, as he surveyed the sylvan group, the glancing firelight, and the tethered animals in the foreground. Suddenly an idea mingled with the alcoholic fumes that disturbed his brain. It was apparently of a jocular nature, for he felt impelled to slap his leg again and cram his fist into his mouth.

As the shadows crept slowly up the mountain, a slight breeze rocked the tops of the pine-trees and moaned through their long and gloomy aisles. The ruined cabin, patched and covered with pine boughs, was set apart for the ladies. As the lovers parted, they unaffectedly exchanged a kiss, so honest and sincere that it might have been heard above the swaying pines. The frail Duchess and the malevolent Mother Shipton were probably too stunned to remark upon this last evidence of simplicity, and so turned without

a word to the hut. The fire was replenished, the men lay down before the door, and in a few minutes were asleep.

Mr. Oakhurst was a light sleeper. Toward morning he awoke benumbed and cold. As he stirred the dying fire, the wind, which was now blowing strongly, brought to his cheek that which caused the blood to leave it, — snow!

He started to his feet with the intention of awakening the sleepers, for there was no time to lose. But turning to where Uncle Billy had been lying, he found him gone. A suspicion leaped to his brain, and a curse to his lips. He ran to the spot where the mules had been tethered — they were no longer there. The tracks were already rapidly disappearing in the snow.

The momentary excitement brought Mr. Oakhurst back to the fire with his usual calm. He did not waken the sleepers. The Innocent slumbered peacefully, with a smile on his good-humored, freckled face; the virgin Piney slept beside her frailer sisters as sweetly as though attended by celestial guardians; and Mr. Oakhurst, drawing his blanket over his shoulders, stroked his mustaches and waited for the dawn. It came slowly in a whirling mist of snowflakes that dazzled and confused the eye. What could be seen of the landscape appeared magically changed. He looked over the valley, and summed up the present and future in two words, "Snowed in!"

A careful inventory of the provisions, which, fortunately for the party, had been stored within the hut, and so escaped the felonious fingers of Uncle Billy, disclosed the fact that with care and prudence they might last ten days longer. "That is," said Mr. Oakhurst *sotto voce* to the Innocent, "if you're willing to board us. If you ain't — and perhaps you'd better not — you can wait till Uncle Billy gets back with provisions." For some occult reason, Mr. Oakhurst could not bring himself to disclose Uncle Billy's rascality, and so offered the hypothesis that he had wandered from the camp and had accidentally stampeded the animals. He dropped a warning to the Duchess and Mother Shipton, who of course knew the facts of their associate's defection. "They'll find out the truth about us *all* when they find out anything," he added significantly, "and there's no good frightening them now."

Tom Simson not only put all his worldly store at the disposal of Mr. Oakhurst, but seemed to enjoy the prospect of their enforced seclusion. "We'll have a good camp for a week, and then the snow'll melt, and we'll all go back together." The cheerful gayety of the young man and Mr. Oakhurst's calm infected the others. The Innocent, with the aid of pine boughs, extemporized a thatch for the roofless cabin, and the Duchess directed Piney in the rearrangement of the interior with a taste and tact that opened the blue eyes of that provincial maiden to their fullest extent. "I reckon now you're used to fine things at Poker Flat," said Piney. The Duchess turned away sharply to conceal something that reddened her cheeks through their professional tint, and Mother Shipton requested Piney not to "chatter." But when Mr. Oakhurst returned from a weary search for the trail, he heard the sound of happy laughter echoed from the rocks. He stopped in some alarm, and his thoughts first naturally reverted to the whiskey, which he had prudently cachéd. "And yet it don't somehow sound like whiskey," said the gambler. It was not until he caught sight of the blazing fire through the still blinding storm, and the group around it, that he settled to the conviction that it was "square fun."

Whether Mr. Oakhurst had cachéd his cards with the whiskey as something debarred the free access of the community, I cannot say. It was certain that, in Mother Shipton's words, he "didn't say 'cards' once" during that evening. Haply the time was beguiled by an accordion, produced somewhat ostentatiously by Tom Simson from his pack. Notwithstanding some difficulties attending the manipulation of this instrument, Piney Woods managed to pluck several reluctant melodies from its keys, to an accompaniment by the Innocent on a pair of bone castanets. But the crowning festivity of the evening was reached in a rude camp-meeting hymn, which the lovers, joining hands, sang with great earnestness and vociferation. I fear that a certain defiant tone and Covenanter's swing to its chorus, rather than any devotional quality, caused it speedily to infect the others, who at last joined in the refrain: —

"I'm proud to live in the service of the Lord,
And I'm bound to die in His army."

The pines rocked, the storm eddied and whirled above the miserable group, and the flames of their altar leaped heavenward, as if in token of the vow.

At midnight the storm abated, the rolling clouds parted, and the stars glittered keenly above the sleeping camp. Mr. Oakhurst, whose professional habits had enabled him to live on the smallest possible amount of sleep, in dividing the watch with Tom Simson somehow managed to take upon himself the greater part of that duty. He excused himself to the Innocent by saying that he had "often been a week without sleep." "Doing what?" asked Tom. "Poker!" replied Oakhurst sententiously. "When a man gets a streak of luck, — nigger-luck, — he don't get tired. The luck gives in first. Luck," continued the gambler reflectively, "is a mighty queer thing. All you know about it for certain is that it's bound to change. And it's finding out when it's going to change that makes you. We've had a streak of bad luck since we left Poker Flat, — you came along, and slap you get into it, too. If you can hold your cards right along you're all right. For," added the gambler, with cheerful irrelevance —

" 'I'm proud to live in the service of the Lord,
And I'm bound to die in His army.' "

The third day came, and the sun, looking through the white-curtained valley, saw the outcasts divide their slowly decreasing store of provisions for the morning meal. It was one of the peculiarities of that mountain climate that its rays diffused a kindly warmth over the wintry landscape, as if in regretful commiseration of the past. But it revealed drift on drift of snow piled high around the hut, — a hopeless, uncharted, trackless sea of white lying below the rocky shores to which the castaways still clung. Through the marvelously clear air the smoke of the pastoral village of Poker Flat rose miles away. Mother Shipton saw it, and from a remote pinnacle of her rocky fastness hurled in that direction a final malediction. It was her last vituperative attempt, and perhaps for that reason was invested with a certain degree of sublimity. It did her good, she privately informed the Duchess. "Just you go out there and cuss, and see." She then set herself to the task of amusing "the child," as she and the Duchess were pleased to call Piney. Piney was no chicken, but it was a soothing and original theory of the pair thus to account for the fact that she didn't swear and wasn't improper.

When night crept up again through the gorges, the reedy notes of the accordion rose and fell in fitful spasms and long-drawn gasps by the flickering campfire. But music failed to fill entirely the aching void left by insufficient food, and a new diversion was proposed by Piney, — story-telling. Neither Mr. Oakhurst nor his female companions caring to relate their personal experiences, this plan would have failed too, but for the Innocent. Some months before he had chanced upon a stray copy of Mr. Pope's ingenious translation of the Iliad. He now proposed to narrate the principal incidents of that poem — having thoroughly mastered the argument and fairly forgotten the words — in the current vernacular of Sandy Bar. And so for the rest of that night the Homeric demigods again walked the earth. Trojan bully and wily Greek wrestled in the winds, and the great pines in the cañon seemed to bow to the wrath of the son of Peleus. Mr. Oakhurst listened with quiet satisfaction. Most especially was he interested in the fate of "Ashheels," as the Innocent persisted in denominating the "swift-footed Achilles."

So, with small food and much of Homer and the accordion, a week passed over the heads of the outcasts. The sun again forsook them, and again from leaden skies the snowflakes were sifted over the land. Day by day closer around them drew the snowy circle, until at last they looked from their prison over drifted walls of dazzling white, that towered twenty feet above their heads. It became more and more difficult to replenish their fires, even from the fallen trees beside them, now half hidden in the drifts. And yet no one complained. The lovers turned from the dreary prospect and looked into each other's eyes, and were happy. Mr. Oakhurst settled himself coolly to the losing game before him. The Duchess, more cheerful than she had been, assumed the care of Piney. Only Mother Shipton — once the strongest of the party — seemed to sicken and fade. At midnight on the tenth day she called Oakhurst to her side. "I'm going," she said, in a voice of querulous weakness, "but don't say anything about it. Don't waken the kids. Take the bundle from under my head, and open it." Mr. Oakhurst did so. It contained Mother Shipton's rations for the last week, untouched. "Give 'em to the child," she said, pointing to the sleeping Piney. "You've starved yourself," said the gambler. "That's what they call it," said the woman querulously, as she lay down again, and turning her face to the wall, passed quietly away.

The accordion and the bones were put aside that day, and Homer was forgotten. When the body of Mother Shipton had been committed to the snow, Mr. Oakhurst took the Innocent aside, and showed him a pair of snowshoes, which he had fashioned from the old pack-saddle. "There's one chance in a hundred to save her yet," he said, pointing to Piney; "but it's there," he added, pointing toward Poker Flat. "If you can reach there in two days she's safe." "And you?" asked Tom Simson. "I'll stay here," was the curt reply.

The lovers parted with a long embrace. "You are not going, too?" said the Duchess, as she saw Mr. Oakhurst apparently waiting to accompany him. "As far as the cañon," he replied. He turned suddenly and kissed the Duchess, leaving her pallid face aflame, and her trembling limbs rigid with amazement.

Night came, but not Mr. Oakhurst. It brought the storm again and the whirling snow. Then the Duchess, feeding the fire, found that some one had quietly piled beside the hut enough fuel to last a few days longer. The tears rose to her eyes, but she hid them from Piney.

The women slept but little. In the morning, looking into each other's faces, they read their fate. Neither spoke, but Piney, accepting the position of the stronger, drew near and placed her arm around the Duchess's waist. They kept this attitude for the rest of the day. That night the storm reached its greatest fury, and, rending asunder the protecting vines, invaded the very hut.

Toward morning they found themselves unable to feed the fire, which gradually died away. As the embers slowly blackened, the Duchess crept closer to Piney, and broke the silence of many hours: "Piney, can you pray?" "No, dear," said Piney simply. The Duchess, without knowing exactly why, felt relieved, and, putting her head upon Piney's shoulder, spoke no more. And so reclining, the younger and purer pillowing the head of her soiled sister upon her virgin breast, they fell asleep.

The wind lulled as if it feared to waken them. Feathery drifts of snow, shaken from the long pine boughs, flew like white winged birds, and settled about them as they slept. The moon through the

rifted clouds looked down upon what had been the camp. But all human stain, all trace of earthly travail, was hidden beneath the spotless mantle mercifully flung from above.

They slept all that day and the next, nor did they waken when voices and footsteps broke the silence of the camp. And when pitying fingers brushed the snow from their wan faces, you could scarcely have told from the equal peace that dwelt upon them which was she that had sinned. Even the law of Poker Flat recognized this, and turned away, leaving them still locked in each other's arms.

But at the head of the gulch, on one of the largest pine-trees, they found the deuce of clubs pinned to the bark with a bowie-knife. It bore the following, written in pencil in a firm hand:—

†

BENEATH THIS TREE

LIES THE BODY

OF

JOHN OAKHURST,

WHO STRUCK A STREAK OF BAD LUCK

ON THE 23D OF NOVEMBER 1850,

AND

HANDED IN HIS CHECKS

ON THE 7TH DECEMBER, 1850.

♣

And pulseless and cold, with a derringer by his side and a bullet in his heart, though still calm as in life, beneath the snow lay he who was at once the strongest and yet the weakest of the outcasts of Poker Flat.

MIGGLES

WE WERE EIGHT including the driver. We had not spoken during the passage of the last six miles, since the jolting of the heavy vehicle over the roughening road had spoiled the Judge's last poetical quotation. The tall man beside the Judge was asleep, his arm passed through the swaying strap and his head resting upon it, — altogether a limp, helpless looking object, as if he had hanged himself and been cut down too late. The French lady on the back seat was asleep too, yet in a half-conscious propriety of attitude, shown even in the disposition of the handkerchief which she held to her forehead and which partially veiled her face. The lady from Virginia City, traveling with her husband, had long since lost all individuality in a wild confusion of ribbons, veils, furs, and shawls. There was no sound but the rattling of wheels and the dash of rain upon the roof. Suddenly the stage stopped and we became dimly aware of voices. The driver was evidently in the midst of an exciting colloquy with some one in the road, — a colloquy of which such fragments as "bridge gone," "twenty feet of water," "can't pass," were occasionally distinguishable above the storm. Then came a lull, and a mysterious voice from the road shouted the parting adjuration —

"Try Miggles's."

We caught a glimpse of our leaders as the vehicle slowly turned, of a horseman vanishing through the rain, and we were evidently on our way to Miggles's.

Who and where was Miggles? The Judge, our authority, did not remember the name, and he knew the country thoroughly. The Washoe traveler thought Miggles must keep a hotel. We only knew that we were stopped by high water in front and rear, and that Miggles was our rock of refuge. A ten minutes' splashing through a tangled byroad, scarcely wide enough for the stage, and we drew up before a barred and boarded gate in a wide stone wall or fence about eight feet high. Evidently Miggles's, and evidently Miggles did not keep a hotel.

The driver got down and tried the gate. It was securely locked.

"Miggles! O Miggles!"

No answer.

"Migg-ells! You Miggles!" continued the driver, with rising wrath.

"Migglesy!" joined in the expressman persuasively. "O Miggy! Mig!"

But no reply came from the apparently insensate Miggles. The Judge, who had finally got the window down, put his head out and propounded a series of questions, which if answered categorically would have undoubtedly elucidated the whole mystery, but which the driver evaded by replying that "if we didn't want to sit in the coach all night we had better rise up and sing out for Miggles."

So we rose up and called on Miggles in chorus, then separately. And when we had finished, a Hibernian fellow passenger from the roof called for "Maygells!" whereat we all laughed. While we were laughing the driver cried "Shoo!"

We listened. To our infinite amazement the chorus of "Miggles" was repeated from the other side of the wall, even to the final and supplemental "Maygells."

"Extraordinary echo!" said the Judge.

"Extraordinary d—d skunk!" roared the driver contemptuously. "Come out of that, Miggles, and show yourself! Be a man, Miggles! Don't hide in the dark; I wouldn't if I were you, Miggles," continued Yuba Bill, now dancing about in an excess of fury.

"Miggles!" continued the voice, "O Miggles!"

"My good man! Mr. Myghail!" cried the Judge, softening the

asperities of the name as much as possible. "Consider the inhospitality of refusing shelter from the inclemency of the weather to helpless females. Really, my dear sir"— But a succession of "Miggles," ending in a burst of laughter, drowned his voice.

Yuba Bill hesitated no longer. Taking a heavy stone from the road, he battered down the gate, and with the expressman entered the inclosure. We followed. Nobody was to be seen. In the gathering darkness all that we could distinguish was that we were in a garden — from the rose bushes that scattered over us a minute spray from their dripping leaves — and before a long, rambling wooden building.

"Do you know this Miggles?" asked the Judge of Yuba Bill.

"No, nor don't want to," said Bill shortly, who felt the Pioneer Stage Company insulted in his person by the contumacious Miggles.

"But, my dear sir," expostulated the Judge, as he thought of the barred gate.

"Lookee here," said Yuba Bill, with fine irony, "hadn't you better go back and sit in the coach till yer introduced? I'm going in," and he pushed open the door of the building.

A long room, lighted only by the embers of a fire that was dying on the large hearth at its farther extremity; the wall curiously papered, and the flickering firelight bringing out its grotesque pattern; somebody sitting in a large armchair by the fireplace. All this we saw as we crowded together into the room after the driver and expressman.

"Hello! be you Miggles?" said Yuba Bill to the solitary occupant.

The figure neither spoke nor stirred. Yuba Bill walked wrathfully toward it and turned the eye of his coach-lantern upon its face. It was a man's face, prematurely old and wrinkled, with very large eyes, in which there was that expression of perfectly gratuitous solemnity which I had sometimes seen in an owl's. The large eyes wandered from Bill's face to the lantern, and finally fixed their gaze on that luminous object without further recognition.

Bill restrained himself with an effort.

"Miggles! be you deaf? You ain't dumb anyhow, you know," and Yuba Bill shook the insensate figure by the shoulder.

To our great dismay, as Bill removed his hand, the venerable stranger apparently collapsed, sinking into half his size and an undistinguishable heap of clothing.

"Well, dern my skin," said Bill, looking appealingly at us, and hopelessly retiring from the contest.

The Judge now stepped forward, and we lifted the mysterious invertebrate back into his original position. Bill was dismissed with

the lantern to reconnoitre outside, for it was evident that, from the helplessness of this solitary man, there must be attendants near at hand, and we all drew around the fire. The Judge, who had regained his authority, and had never lost his conversational amiability, — standing before us with his back to the hearth, — charged us, as an imaginary jury, as follows: —

"It is evident that either our distinguished friend here has reached that condition described by Shakespeare as 'the sere and yellow leaf,' or has suffered some premature abatement of his mental and physical faculties. Whether he is really the Miggles" —

Here he was interrupted by "Miggles! O Miggles! Migglesy! Mig!" and, in fact, the whole chorus of Miggles in very much the same key as it had once before been delivered unto us.

We gazed at each other for a moment in some alarm. The Judge, in particular, vacated his position quickly, as the voice seemed to come directly over his shoulder. The cause, however, was soon discovered in a large magpie who was perched upon a shelf over the fireplace, and who immediately relapsed into a sepulchral silence, which contrasted singularly with his previous volubility. It was, undoubtedly, his voice which we had heard in the road, and our friend in the chair was not responsible for the discourtesy. Yuba Bill, who reëntered the room after an unsuccessful search, was loth to accept the explanation, and still eyed the helpless sitter with suspicion. He had found a shed in which he had put up his horses, but he came back dripping and skeptical. "Thar ain't nobody but him within ten mile of the shanty, and that ar d—d old skeesicks knows it."

But the faith of the majority proved to be securely based. Bill had scarcely ceased growling before we heard a quick step upon the porch, the trailing of a wet skirt, the door was flung open, and with a flash of white teeth, a sparkle of dark eyes, and an utter absence of ceremony or diffidence, a young woman entered, shut the door, and, panting, leaned back against it.

"Oh, if you please, I'm Miggles!"

And this was Miggles! this bright-eyed, full-throated young woman, whose wet gown of coarse blue stuff could not hide the beauty of the feminine curves to which it clung; from the chestnut crown of whose head, topped by a man's oil-skin sou'wester, to the little feet and ankles, hidden somewhere in the recesses of her boy's brogans, all was grace, — this was Miggles, laughing at us, too, in the most airy, frank, off-hand manner imaginable.

"You see, boys," said she, quite out of breath, and holding one little hand against her side, quite unheeding the speechless discomfiture of our party or the complete demoralization of Yuba Bill, whose features had relaxed into an expression of gratuitous and imbecile cheerfulness, — "you see, boys, I was mor'n two miles away when you passed down the road. I thought you might pull up here, and so I ran the whole way, knowing nobody was home but Jim, — and — and — I'm out of breath — and — that lets me out." And here Miggles caught her dripping oil-skin hat from her head, with a mischievous swirl that scattered a shower of raindrops over us; attempted to put back her hair; dropped two hairpins in the attempt; laughed, and sat down beside Yuba Bill, with her hands crossed lightly on her lap.

The Judge recovered himself first and essayed an extravagant compliment.

"I'll trouble you for that ha'rpin," said Miggles gravely. Half a dozen hands were eagerly stretched forward; the missing hairpin was restored to its fair owner; and Miggles, crossing the room, looked keenly in the face of the invalid. The solemn eyes looked back at hers with an expression we had never seen before. Life and intelligence seemed to struggle back into the rugged face. Miggles laughed again, — it was a singularly eloquent laugh, — and turned her black eyes and white teeth once more towards us.

"This afflicted person is" — hesitated the Judge.

"Jim!" said Miggles.

"Your father?"

"No!"

"Brother?"

"No!"

"Husband?"

Miggles darted a quick, half-defiant glance at the two lady passengers, who I had noticed did not participate in the general masculine admiration of Miggles, and said gravely, "No; it's Jim!"

There was an awkward pause. The lady passengers moved closer to each other; the Washoe husband looked abstractedly at the fire, and the tall man apparently turned his eyes inward for self-support at this emergency. But Miggles's laugh, which was very infectious, broke the silence.

"Come," she said briskly, "you must be hungry. Who'll bear a hand to help me get tea?"

She had no lack of volunteers. In a few moments Yuba Bill was engaged like Caliban in bearing logs for this Miranda; the expressman was grinding coffee on the veranda; to myself the arduous duty of slicing bacon was assigned; and the Judge lent each man his good-humored and voluble counsel. And when Miggles, assisted by the Judge and our Hibernian "deck-passenger," set the table with all the available crockery, we had become quite joyous, in spite of the rain that beat against the windows, the wind that whirled down the chimney, the two ladies who whispered together in the corner, or the magpie, who uttered a satirical and croaking commentary on their conversation from his perch above. In the now bright, blazing fire we could see that the walls were papered with illustrated journals, arranged with feminine taste and discrimination. The furniture was extemporized and adapted from candle-boxes and packing-cases, and covered with gay calico or the skin of some animal. The armchair of the helpless Jim was an ingenious variation of a flour-barrel. There was neatness, and even taste for the picturesque, to be seen in the few details of the long, low room.

The meal was a culinary success. But more, it was a social triumph, — chiefly, I think, owing to the rare tact of Miggles in guiding the conversation, asking all the questions herself, yet bearing throughout a frankness that rejected the idea of any concealment on her own part, so that we talked of ourselves, of our prospects, of the journey, of the weather, of each other, — of everything but our host and hostess. It must be confessed that Miggles's conversation was never elegant, rarely grammatical, and that at times she employed expletives the use of which had generally been yielded to our sex. But they were delivered with such a lighting up of teeth and eyes, and were usually followed by a laugh — a laugh peculiar to Miggles — so frank and honest that it seemed to clear the moral atmosphere.

Once during the meal we heard a noise like the rubbing of a heavy body against the outer walls of the house. This was shortly followed by a scratching and sniffling at the door. "That's Joaquin," said Miggles, in reply to our questioning glances; "would you like to see him?" Before we could answer she had opened the door, and disclosed a half-grown grizzly, who instantly raised himself on his haunches, with his fore paws hanging down in the popular attitude of mendicancy, and looked admiringly at Miggles, with a very singular resemblance in his manner to Yuba Bill. "That's my watch-dog," said Miggles, in explanation. "Oh, he don't bite," she added, as the two lady passengers fluttered into a corner. "Does he, old Toppy?" (the latter remark being addressed directly to the

sagacious Joaquin). "I tell you what, boys," continued Miggles, after she had fed and closed the door on Ursa Minor, "you were in big luck that Joaquin wasn't hanging round when you dropped in to-night."

"Where was he?" asked the Judge.

"With me," said Miggles. "Lord love you! he trots round with me nights like as if he was a man."

We were silent for a few moments, and listened to the wind. Perhaps we all had the same picture before us, — of Miggles walking through the rainy woods with her savage guardian at her side. The Judge, I remember, said something about Una and her lion; but Miggles received it, as she did other compliments, with quiet gravity. Whether she was altogether unconscious of the admiration she excited, — she could hardly have been oblivious of Yuba Bill's adoration, — I know not; but her very frankness suggested a perfect sexual equality that was cruelly humiliating to the younger members of our party.

The incident of the bear did not add anything in Miggles's favor to the opinions of those of her own sex who were present. In fact, the repast over, a chillness radiated from the two lady passengers that no pine boughs brought in by Yuba Bill and cast as a sacrifice upon the hearth could wholly overcome. Miggles felt it; and suddenly declaring that it was time to "turn in," offered to show the ladies to their bed in an adjoining room. "You, boys, will have to camp out here by the fire as well as you can," she added, "for thar ain't but the one room."

Our sex — by which, my dear sir, I allude of course to the stronger portion of humanity — has been generally relieved from the imputation of curiosity or a fondness for gossip. Yet I am constrained to say, that hardly had the door closed on Miggles than we crowded together, whispering, snickering, smiling, and exchanging suspicions, surmises, and a thousand speculations in regard to our pretty hostess and her singular companion. I fear that we even hustled that imbecile paralytic, who sat like a voiceless Memnon in our midst, gazing with the serene indifference of the Past in his passionless eyes upon our wordy counsels. In the midst of an exciting discussion the door opened again and Miggles reentered.

But not, apparently, the same Miggles who a few hours before had flashed upon us. Her eyes were downcast, and as she hesitated for a moment on the threshold, with a blanket on her arm, she seemed to have left behind her the frank fearlessness which had charmed us a moment before. Coming into the room, she drew a low stool beside the paralytic's chair, sat down, drew the blanket over her shoulders, and saying, "If it's all the same to you, boys, as we're rather crowded, I'll stop here to-night," took the invalid's withered hand in her own, and turned her eyes upon the dying fire. An instinctive feeling that this was only premonitory to more confidential relations, and perhaps some shame at our previous curiosity, kept us silent. The rain still beat upon the roof, wandering gusts of wind stirred the embers into momentary brightness, until, in a lull of the elements, Miggles suddenly lifted up her head, and, throwing her hair over her shoulder, turned her face upon the group and asked, —

"Is there any of you that knows me?"

There was no reply.

"Think again! I lived at Marysville in '53. Everybody knew me there, and everybody had the right to know me. I kept the Polka Saloon until I came to live with Jim. That's six years ago. Perhaps I've changed some."

The absence of recognition may have disconcerted her. She turned her head to the fire again, and it was some seconds before she again spoke, and then more rapidly —

"Well, you see I thought some of you must have known me. There's no great harm done anyway. What I was going to say was this: Jim here" — she took his hand in both of hers as she spoke — "used to know me, if you didn't, and spent a heap of money upon me. I reckon he spent all he had. And one day — it's six years ago this winter — Jim came into my back room, sat down on my sofy, like as you see him in that chair, and never moved again without help. He was struck all of a heap, and never seemed to know what ailed him. The doctors came and said as how it was caused all along of his way of life, — for Jim was mighty free and wild-like, — and that he would never get better, and couldn't last long anyway. They advised me to send him to Frisco to the hospital, for he was no good to any one and would be a baby all his life. Perhaps it was something in Jim's eye, perhaps it was that I never had a baby, but I said 'No.' I was rich then, for I was popular with everybody, — gentlemen like yourself, sir, came to see me, — and I sold out my business and bought this yer place, because it was sort of out of the way of travel, you see, and I brought my baby here."

With a woman's intuitive tact and poetry, she had, as she spoke, slowly shifted her position so as to bring the mute figure of the ruined man between her and her audience, hiding in the shadow behind it, as if she offered it as a tacit apology for her actions. Silent and expressionless, it yet spoke for her; helpless, crushed, and smitten with the Divine thunderbolt, it still stretched an invisible arm around her.

Hidden in the darkness, but still holding his hand, she went on: —

"It was a long time before I could get the hang of things about yer, for I was used to company and excitement. I couldn't get any woman to help me, and a man I dursn't trust; but what with the Indians hereabout, who'd do odd jobs for me, and having everything sent from the North Fork, Jim and I managed to worry through. The Doctor would run up from Sacramento once in a while. He'd ask to see 'Miggles's baby,' as he called Jim, and when he'd go away, he'd say, 'Miggles, you're a trump, — God bless you,' and it didn't seem so lonely after that. But the last time he was here he said, as he opened the door to go, 'Do you know, Miggles, your baby will grow up to be a man yet and an honor to his mother; but not here, Miggles, not here!' And I thought he went away sad, — and — and" — and here Miggles's voice and head were somehow both lost completely in the shadow.

"The folks about here are very kind," said Miggles, after a pause, coming a little into the light again. "The men from the Fork used to hang around here, until they found they wasn't wanted, and the women are kind, and don't call. I was pretty lonely until I picked up Joaquin in the woods yonder one day, when he wasn't so high, and taught him to beg for his dinner; and then thar's Polly — that's the magpie — she knows no end of tricks, and makes it quite sociable of evenings with her talk, and so I don't feel like I was the only living being about the ranch. And Jim here," said Miggles, with her old laugh again, and coming out quite into the firelight, — "Jim — Why, boys, you would admire to see how much he knows for a man like him. Sometimes I bring him flowers, and he looks at 'em just as natural as if he knew 'em; and times, when we're sitting alone, I read him those things on the wall. Why, Lord!" said Miggles, with her frank laugh, "I've read him that whole side of the house this winter. There never was such a man for reading as Jim."

"Why," asked the Judge, "do you not marry this man to whom you have devoted your youthful life?"

"Well, you see," said Miggles, "it would be playing it rather low down on Jim to take advantage of his being so helpless. And then, too, if we were man and wife, now, we'd both know that I was *bound* to do what I do now of my own accord."

"But you are young yet and attractive" —

"It's getting late," said Miggles gravely, "and you'd better all turn in. Good-night, boys;" and throwing the blanket over her head, Miggles laid herself down beside Jim's chair, her head pillowed on the low stool that held his feet, and spoke no more. The fire slowly faded from the hearth; we each sought our blankets in silence; and presently there was no sound in the long room but the pattering of the rain upon the roof and the heavy breathing of the sleepers.

It was nearly morning when I awoke from a troubled dream. The storm had passed, the stars were shining, and through the shutterless window the full moon, lifting itself over the solemn pines without, looked into the room. It touched the lonely figure in the chair with an infinite compassion, and seemed to baptize with a shining flood the lowly head of the woman whose hair, as in the sweet old story, bathed the feet of him she loved. It even lent a kindly poetry to the rugged outline of Yuba Bill, half reclining on his elbow between them and his passengers, with savagely patient eyes keeping watch and ward. And then I fell asleep and only woke at broad day, with Yuba Bill standing over me, and "All aboard" ringing in my ears.

Coffee was waiting for us on the table, but Miggles was gone.

We wandered about the house and lingered long after the horses were harnessed, but she did not return. It was evident that she wished to avoid a formal leave-taking, and had so left us to depart as we had come. After we had helped the ladies into the coach, we returned to the house and solemnly shook hands with the paralytic Jim, as solemnly setting him back into position after each handshake. Then we looked for the last time around the long low room, at the stool where Miggles had sat, and slowly took our seats in the waiting coach. The whip cracked, and we were off!

But as we reached the highroad, Bill's dexterous hand laid the six horses back on their haunches, and the stage stopped with a jerk. For there, on a litle eminence beside the road, stood Miggles, her hair flying, her eyes sparkling, her white handkerchief waving, and her white teeth flashing a last "good-by." We waved our hats in return. And then Yuba Bill, as if fearful of further fascination, madly lashed his horses forward, and we sank back in our seats.

We exchanged not a word until we reached the North Fork and the stage drew up at the Independence House. Then, the Judge leading, we walked into the bar-room and took our places gravely at the bar.

"Are your glasses charged, gentlemen?" said the Judge, solemnly taking off his white hat.

They were.

"Well, then, here's to *Miggles* — GOD BLESS HER!"

Perhaps He had. Who knows?

TENNESSEE'S
PARTNER

I DO NOT THINK that we ever knew his real name. Our ignorance of it certainly never gave us any social inconvenience, for at Sandy Bar in 1854 most men were christened anew. Sometimes these appellatives were derived from some distinctiveness of dress, as in the case of "Dungaree Jack;" or from some peculiarity of habit, as shown in "Saleratus Bill," so called from an undue proportion of that chemical in his daily bread; or from some unlucky slip, as exhibited in "The Iron Pirate," a mild, inoffensive man, who earned that baleful title by his unfortunate mispronunciation of the term "iron pyrites." Perhaps this may have been the beginning of a rude heraldry; but I am constrained to think that it was because a man's real name in that day rested solely upon his own unsupported statement. "Call yourself Clifford, do you?" said Boston, addressing a timid newcomer with infinite scorn; "hell is full of such Cliffords!" He then introduced the unfortunate man, whose name happened to be really Clifford, as "Jaybird Charley," — an unhallowed inspiration of the moment that clung to him ever after.

But to return to Tennessee's Partner, whom we never knew by any other than this relative title. That he had ever existed as a separate and distinct individuality we only learned later. It seems that in 1853 he left Poker Flat to go to San Francisco, ostensibly to procure a wife. He never got any farther than Stockton. At that place he was attracted by a young person who waited upon the table at the hotel where he took his meals. One morning he said something to her which caused her to smile not unkindly, to somewhat coquettishly break a plate of toast over his upturned, serious, simple face, and to retreat to the kitchen. He followed her, and emerged a few moments later, covered with more toast and victory. That day week they were married by a justice of the peace, and returned to Poker Flat. I am aware that something more might be made of this episode, but I prefer to tell it as it was current at Sandy Bar, — in the gulches and bar-rooms, — where all sentiment was modified by a strong sense of humor.

Of their married felicity but little is known, perhaps for the reason that Tennessee, then living with his partner, one day took occasion to say something to the bride on his own account, at which, it is said, she smiled not unkindly and chastely retreated, — this time as far as Marysville, where Tennessee followed her, and where they went to housekeeping without the aid of a justice of the peace. Tennessee's Partner took the loss of his wife simply and seriously, as was his fashion. But to everybody's surprise, when Tennessee one day returned from Marysville, without his partner's wife, — she having smiled and retreated with somebody else, — Tennessee's Partner was the first man to shake his hand and greet him with affection. The boys who had gathered in the cañon to see the shooting were naturally indignant. Their indignation might have found vent in sarcasm but for a certain look in Tennessee's Partner's eye that indicated a lack of humorous appreciation. In fact, he was a grave man, with a steady application to practical detail which was unpleasant in a difficulty.

Meanwhile a popular feeling against Tennessee had grown up on the Bar. He was known to be a gambler; he was suspected to be a thief. In these suspicions Tennessee's Partner was equally compromised; his continued intimacy with Tennessee after the affair above quoted could only be accounted for on the hypothesis of a copartnership of crime. At last Tennessee's guilt became flagrant. One day he overtook a stranger on his way to Red Dog. The stranger afterward related that Tennessee beguiled the time with interesting anecdote and reminiscence, but illogically concluded the interview in the following words: "And now, young man, I'll trouble you for your knife, your pistols, and your money. You see your weppings might get you into trouble at Red Dog, and your money's a temptation to the evilly disposed. I think you said your address was San Francisco. I shall endeavor to call." It may be stated here that Tennessee had a fine flow of humor, which no business preoccupation could wholly subdue.

This exploit was his last. Red Dog and Sandy Bar made common cause against the highwayman. Tennessee was hunted in very much the same fashion as his prototype, the grizzly. As the toils closed around him, he made a desperate dash through the Bar, emptying his revolver at the crowd before the Arcade Saloon, and so on up Grizzly Cañon; but at its farther extremity he was stopped by a small man on a gray horse. The men looked at each other a moment in silence. Both were fearless, both self-possessed and independent, and both types of a civilization that in the seventeenth century would have been called heroic, but in the nineteenth simply "reckless."

"What have you got there? — I call," said Tennessee quietly.

"Two bowers and an ace," said the stranger as quietly, showing two revolvers and a bowie-knife.

"That takes me," returned Tennessee; and, with this gambler's epigram, he threw away his useless pistol and rode back with his captor.

It was a warm night. The cool breeze which usually sprang up with the going down of the sun behind the chaparral-crested mountain was that evening withheld from Sandy Bar. The little cañon was stifling with heated resinous odors, and the decaying driftwood on the Bar sent forth faint sickening exhalations. The feverishness of day and its fierce passions still filled the camp. Lights moved restlessly along the bank of the river, striking no answering reflection from its tawny current. Against the blackness of the pines the windows of the old loft above the express-office stood out staringly bright; and through their curtainless panes the loungers below could see the forms of those who were even then deciding the fate of Tennessee. And above all this, etched on the dark firmament, rose the Sierra, remote and passionless, crowned with remoter passionless stars.

The trial of Tennessee was conducted as fairly as was consistent with a judge and jury who felt themselves to some extent obliged to justify, in their verdict, the previous irregularities of arrest and indictment. The law of Sandy Bar was implacable, but not vengeful. The excitement and personal feeling of the chase were over; with Tennessee safe in their hands, they were ready to listen patiently to any defense, which they were already satisfied was insufficient. There being no doubt in their own minds, they were willing to give the prisoner the benefit of any that might exist. Secure in the hypothesis that he ought to be hanged on general principles, they indulged him with more latitude of defense than his reckless hardihood seemed to ask. The Judge appeared to be more anxious than the prisoner, who, otherwise unconcerned, evidently took a grim pleasure in the responsibility he had created. "I don't take any hands in this yer game," had been his invariable but good-humored reply to all questions. The Judge — who was also his captor — for a moment vaguely regretted that he had not shot him "on sight" that morning, but presently dismissed this human weakness as unworthy of the judicial mind. Nevertheless, when there was a tap at the door, and it was said that Tennessee's Partner was there on behalf of the prisoner, he was admitted at once without question. Perhaps the younger members of the jury, to whom the proceedings were becoming irksomely thoughtful, hailed him as a relief.

For he was not, certainly, an imposing figure. Short and stout, with a square face, sunburned into a preternatural redness, clad in a loose duck "jumper" and trousers streaked and splashed with red soil, his aspect under any circumstances would have been quaint, and was now even ridiculous. As he stooped to deposit at his feet a heavy carpetbag he was carrying, it became obvious, from partially developed legends and inscriptions, that the material with which his trousers had been patched had been originally intended for a less ambitious covering. Yet he advanced with great gravity, and after shaking the hand of each person in the room with labored cordiality, he wiped his serious perplexed face on a red bandana handkerchief, a shade lighter than his complexion, laid his powerful hand upon the table to steady himself, and thus addressed the Judge: —

"I was passin' by," he began, by way of apology, "and I thought I'd just step in and see how things was gittin' on with Tennessee thar,—my pardner. It's a hot night. I disremember any sich weather before on the Bar."

He paused a moment, but nobody volunteering any other meteorological recollection, he again had recourse to his pocket-handkerchief, and for some moments mopped his face diligently.

"Have you anything to say on behalf of the prisoner?" said the Judge finally.

"That's it," said Tennessee's Partner, in a tone of relief. "I come yar as Tennessee's pardner,—knowing him nigh on four year, off and on, wet and dry, in luck and out o' luck. His ways ain't aller my ways, but thar ain't any p'ints in that young man, thar ain't any liveliness as he's been up to, as I don't know. And you sez to me, sez you,—confidential-like, and between man and man,—sez you, 'Do you know anything in his behalf?' and I sez to you, sez I,—confidential-like, as between man and man,—'What should a man know of his pardner?'"

"Is this all you have to say?" asked the Judge impatiently, feeling, perhaps, that a dangerous sympathy of humor was beginning to humanize the court.

"That's so," continued Tennessee's Partner. "It ain't for me to say anything ag'in' him. And now, what's the case? Here's Tennessee wants money, wants it bad, and doesn't like to ask it of his old pardner. Well, what does Tennessee do? He lays for a stranger, and he fetches that stranger; and you lays for *him*, and you fetches *him*; and the honors is easy. And I put it to you, bein' a fa'r-minded man, and to you, gentleman all, as fa'r-minded men, ef this isn't so."

"Prisoner," said the Judge, interrupting, "have you any questions to ask this man?"

"No! no!" continued Tennessee's Partner hastily. "I play this yer hand alone. To come down to the bed-rock, it's just this: Tennessee, thar, has played it pretty rough and expensive-like on a stranger, and on this yer camp. And now, what's the fair thing? Some would say more, some would say less. Here's seventeen hundred dollars in coarse gold and a watch,—it's about all my pile, —and call it square!" And before a hand could be raised to prevent

him, he had emptied the contents of the carpetbag upon the table.

For a moment his life was in jeopardy. One or two men sprang to their feet, several hands groped for hidden weapons, and a suggestion to "throw him from the window" was only overridden by a gesture from the Judge. Tennessee laughed. And apparently oblivious of the excitement, Tennessee's Partner improved the opportunity to mop his face again with his handkerchief.

When order was restored, and the man was made to understand, by the use of forcible figures and rhetoric, that Tennessee's offense could not be condoned by money, his face took a more serious and sanguinary hue, and those who were nearest to him noticed that his rough hand trembled slightly on the table. He hesitated a moment as he slowly returned the gold to the carpetbag, as if he had not yet entirely caught the elevated sense of justice which swayed the tribunal, and was perplexed with the belief that he had not offered enough. Then he turned to the Judge, and saying, "This yer is a lone hand, played alone, and without my pardner," he bowed to the jury and was about to withdraw, when the Judge called him back: — "If you have anything to say to Tennessee, you had better say it now."

For the first time that evening the eyes of the prisoner and his strange advocate met. Tennessee smiled, showed his white teeth, and saying, "Euchred, old man!" held out his hand.

Tennessee's Partner took it in his own, and saying, "I just dropped in as I was passin' to see how things was gettin' on," let the hand passively fall, and adding that "it was a warm night," again mopped his face with his handkerchief, and without another word withdrew.

The two men never again met each other alive. For the unparalleled insult of a bribe offered to Judge Lynch — who, whether bigoted, weak, or narrow, was at least incorruptible — firmly fixed in the mind of that mythical personage any wavering determination of Tennessee's fate; and at the break of day he was marched, closely guarded, to meet it at the top of Marley's Hill.

How he met it, how cool he was, how he refused to say anything, how perfect were the arrangements of the committee, were all duly reported, with the addition of a warning moral and example to all future evil-doers, in the "Red Dog Clarion," by its editor, who was present, and to whose vigorous English I cheerfully refer the reader. But the beauty of that midsummer morning, the blessed amity of earth and air and sky, the awakened life of the free woods and hills, the joyous renewal and promise of Nature, and above all, the infinite serenity that thrilled through each, was not reported, as not being a part of the social lesson. And yet, when the weak and foolish deed was done, and a life, with its possibilities and responsibilities, had passed out of the misshapen thing that dangled between earth and sky, the birds sang, the flowers bloomed, the sun shone, as cheerily as before; and possibly the "Red Dog Clarion" was right.

Tennessee's Partner was not in the group that surrounded the ominous tree. But as they turned to disperse, attention was drawn to the singular appearance of a motionless donkey-cart halted at the side of the road. As they approached, they at once recognized the venerable "Jenny" and the two-wheeled cart as the property of Tennessee's Partner, used by him in carrying dirt from his claim; and a few paces distant the owner of the equipage himself, sitting under a buckeye-tree, wiping the perspiration from his glowing face. In answer to an inquiry, he said he had come for the body of the "diseased," "if it was all the same to the committee." He didn't wish to "hurry anything;" he could "wait." He was not working that day; and when the gentlemen were done with the "diseased," he would take him. "Ef thar is any present," he added, in his simple, serious way, "as would care to jine in the fun'l, they kin come." Perhaps it was from a sense of humor, which I have already intimated was a feature of Sandy Bar, — perhaps it was from something even better than that, but two thirds of the loungers accepted the invitation at once.

It was noon when the body of Tennessee was delivered into the hands of his partner. As the cart drew up to the fatal tree, we noticed that it contained a rough oblong box, — apparently made from a section of sluicing, — and half filled with bark and the tassels of pine. The cart was further decorated with slips of willow and made fragrant with buckeye-blossoms. When the body was deposited in the box, Tennessee's Partner drew over it a piece of tarred canvas, and gravely mounting the narrow seat in front, with his feet upon the shafts, urged the little donkey forward. The equipage moved slowly on, at that decorous pace which was habitual with Jenny even under less solemn circumstances. The men — half curiously, half jestingly, but all good-humoredly — strolled along beside the cart, some in advance, some a little in the rear of the homely catafalque. But whether from the narrowing of the road or some present sense of decorum, as the cart passed on, the company fell to the rear in couples, keeping step, and otherwise assuming the external show of a formal procession. Jack Folinsbee, who had at the outset played a funeral march in dumb show upon an imaginary trombone, desisted from a lack of sympathy and appreciation, — not having, perhaps, your true humorist's capacity to be content with the enjoyment of his own fun.

The way led through Grizzly Cañon, by this time clothed in funereal drapery and shadows. The redwoods, burying their moccasined feet in the red soil, stood in Indian file along the track, trailing an uncouth benediction from their bending boughs upon the passing bier. A hare, surprised into helpless inactivity, sat upright and pulsating in the ferns by the roadside as the cortége went by. Squirrels hastened to gain a secure outlook from higher boughs; and the blue-jays, spreading their wings, fluttered before them like outriders, until the outskirts of Sandy Bar were reached, and the solitary cabin of Tennessee's Partner.

Viewed under more favorable circumstances, it would not have been a cheerful place. The unpicturesque site, the rude and unlovely outlines, the unsavory details, which distinguish the nest-building of the California miner, were all here with the dreariness of decay superadded. A few paces from the cabin there was a rough inclosure, which, in the brief days of Tennessee's Partner's matrimonial felicity, had been used as a garden, but was now overgrown with fern. As we approached it, we were surprised to find that what we had taken for a recent attempt at cultivation was the broken soil about an open grave.

The cart was halted before the inclosure, and rejecting the offers of assistance with the same air of simple self-reliance he had displayed throughout, Tennessee's Partner lifted the rough coffin on his back, and deposited it unaided within the shallow grave. He then nailed down the board which served as a lid, and mounting the little mound of earth beside it, took off his hat and slowly mopped his face with his handkerchief. This the crowd felt was a preliminary to speech, and they disposed themselves variously on stumps and boulders, and sat expectant.

"When a man," began Tennessee's Partner slowly, "has been running free all day, what's the natural thing for him to do? Why, to come home. And if he ain't in a condition to go home, what can his best friend do? Why, bring him home. And here's Tennessee has been running free, and we brings him home from his wandering." He paused and picked up a fragment of quartz, rubbed it thoughtfully on his sleeve, and went on: "It ain't the first time that I've packed him on my back, as you see'd me now. It ain't the first time that I brought him to this yer cabin when he couldn't help himself; it ain't the first time that I and Jinny have waited for him on yon hill, and picked him up and so fetched him home, when he couldn't speak and didn't know me. And now that it's the last time, why" — he paused and rubbed the quartz gently on his sleeve — "you see it's sort of rough on his pardner. And now, gentlemen," he added abruptly, picking up his long-handled shovel, "the fun'l's over; and my thanks, and Tennessee's thanks, to you for your trouble."

Resisting any proffers of assistance, he began to fill in the grave, turning his back upon the crowd, that after a few moments' hesitation gradually withdrew. As they crossed the little ridge that hid Sandy Bar from view, some, looking back, thought they could see Tennessee's Partner, his work done, sitting upon the grave, his shovel between his knees, and his face buried in his red bandana handkerchief. But it was argued by others that you couldn't tell his face from his handkerchief at that distance, and this point remained undecided.

In the reaction that followed the feverish excitement of that day, Tennessee's Partner was not forgotten. A secret investigation had cleared him of any complicity in Tennessee's guilt, and left only a suspicion of his general sanity. Sandy Bar made a point of calling on him, and proffering various uncouth but well-meant kindnesses. But from that day his rude health and great strength seemed visibly to decline; and when the rainy season fairly set in, and the tiny grass-blades were beginning to peep from the rocky mound above Tennessee's grave, he took to his bed.

One night, when the pines beside the cabin were swaying in the storm and trailing their slender fingers over the roof, and the roar and rush of the swollen river were heard below, Tennessee's Partner lifted his head from the pillow, saying, "It is time to go for Tennessee; I must put Jinny in the cart;" and would have risen from his bed but for the restraint of his attendant. Struggling, he still pursued his singular fancy: "There, now, steady, Jinny, — steady, old girl. How dark it is! Look out for the ruts, — and look out for him, too, old gal. Sometimes, you know, when he's blind drunk, he drops down right in the trail. Keep on straight up to the pine on the top of the hill. Thar! I told you so! — thar he is, — coming this way, too, — all by himself, sober, and his face a-shining. Tennessee! Pardner!"

And so they met.

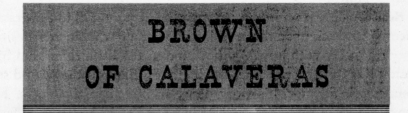

BROWN OF CALAVERAS

A SUBDUED TONE of conversation, and the absence of cigar-smoke and boot-heels at the windows of the Wingdam stagecoach, made it evident that one of the inside passengers was a woman. A disposition on the part of loungers at the stations to congregate before the window, and some concern in regard to the appearance of coats, hats, and collars, further indicated that she was lovely. All of which Mr. Jack Hamlin, on the box-seat, noted with the smile of cynical philosophy. Not that he depreciated the sex, but that he recognized therein a deceitful element, the pursuit of which sometimes drew mankind away from the equally uncertain blandishments of poker, — of which it may be remarked that Mr. Hamlin was a professional exponent.

So that, when he placed his narrow boot on the wheel and leaped down, he did not even glance at the window from which a green veil was fluttering, but lounged up and down with that listless and grave indifference of his class, which was, perhaps the next thing to good-breeding. With his closely buttoned figure and self-contained air he was a marked contrast to the other passengers, with their feverish restlessness and boisterous emotion; and even Bill Masters, a graduate of Harvard, with his slovenly dress, his overflowing vitality, his intense appreciation of lawlessness and barbarism, and his mouth filled with crackers and cheese, I fear cut but an unromantic figure beside this lonely calculator of chances, with his pale Greek face and Homeric gravity.

54

The driver called "All aboard!" and Mr. Hamlin returned to the coach. His foot was upon the wheel, and his face raised to the level of the open window, when, at the same moment, what appeared to him to be the finest eyes in the world suddenly met his. He quietly dropped down again, addressed a few words to one of the inside passengers, effected an exchange of seats, and as quietly took his place inside. Mr. Hamlin never allowed his philosophy to interfere with decisive and prompt action.

I fear that this irruption of Jack cast some restraint upon the other passengers, particularly those who were making themselves most agreeable to the lady. One of them leaned forward, and apparently conveyed to her information regarding Mr. Hamlin's profession in a single epithet. Whether Mr. Hamlin heard it, or whether he recognized in the informant a distinguished jurist, from whom, but a few evenings before, he had won several thousand dollars, I cannot say. His colorless face betrayed no sign; his black eyes, quietly observant, glanced indifferently past the legal gentleman, and rested on the much more pleasing features of his neighbor. An Indian stoicism — said to be an inheritance from his maternal ancestor — stood him in good service, until the rolling wheels rattled upon the river gravel at Scott's Ferry, and the stage drew up at the International Hotel for dinner. The legal gentleman and a member of Congress leaped out, and stood ready to assist the descending goddess, while Colonel Starbottle of Siskiyou took charge of her parasol and shawl. In this multiplicity of attention there was a momentary confusion and delay. Jack Hamlin quietly opened the *opposite* door of the coach, took the lady's hand, with that decision and positiveness which a hesitating and undecided sex know how to admire, and in an instant had dexterously and gracefully swung her to the ground and again lifted her to the platform. An audible chuckle on the box, I fear, came from that other cynic, Yuba Bill, the driver. "Look keerfully arter that baggage, Kernel," said the expressman, with affected concern, as he looked after Colonel Starbottle, gloomily bringing up the rear of the triumphant procession to the waiting-room.

Mr. Hamlin did not stay for dinner. His horse was already saddled and awaiting him. He dashed over the ford, up the gravelly hill, and out into the dusty perspective of the Wingdam road, like one leaving an unpleasant fancy behind him. The inmates of dusty cabins by the roadside shaded their eyes with their hands and looked after him, recognizing the man by his horse, and speculating what "was up with Comanche Jack." Yet much of this interest centred in the horse, in a community where the time made by "French Pete's" mare, in his run from the Sheriff of Calaveras, eclipsed all concern in the ultimate fate of that worthy.

The sweating flanks of his gray at length recalled him to himself. He checked his speed, and turning into a byroad, sometimes used as a cut-off, trotted leisurely along, the reins hanging listlessly from his fingers. As he rode on, the character of the landscape changed and became more pastoral. Openings in groves of pine and sycamore disclosed some rude attempts at cultivation, — a flowering vine trailed over the porch of one cabin, and a woman rocked her cradled babe under the roses of another. A little farther on, Mr. Hamlin came upon some bare-legged children wading in the willowy creek, and so wrought upon them with a badinage peculiar to himself, that they were emboldened to climb up his horse's legs and over his saddle, until he was fain to develop an exaggerated ferocity of demeanor, and to escape, leaving behind some kisses and coin. And then, advancing deeper into the woods, where all signs of habitation failed, he began to sing, uplifting a tenor so singularly sweet, and shaded by a pathos so subdued and tender, that I wot the robins and linnets stopped to listen. Mr. Hamlin's voice was not cultivated; the subject of his song was some sentimental lunacy, borrowed from the negro minstrels; but there thrilled through all some occult quality of tone and expression that was unspeakably touching. Indeed, it was a wonderful sight to see this sentimental blackleg, with a pack of cards in his pocket and a revolver at his back, sending his voice before him through the dim woods with a plaint about his "Nelly's grave," in a way that overflowed the eyes of the listener. A sparrow-hawk, fresh from his sixth victim, possibly recognizing in Mr. Hamlin a kindred spirit, stared at him in surprise, and was fain to confess the superiority of man. With a superior predatory capacity *he* couldn't sing.

But Mr. Hamlin presently found himself again on the high-road and at his former pace. Ditches and banks of gravel, denuded hillsides, stumps, and decayed trunks of trees, took the place of woodland and ravine, and indicated his approach to civilization. Then a church-steeple came in sight, and he knew that he had reached home. In a few moments he was clattering down the single narrow street that lost itself in a chaotic ruin of races, ditches, and tailings at the foot of the hill, and dismounted before the gilded windows of the Magnolia saloon. Passing through the long bar-room, he pushed open a green-baize door, entered a dark passage, opened another door with a pass-key, and found himself in a dimly lighted room, whose furniture, though elegant and costly for the locality, showed signs of abuse. The inlaid centre-table was over-laid with stained disks that were not contemplated in the original design, the embroidered armchairs were discolored, and the green velvet lounge, on which Mr. Hamlin threw himself, was soiled at the foot with the red soil of Wingdam.

Mr. Hamlin did not sing in his cage. He lay still, looking at a highly colored painting above him, representing a young creature of opulent charms. It occurred to him then, for the first time, that he had never seen exactly that kind of a woman, and that, if he should, he would not, probably, fall in love with her. Perhaps he was thinking of another style of beauty. But just then some one knocked at the door. Without rising, he pulled a cord that appar-ently shot back a bolt, for the door swung open, and a man entered.

The new-comer was broad-shouldered and robust, — a vigor not borne out in the face, which, though handsome, was singularly weak and disfigured by dissipation. He appeared to be, also, under the influence of liquor, for he started on seeing Mr. Hamlin, and said, "I thought Kate was here;" stammered, and seemed confused and embarrassed.

Mr. Hamlin smiled the smile which he had before worn on the Wingdam coach, and sat up, quite refreshed and ready for business.

"You didn't come up on the stage," continued the new-comer, "did you?"

"No," replied Hamlin; "I left it at Scott's Ferry. It isn't due for half an hour yet. But how's luck, Brown?"

"D—d bad," said Brown, his face suddenly assuming an expression of weak despair. "I'm cleaned out again, Jack," he continued, in a whining tone, that formed a pitiable contrast to his bulky figure; "can't you help me with a hundred till to-morrow's clean-up? You see I've got to send money home to the old woman, and — you've won twenty times that amount from me."

The conclusion was, perhaps, not entirely logical, but Jack overlooked it, and handed the sum to his visitor. "The old-woman business is about played out, Brown," he added, by way of commentary; "why don't you say you want to buck ag'in' faro? You know you ain't married!"

"Fact, sir," said Brown, with a sudden gravity, as if the mere contact of the gold with the palm of the hand had imparted some dignity to his frame. "I've got a wife—a d—d good one, too, if I do say it — in the States. It's three years since I've seen her, and a year since I've writ to her. When things is about straight, and we get down to the lead, I'm going to send for her."

"And Kate?" queried Mr. Hamlin, with his previous smile.

Mr. Brown of Calaveras essayed an archness of glance to cover his confusion, which his weak frame and whiskey-muddled intellect but poorly carried out, and said, —

"D—n it, Jack, a man must have a little liberty, you know. But come, what do you say to a little game? Give us a show to double this hundred."

Jack Hamlin looked curiously at his fatuous friend. Perhaps he knew that the man was predestined to lose the money, and preferred that it should flow back into his own coffers rather than any other. He nodded his head, and drew his chair toward the table. At the same moment there came a rap upon the door.

"It's Kate," said Mr. Brown.

Mr. Hamlin shot back the bolt and the door opened. But, for the first time in his life, he staggered to his feet utterly unnerved and abashed, and for the first time in his life the hot blood crimsoned his colorless cheeks to his forehead. For before him stood the lady he had lifted from the Wingdam coach, whom Brown, dropping his cards with a hysterical laugh, greeted as, —

"My old woman, by thunder!"

They say that Mrs. Brown burst into tears and reproaches of her husband. I saw her in 1857 at Marysville, and disbelieve the story. And the "Wingdam Chronicle" of the next week, under the head of "Touching Reunion," said: "One of those beautiful and touching incidents, peculiar to California life, occurred last week in our city. The wife of one of Wingdam's eminent pioneers, tired of the effete civilization of the East and its inhospitable climate, resolved to join her noble husband upon these golden shores. Without informing him of her intention, she undertook the long journey, and arrived last week. The joy of the husband may be easier imagined than described. The meeting is said to have been indescribably affecting. We trust her example may be followed."

Whether owing to Mrs. Brown's influence, or to some more successful speculations, Mr. Brown's financial fortune from that day steadily improved. He bought out his partners in the "Nip and Tuck" lead, with money which was said to have been won at poker a week or two after his wife's arrival, but which rumor, adopting Mrs. Brown's theory that Brown had forsworn the gaming-table, declared to have been furnished by Mr. Jack Hamlin. He built and furnished the Wingdam House, which pretty Mrs. Brown's great popularity kept overflowing with guests. He was elected to the Assembly, and gave largess to churches. A street in Wingdam was named in his honor.

Yet it was noted that in proportion as he waxed wealthy and fortunate, he grew pale, thin, and anxious. As his wife's popularity increased, he became fretful and impatient. The most uxorious of husbands, he was absurdly jealous. If he did not interfere with his wife's social liberty, it was because it was maliciously whispered that his first and only attempt was met by an outburst from Mrs. Brown that terrified him into silence. Much of this kind of gossip came from those of her own sex whom she had supplanted in the chivalrous attentions of Wingdam, which, like most popular chivalry, was devoted to an admiration of power, whether of masculine force or feminine beauty. It should be remembered, too, in her extenuation, that, since her arrival, she had been the unconscious priestess of a mythological worship, perhaps not more ennobling to her womanhood than that which distinguished an older Greek democracy. I think that Brown was dimly conscious of this. But his only confidant was Jack Hamlin, whose infelix reputation naturally precluded any open intimacy with the family, and whose visits were infrequent.

It was midsummer and a moonlit night, and Mrs. Brown, very rosy, large-eyed, and pretty, sat upon the piazza, enjoying the fresh incense of the mountain breeze, and, it is to be feared, another incense which was not so fresh nor quite as innocent. Beside her sat Colonel Starbottle and Judge Boompointer, and a later addition to her court in the shape of a foreign tourist. She was in good spirits.

"What do you see down the road?" inquired the gallant Colonel, who had been conscious, for the last few minutes, that Mrs. Brown's attention was diverted.

"Dust," said Mrs. Brown, with a sigh. "Only Sister Anne's 'flock of sheep.'"

The colonel, whose literary recollections did not extend farther back than last week's paper, took a more practical view. "It ain't sheep," he continued; "it's a horseman. Judge, ain't that Jack Hamlin's gray?"

But the Judge didn't know; and, as Mrs. Brown suggested the air was growing too cold for further investigations, they retired to the parlor.

Mr. Brown was in the stable, where he generally retired after dinner. Perhaps it was to show his contempt for his wife's companions; perhaps, like other weak natures, he found pleasure in the exercise of absolute power over inferior animals. He had a certain gratification in the training of a chestnut mare, whom he could beat or caress as pleased him, which he couldn't do with Mrs. Brown. It was here that he recognized a certain gray horse which had just come in, and, looking a little farther on, found his rider. Brown's greeting was cordial and hearty; Mr. Hamlin's somewhat restrained. But, at Brown's urgent request, he followed him up the back stairs to a narrow corridor, and thence to a small room looking out upon the stable-yard. It was plainly furnished with a bed, a table, a few chairs, and a rack of guns and whips.

"This yer's my home, Jack," said Brown with a sigh, as he threw himself upon the bed and motioned his companion to a chair. "Her room's t' other end of the hall. It's more'n six months since we've lived together, or met, except at meals. It's mighty rough papers on the head of the house, ain't it?" he said with a forced laugh. "But I'm glad to see you, Jack, d—d glad," and he reached from the bed, and again shook the unresponsive hand of Jack Hamlin.

"I brought ye up here, for I didn't want to talk in the stable; though, for the matter of that, it's all round town. Don't strike a light. We can talk here in the moonshine. Put up your feet on that winder and sit here beside me. Thar's whiskey in that jug."

Mr. Hamlin did not avail himself of the information. Brown of Calaveras turned his face to the wall, and continued, —

"If I didn't love the woman, Jack, I wouldn't mind. But it's loving her, and seeing her day arter day goin' on at this rate, and no one to put down the brake; that's what gits me! But I'm glad to see ye, Jack, d—d glad."

In the darkness he groped about until he had found and wrung his companion's hand again. He would have detained it, but Jack slipped it into the buttoned breast of his coat, and asked listlessly, "How long has this been going on?"

"Ever since she came here; ever since the day she walked into the Magnolia. I was a fool then; Jack, I'm a fool now; but I didn't know how much I loved her till then. And she hasn't been the same woman since.

"But that ain't all, Jack; and it's what I wanted to see you about, and I'm glad you've come. It ain't that she doesn't love me any more; it ain't that she fools with every chap that comes along; for perhaps I staked her love and lost it, as I did everything else at the Magnolia; and perhaps foolin' is nateral to some women, and thar ain't no great harm done, 'cept to the fools. But, Jack, I think, — I think she loves somebody else. Don't move, Jack! don't move; if your pistol hurts ye, take it off.

"It's been more'n six months now that she's seemed unhappy and lonesome, and kinder nervous and scared-like. And sometimes I've ketched her lookin' at me sort of timid and pitying. And she writes to somebody. And for the last week she's been gathering her own things, — trinkets, and furbelows, and jew'lry, — and, Jack, I think she's goin' off. I could stand all but that. To have her steal away like a thief!" He put his face downward to the pillow, and for a few moments there was no sound but the ticking of a clock on the mantel. Mr. Hamlin lit a cigar, and moved to the open window. The moon no longer shone into the room, and the bed and its occupant were in shadow. "What shall I do, Jack?" said the voice from the darkness.

The answer came promptly and clearly from the window-side, "Spot the man, and kill him on sight."

"But, Jack" —

"He's took the risk!"

"But will that bring *her* back?"

Jack did not reply, but moved from the window towards the door.

"Don't go yet, Jack; light the candle and sit by the table. It's a comfort to see ye, if nothin' else."

Jack hesitated and then complied. He drew a pack of cards from his pocket and shuffled them, glancing at the bed. But Brown's face was turned to the wall. When Mr. Hamlin had shuffled the cards, he cut them, and dealt one card on the opposite side of the table towards the bed, and another on his side of the table for himself. The first was a deuce; his own card a king. He then shuffled and cut again. This time "dummy" had a queen and himself a four-spot. Jack brightened up for the third deal. It brought his adversary a deuce and himself a king again. "Two out of three," said Jack audibly.

"What's that, Jack?" said Brown.

"Nothing."

Then Jack tried his hand with dice; but he always threw sixes and his imaginary opponent aces. The force of habit is sometimes confusing.

Meanwhile some magnetic influence in Mr. Hamlin's presence, or the anodyne of liquor, or both, brought surcease of sorrow, and Brown slept. Mr. Hamlin moved his chair to the window and looked out on the town of Wingdam, now sleeping peacefully, its harsh outlines softened and subdued, its glaring colors mellowed and sobered in the moonlight that flowed over all. In the hush he could hear the gurgling of water in the ditches and the sighing of the pines beyond the hill. Then he looked up at the firmament, and as he did so a star shot across the twinkling field. Presently another, and then another. The phenomenon suggested to Mr. Hamlin a fresh augury. If in another fifteen minutes another star should fall— He sat there, watch in hand, for twice that time, but the phenomenon was not repeated.

The clock struck two, and Brown still slept. Mr. Hamlin approached the table and took from his pocket a letter, which he read by the flickering candlelight. It contained only a single line, written in pencil, in a woman's hand, —

"Be at the corral with the buggy at three."

The sleeper moved uneasily and then awoke. "Are you there, Jack?"

"Yes."

"Don't go yet. I dreamed just now, Jack, — dreamed of old times. I thought that Sue and me was being married agin, and that the parson, Jack, was — who do you think? — you!"

The gambler laughed, and seated himself on the bed, the paper still in his hand.

"It's a good sign, ain't it?" queried Brown.

"I reckon! Say, old man, hadn't you better get up?"

The "old man," thus affectionately appealed to, rose, with the assistance of Hamlin's outstretched hand.

"Smoke?"

Brown mechanically took the proffered cigar.

"Light?"

Jack had twisted the letter into a spiral, lit it, and held it for his companion. He continued to hold it until it was consumed, and dropped the fragment — a fiery star — from the open window. He watched it as it fell, and then returned to his friend.

"Old man," he said, placing his hands upon Brown's shoulders, "in ten minutes I'll be on the road, and gone like that spark. We won't see each other agin; but, before I go, take a fool's advice: sell out all you've got, take your wife with you, and quit the country. It ain't no place for you nor her. Tell her she must go; make her go if she won't. Don't whine because you can't be a saint and she ain't an angel. Be a man, and treat her like a woman. Don't be a d—d fool. Good-by."

He tore himself from Brown's grasp and leaped down the stairs like a deer. At the stable-door he collared the half-sleeping hostler, and backed him against the wall. "Saddle my horse in two minutes, or I'll" — The ellipsis was frightfully suggestive.

"The missis said you was to have the buggy," stammered the man.

"D—n the buggy!"

The horse was saddled as fast as the nervous hands of the astounded hostler could manipulate buckle and strap.

"Is anything up, Mr. Hamlin?" said the man, who, like all his class, admired the élan of his fiery patron, and was really concerned in his welfare.

"Stand aside!"

The man fell back. With an oath, a bound, and clatter, Jack was into the road. In another moment, to the man's half-awakened eyes, he was but a moving cloud of dust in the distance, towards which a star just loosed from its brethren was trailing a stream of fire.

But early that morning the dwellers by the Wingdam turnpike, miles away, heard a voice, pure as a sky-lark's, singing afield.

They who were asleep turned over on their rude couches to dream of youth, and love, and olden days. Hard-faced men and anxious gold-seekers, already at work, ceased their labors and leaned upon their picks to listen to a romantic vagabond ambling away against the rosy sunrise.

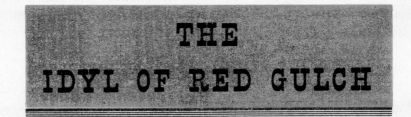

THE
IDYL OF RED GULCH

Sandy was very drunk. He was lying under an azalea bush, in pretty much the same attitude in which he had fallen some hours before. How long he had been lying there he could not tell, and didn't care; how long he should lie there was a matter equally indefinite and unconsidered. A tranquil philosophy, born of his physical condition, suffused and saturated his moral being.

The spectacle of a drunken man, and of this drunken man in particular, was not, I grieve to say, of sufficient novelty in Red Gulch to attract attention. Earlier in the day some local satirist had erected a temporary tombstone at Sandy's head, bearing the inscription, "Effects of McCorkle's whiskey — kills at forty rods," with a hand pointing to McCorkle's saloon. But this, I imagine, was, like most local satire, personal; and was a reflection upon the unfairness of the process rather than a commentary upon the impropriety of the result. With this facetious exception, Sandy had been undisturbed. A wandering mule, released from his pack, had cropped the scant herbage beside him, and sniffed curiously at the prostrate man; a vagabond dog, with that deep sympathy which the species have for drunken men, had licked his dusty boots and curled himself up at his feet, and lay there, blinking one eye in the sunlight, with a simulation of dissipation that was ingenious and dog-like in its implied flattery of the unconscious man beside him.

Meanwhile the shadows of the pine-trees had slowly swung around until they crossed the road, and their trunks barred the

68

open meadow with gigantic parallels of black and yellow. Little puffs of red dust, lifted by the plunging hoofs of passing teams, dispersed in a grimy shower upon the recumbent man. The sun sank lower and lower, and still Sandy stirred not. And then the repose of this philosopher was disturbed, as other philosophers have been, by the intrusion of an unphilosophical sex.

"Miss Mary," as she was known to the little flock that she had just dismissed from the log schoolhouse beyond the pines, was taking her afternoon walk. Observing an unusually fine cluster of blossoms on the azalea-bush opposite, she crossed the road to pluck it, picking her way through the red dust, not without certain fierce little shivers of disgust and some feline circumlocution. And then she came suddenly upon Sandy!

Of course she uttered the little staccato cry of her sex. But when she had paid that tribute to her physical weakness she became overbold and halted for a moment, — at least six feet from this prostrate monster, — with her white skirts gathered in her hand, ready for flight. But neither sound nor motion came from the bush. With one little foot she then overturned the satirical headboard, and muttered "Beasts!" — an epithet which probably, at that moment, conveniently classified in her mind the entire male population of Red Gulch. For Miss Mary, being possessed of certain rigid notions of her own, had not, perhaps, properly appreciated the demonstrative gallantry for which the Californian has been so justly celebrated by his brother Californians, and had, as a newcomer, perhaps fairly earned the reputation of being "stuck up."

As she stood there she noticed, also, that the slant sunbeams were heating Sandy's head to what she judged to be an unhealthy temperature, and that his hat was lying uselessly at his side. To pick it up and to place it over his face was a work requiring some courage, particularly as his eyes were open. Yet she did it and made good her retreat. But she was somewhat concerned, on looking back, to see that the hat was removed, and that Sandy was sitting up and saying something.

The truth was, that in the calm depths of Sandy's mind he was satisfied that the rays of the sun were beneficial and healthful; that from childhood he had objected to lying down in a hat; that no people but condemned fools, past redemption, ever wore hats; and that his right to dispense with them when he pleased was inalienable. This was the statement of his inner consciousness. Unfortunately, its outward expression was vague, being limited to a repetition of the following formula: "Su'shine all ri'! Wasser maär, eh? Wass up, su'shine?"

Miss Mary stopped, and, taking fresh courage from her vantage of distance, asked him if there was anything that he wanted.

"Wass up? Wasser maär?" continued Sandy, in a very high key.

"Get up, you horrid man!" said Miss Mary, now thoroughly incensed; "get up and go home."

Sandy staggered to his feet. He was six feet high, and Miss Mary trembled. He started forward a few paces and then stopped.

"Wass I go home for?" he suddenly asked, with great gravity.

"Go and take a bath," replied Miss Mary, eying his grimy person with great disfavor.

To her infinite dismay, Sandy suddenly pulled off his coat and vest, threw them on the ground, kicked off his boots, and, plunging wildly forward, darted headlong over the hill in the direction of the river.

"Goodness heavens! the man will be drowned!" said Miss Mary; and then, with feminine inconsistency, she ran back to the school-house and locked herself in.

That night, while seated at supper with her hostess, the black-smith's wife, it came to Miss Mary to ask, demurely, if her husband ever got drunk. "Abner," responded Mrs. Stidger reflectively, — "let's see! Abner hasn't been tight since last 'lection." Miss Mary would have liked to ask if he preferred lying in the sun on these occasions, and if a cold bath would have hurt him; but this would have involved an explanation, which she did not then care to give. So she contented herself with opening her gray eyes widely at the red-cheeked Mrs. Stidger, — a fine specimen of Southwestern efflorescence, — and then dismissed the subject altogether. The next day she wrote to her dearest friend in Boston: "I think I find the intoxicated portion of this community the least objectionable. I refer, my dear, to the men, of course. I do not know anything that could make the women tolerable."

In less than a week Miss Mary had forgotten this episode, except that her afternoon walks took thereafter, almost unconsciously, another direction. She noticed, however, that every morning a fresh cluster of azalea blossoms appeared among the flowers on her desk. This was not strange, as her little flock were aware of her fondness for flowers, and invariably kept her desk bright with anemones, syringas, and lupines; but, on questioning them, they one and all professed ignorance of the azaleas. A few days later, Master Johnny Stidger, whose desk was nearest to the window, was suddenly taken with spasms of apparently gratuitous laughter, that threatened the discipline of the school. All that Miss Mary could get from him was, that some one had been "looking in the winder." Irate and indignant, she sallied from her hive to do battle with the intruder. As she turned the corner of the schoolhouse she came plump upon the quondam drunkard, now perfectly sober, and inexpressibly sheepish and guilty-looking.

These facts Miss Mary was not slow to take a feminine advantage of, in her present humor. But it was somewhat confusing to observe, also, that the beast, despite some faint signs of past dissipation, was amiable-looking, — in fact, a kind of blond Samson, whose corn-colored silken beard apparently had never yet known the touch of barber's razor or Delilah's shears. So that the cutting speech which quivered on her ready tongue died upon her lips, and she contented herself with receiving his stammering apology with supercilious eyelids and the gathered skirts of uncontamination. When she reëntered the schoolroom, her eyes fell upon the azaleas with a new sense of revelation; and then she laughed, and the little people all laughed, and they were all unconsciously very happy.

It was a hot day, and not long after this, that two short-legged boys came to grief on the threshold of the school with a pail of water, which they had laboriously brought from the spring, and that Miss Mary compassionately seized the pail and started for the spring herself. At the foot of the hill a shadow crossed her path, and a blue-shirted arm dexterously but gently relieved her of her burden. Miss Mary was both embarrassed and angry. "If you carried more of that for yourself," she said spitefully to the blue arm, without deigning to raise her lashes to its owner, "you'd do better." In the submissive silence that followed she regretted the speech, and thanked him so sweetly at the door that he stumbled. Which caused the children to laugh again, — a laugh in which Miss Mary joined, until the color came faintly into her pale cheek. The next day a barrel was mysteriously placed beside the door, and as mysteriously filled with fresh spring-water every morning.

Nor was this superior young person without other quiet attentions. "Profane Bill," driver of the Slumgullion Stage, widely known in the newspapers for his "gallantry" in invariably offering the box-seat to the fair sex, had excepted Miss Mary from this attention, on the ground that he had a habit of "cussin' on up grades," and gave her half the coach to herself. Jack Hamlin, a gambler, having once silently ridden with her in the same coach, afterward threw a decanter at the head of a confederate for mentioning her name in a bar-room. The over-dressed mother of a pupil whose paternity was doubtful had often lingered near this astute Vestal's temple, never daring to enter its sacred precincts, but content to worship the priestess from afar.

With such unconscious intervals the monotonous procession of blue skies, glittering sunshine, brief twilights, and starlit nights passed over Red Gulch. Miss Mary grew fond of walking in the sedate and proper woods. Perhaps she believed, with Mrs. Stidger, that the balsamic odors of the firs "did her chest good," for certainly her slight cough was less frequent and her step was firmer; perhaps she had learned the unending lesson which the patient pines are never weary of repeating to heedful or listless ears. And so one day she planned a picnic on Buckeye Hill, and took the children with her. Away from the dusty road, the straggling shanties, the yellow ditches, the clamor of restless engines, the cheap finery of shop-windows, the deeper glitter of paint and colored glass, and the thin veneering which barbarism takes upon itself in such localities, what infinite relief was theirs! The last heap of ragged rock and clay passed, the last unsightly chasm crossed, — how the waiting woods opened their long files to receive them! How the children — perhaps because they had not yet grown quite away from the breast of the bounteous Mother — threw themselves face downward on her brown bosom with uncouth caresses, filling the air with their laughter; and how Miss Mary herself — felinely fastidious and intrenched as she was in the purity of spotless skirts, collar, and cuffs — forgot all, and ran like a crested quail at the head of her brood, until, romping, laughing, and panting, with a loosened braid of brown hair, a hat hanging by a knotted ribbon from her throat, she came suddenly and violently, in the heart of the forest, upon the luckless Sandy!

The explanations, apologies, and not overwise conversation that ensued need not be indicated here. It would seem, however, that Miss Mary had already established some acquaintance with this ex-drunkard. Enough that he was soon accepted as one of the party; that the children, with that quick intelligence which Providence gives the helpless, recognized a friend, and played with his blond beard and long silken mustache, and took other liberties, — as the helpless are apt to do. And when he had built a fire against a tree, and had shown them other mysteries of woodcraft, their admiration knew no bounds. At the close of two such foolish, idle, happy hours he found himself lying at the feet of the schoolmistress, gazing dreamily in her face as she sat upon the sloping hillside weaving wreaths of laurel and syringa, in very much the same attitude as he had lain when first they met. Nor was the similitude greatly forced. The weakness of an easy, sensuous nature, that had found a dreamy exaltation in liquor, it is to be feared was now finding an equal intoxication in love.

I think that Sandy was dimly conscious of this himself. I know that he longed to be doing something, — slaying a grizzly, scalping a savage, or sacrificing himself in some way for the sake of this sallow-faced, gray-eyed schoolmistress. As I should like to present him in an heroic attitude, I stay my hand with great difficulty at this moment, being only withheld from introducing such an episode by a strong conviction that it does not usually occur at such times. And I trust that my fairest reader, who remembers that, in a real crisis, it is always some uninteresting stranger or unromantic policeman, and not Adolphus, who rescues, will forgive the omission.

So they sat there undisturbed, — the woodpeckers chattering overhead and the voices of the children coming pleasantly from the hollow below. What they said matters little. What they thought — which might have been interesting — did not transpire. The woodpeckers only learned how Miss Mary was an orphan; how she left her uncle's house to come to California for the sake of health and independence; how Sandy was an orphan too; how he came to California for excitement; how he had lived a wild life, and how he was trying to reform; and other details, which, from a woodpecker's view-point, undoubtedly must have seemed stupid and a waste of time. But even in such trifles was the afternoon spent; and when the children were again gathered, and Sandy, with a delicacy which the schoolmistress well understood, took leave of them quietly at the outskirts of the settlement, it had seemed the shortest day of her weary life.

As the long, dry summer withered to its roots, the school term of Red Gulch — to use a local euphuism — "dried up" also. In another day Miss Mary would be free, and for a season, at least, Red Gulch would know her no more. She was seated alone in the schoolhouse, her cheek resting on her hand, her eyes half closed in one of those day-dreams in which Miss Mary, I fear, to the danger of

school discipline, was lately in the habit of indulging. Her lap was full of mosses, ferns, and other woodland memories. She was so preoccupied with these and her own thoughts that a gentle tapping at the door passed unheard, or translated itself into the remembrance of far-off woodpeckers. When at last it asserted itself more distinctly, she started up with a flushed cheek and opened the door. On the threshold stood a woman, the self-assertion and audacity of whose dress were in singular contrast to her timid, irresolute bearing.

Miss Mary recognized at a glance the dubious mother of her anonymous pupil. Perhaps she was disappointed, perhaps she was only fastidious, but as she coldly invited her to enter, she half unconsciously settled her white cuffs and collar, and gathered closer her own chaste skirts. It was, perhaps, for this reason that the embarrassed stranger, after a moment's hesitation, left her gorgeous parasol open and sticking in the dust beside the door, and then sat down at the farther end of a long bench. Her voice was husky as she began, —

"I heerd tell that you were goin' down to the Bay tomorrow, and I couldn't let you go until I came to thank you for your kindness to my Tommy."

Tommy, Miss Mary said, was a good boy, and deserved more than the poor attention she could give him.

"Thank you, miss; thank ye!" cried the stranger, brightening even through the color which Red Gulch knew facetiously as her "war paint," and striving, in her embarrassment, to drag the long bench nearer the schoolmistress. "I thank you, miss, for that; and if I am his mother, there ain't a sweeter, dearer, better boy lives than him. And if I ain't much as says it, thar ain't a sweeter, dearer, angeler teacher lives than he's got."

Miss Mary, sitting primly behind her desk, with a ruler over her shoulder, opened her gray eyes widely at this, but said nothing.

"It ain't for you to be complimented by the like of me, I know," she went on hurriedly. "It ain't for me to be comin' here, in broad day, to do it, either; but I come to ask a favor, — not for me, miss, — not for me, but for the darling boy."

Encouraged by a look in the young schoolmistress's eye, and

putting her lilac-gloved hands together, the fingers downward, between her knees, she went on, in a low voice: —

"You see, miss, there's no one the boy has any claim on but me, and I ain't the proper person to bring him up. I thought some, last year, of sending him away to Frisco to school, but when they talked of bringing a schoolma'am here, I waited till I saw you, and then I knew it was all right, and I could keep my boy a little longer. And, oh! miss, he loves you so much; and if you could hear him talk about you in his pretty way, and if he could ask you what I ask you now, you couldn't refuse him.

"It is natural," she went on rapidly, in a voice that trembled strangely between pride and humility, — "it's natural that he should take to you, miss, for his father, when I first knew him, was a gentleman, — and the boy must forget me, sooner or later, — and so I ain't a-goin' to cry about that. For I come to ask you to take my Tommy, — God bless him for the bestest, sweetest boy that lives, — to — to — take him with you."

She had risen and caught the young girl's hand in her own, and had fallen on her knees beside her.

"I've money plenty, and it's all yours and his. Put him in some good school, where you can go and see him, and help him to — to — to forget his mother. Do with him what you like. The worst you can do will be kindness to what he will learn with me. Only take him out of this wicked life, this cruel place, this home of shame and sorrow. You will! I know you will, — won't you? You will, — you must not, you cannot say no! You will make him as pure, as gentle as yourself; and when he has grown up, you will tell him his father's name, — the name that hasn't passed my lips for years, — the name of Alexander Morton, whom they call here Sandy! Miss Mary! — do not take your hand away! Miss Mary, speak to me! You will take my boy? Do not put your face from me. I know it ought not to look on such as me. Miss Mary! — my God, be merciful! — she is leaving me!"

Miss Mary had risen, and, in the gathering twilight, had felt her way to the open window. She stood there, leaning against the casement, her eyes fixed on the last rosy tints that were fading from the western sky. There was still some of its light on her pure young forehead, on her white collar, on her clasped white hands, but all fading slowly away. The suppliant had dragged herself, still on her knees, beside her.

"I know it takes time to consider. I will wait here all night; but I cannot go until you speak. Do not deny me now. You will! — I see it in your sweet face, — such a face as I have seen in my dreams. I see it in your eyes, Miss Mary! — you will take my boy!"

The last red beam crept higher, suffused Miss Mary's eyes with something of its glory, flickered, and faded, and went out. The sun had set on Red Gulch. In the twilight and silence Miss Mary's voice sounded pleasantly. "I will take the boy. Send him to me to-night."

The happy mother raised the hem of Miss Mary's skirts to her lips. She would have buried her hot face in its virgin folds, but she dared not. She rose to her feet. "Does — this man — know of your intention?" asked Miss Mary suddenly.

"No, nor cares. He has never even seen the child to know it."

"Go to him at once — to-night — now! Tell him what you have done. Tell him I have taken his child, and tell him — he must never see — see — the child again. Wherever it may be, he must not come; wherever I may take it, he must not follow! There, go now, please, — I'm weary, and — have much yet to do!"

They walked together to the door. On the threshold the woman turned. "Good-night!" She would have fallen at Miss Mary's feet. But at the same moment the young girl reached out her arms, caught the sinful woman to her own pure breast for one brief moment, and then closed and locked the door.

It was with a sudden sense of great responsibility that Profane Bill took the reins of the Slumgullion stage the next morning, for the schoolmistress was one of his passengers. As he entered the highroad, in obedience to a pleasant voice from the "inside," he suddenly reined up his horses and respectfully waited, as Tommy hopped out at the command of Miss Mary.

"Not that bush, Tommy, — the next."

Tommy whipped out his new pocket-knife, and cutting a branch from a tall azalea-bush, returned with it to Miss Mary.

"All right now?" "All right!"

And the stage-door closed on the Idyl of Red Gulch.

THE ILIAD OF SANDY BAR

BEFORE NINE O'CLOCK it was pretty well known all along the river that the two parties of the "Amity Claim" had quarreled and separated at daybreak. At that time the attention of their nearest neighbor had been attracted by the sounds of altercations and two consecutive pistol-shots. Running out, he had seen dimly in the gray mist that rose from the river the tall form of Scott, one of the partners, descending the hill towards the cañon; a moment later, York, the other partner, had appeared from the cabin, and walked in an opposite direction towards the river, passing within a few feet of the curious watcher. Later it was discovered that a serious Chinaman, cutting wood before the cabin, had witnessed part of the quarrel. But John was stolid, indifferent, and reticent. "Me choppee wood, me no fightee," was his serene response to all anxious queries. "But what did they *say*, John?" John did not *sabe*. Colonel Starbottle deftly ran over the various popular epithets which a generous public sentiment might accept as reasonable provocation for an assault. But John did not recognize them. "And this yer's the cattle," said the Colonel, with some severity, "that some thinks oughter be allowed to testify agin a White Man! Git — you heathen!"

Still the quarrel remained inexplicable. That two men, whose amiability and grave tact had earned for them the title of "The Peacemakers," in a community not greatly given to the passive virtues, — that these men, singularly devoted to each other, should

80

suddenly and violently quarrel, might well excite the curiosity of the camp. A few of the more inquisitive visited the late scene of conflict, now deserted by its former occupants. There was no trace of disorder or confusion in the neat cabin. The rude table was arranged as if for breakfast; the pan of yellow biscuit still sat upon that hearth whose dead embers might have typified the evil passions that had raged there but an hour before. But Colonel Starbottle's eye, albeit somewhat bloodshot and rheumy, was more intent on practical details. On examination, a bullet-hole was found in the doorpost, and another nearly opposite in the casing of the window. The Colonel called attention to the fact that the one "agreed with" the bore of Scott's revolver, and the other with that of York's derringer. "They must hev stood about yer," said the Colonel, taking position; "not more'n three feet apart, and — missed!" There was a fine touch of pathos in the falling inflection of the Colonel's voice, which was not without effect. A delicate perception of wasted opportunity thrilled his auditors.

But the Bar was destined to experience a greater disappointment. The two antagonists had not met since the quarrel, and it was vaguely rumored that, on the occasion of a second meeting, each had determined to kill the other "on sight." There was, consequently, some excitement — and, it is to be feared, no little gratification — when, at ten o'clock, York stepped from the Magnolia Saloon into the one long straggling street of the camp, at the same moment that Scott left the blacksmith's shop at the forks of the road. It was evident, at a glance, that a meeting could only be avoided by the actual retreat of one or the other.

In an instant the doors and windows of the adjacent saloons were filled with faces. Heads unaccountably appeared above the river banks and from behind boulders. An empty wagon at the crossroad was suddenly crowded with people, who seemed to have sprung from the earth. There was much running and confusion on the hillside. On the mountain-road, Mr. Jack Hamlin had reined up his horse and was standing upright on the seat of his buggy. And the two objects of this absorbing attention approached each other.

"York's got the sun," "Scott'll line him on that tree," "He's waiting to draw his fire," came from the cart; and then it was silent. But above this human breathlessness the river rushed and sang, and the wind rustled the tree-tops with an indifference that seemed obtrusive. Colonel Starbottle felt it, and in a moment of sublime preoccupation, without looking around, waved his cane behind him warningly to all Nature, and said, "Shu!"

The men were now within a few feet of each other. A hen ran across the road before one of them. A feathery seed vessel, wafted from a wayside tree, fell at the feet of the other. And, unheeding this irony of Nature, the two opponents came nearer, erect and rigid, looked in each other's eyes, and — passed!

Colonel Starbottle had to be lifted from the cart. "This yer camp is played out," he said gloomily, as he affected to be supported into the Magnolia. With what further expression he might have indicated his feelings it was impossible to say, for at that moment Scott joined the group. "Did you speak to me?" he asked of the Colonel, dropping his hand, as if with accidental familiarity, on that gentleman's shoulder. The Colonel, recognizing some occult quality in the touch, and some unknown quantity in the glance of his questioner, contented himself by replying, "No, sir," with dignity. A few rods away, York's conduct was as characteristic and peculiar. "You had a mighty fine chance; why didn't you plump him?" said Jack Hamlin, as York drew near the buggy. "Because I hate him," was the reply, heard only by Jack. Contrary to popular belief, this reply was not hissed between the lips of the speaker, but was said in an ordinary tone. But Jack Hamlin, who was an observer of mankind, noticed that the speaker's hands were cold and his lips dry, as he helped him into the buggy, and accepted the seeming paradox with a smile.

When Sandy Bar became convinced that the quarrel between York and Scott could not be settled after the usual local methods, it gave no further concern thereto. But presently it was rumored that the "Amity Claim" was in litigation, and that its possession would be expensively disputed by each of the partners. As it was well known that the claim in question was "worked out" and worthless, and that the partners whom it had already enriched had talked of abandoning it but a day or two before the quarrel, this proceeding could only be accounted for as gratuitous spite. Later, two San Francisco lawyers made their appearance in this guileless Arcadia, and were eventually taken into the saloons, and — what was pretty much the same thing — the confidence of the inhabitants. The results of this unhallowed intimacy were many subpœnas; and, indeed, when the "Amity Claim" came to trial, all of Sandy Bar that was not in compulsory attendance at the county seat came there from curiosity. The gulches and ditches for miles around were deserted. I do not propose to describe that already famous trial. Enough that, in the language of the plaintiff's counsel, "it was one of no ordinary significance, involving the inherent rights of that untiring industry which had developed the Pactolian resources of this golden land;" and, in the homelier phrase of Colonel Starbottle, "a fuss that gentlemen might hev settled in ten minutes over a social glass, ef they meant business; or in ten seconds with a revolver, ef they meant fun." Scott got a verdict, from which York instantly appealed. It was said that he had sworn to spend his last dollar in the struggle.

In this way Sandy Bar began to accept the enmity of the former partners as a lifelong feud, and the fact that they had ever been friends was forgotten. The few who expected to learn from the trial the origin of the quarrel were disappointed. Among the various conjectures, that which ascribed some occult feminine influence as the cause was naturally popular in a camp given to dubious compliment of the sex. "My word for it, gentlemen," said Colonel Starbottle, who had been known in Sacramento as a Gentleman of the Old School, "there's some lovely creature at the bottom of this." The gallant Colonel then proceeded to illustrate his theory by divers sprightly stories, such as Gentlemen of the Old School are in the habit of repeating, but which, from deference to the prejudices of gentlemen of a more recent school, I refrain from transcribing here. But it would appear that even the Colonel's theory was fallacious. The only woman who personally might have exercised any influence over the partners was the pretty daughter of "old man Folinsbee," of Poverty Flat, at whose hospitable house — which exhibited some comforts and refinements rare in that crude civilization — both York and Scott were frequent visitors. Yet into this charming retreat York strode one evening a month after the quarrel, and, beholding Scott sitting there, turned to the fair hostess with the abrupt query, "Do you love this man?" The young woman thus addressed returned that answer — at once spirited and evasive — which would occur to most of my fair readers in such an emergency. Without another word, York left the house. "Miss Jo" heaved the least possible sigh as the door closed on York's curls and square shoulders, and then, like a good girl, turned to her insulted guest. "But would you believe it, dear?" she afterwards related to an intimate friend, "the other creature, after glowering at me for a moment, got upon its hind legs, took its hat, and left too; and that's the last I've seen of either."

The same hard disregard of all other interests or feelings in the gratification of their blind rancor characterized all their actions. When York purchased the land below Scott's new claim, and obliged the latter, at a great expense, to make a long détour to carry a "tail-race" around it, Scott retaliated by building a dam that overflowed York's claim on the river. It was Scott, who in conjunction with Colonel Starbottle, first organized that active opposition to the Chinamen which resulted in the driving off of York's Mongolian laborers; it was York who built the wagon-road and established the express which rendered Scott's mules and pack-trains obsolete; it was Scott who called into life the Vigilance Committee which expatriated York's friend, Jack Hamlin; it was York who created the "Sandy Bar Herald," which characterized the act as "a lawless outrage" and Scott as a "Border Ruffian;" it was Scott, at the head of twenty masked men, who, one moonlight night, threw the offending "forms" into the yellow river, and scattered the types in the dusty road. These proceedings were received in the distant and more civilized outlying towns as vague indications of progress and vitality. I have before me a copy of the "Poverty Flat Pioneer" for the week ending August 12, 1856, in which the editor, under the head of "County Improvements," says: "The new Presbyterian Church on C Street, at Sandy Bar, is completed. It stands upon the lot formerly occupied by the Magnolia Saloon, which was so mysteriously burnt last month. The temple, which now rises like a Phœnix from the ashes of the Magnolia, is virtually the free gift of H. J. York, Esq., of Sandy Bar, who purchased the lot and donated the lumber. Other buildings are going up in the vicinity, but the most noticeable is the 'Sunny South Saloon,' erected by Captain Mat. Scott, nearly opposite the church. Captain Scott has spared no expense in the furnishing of this saloon, which promises to be one of the most agreeable places of resort in old Tuolumne. He has recently imported two new first-class billiard-tables with cork cushions. Our old friend, 'Mountain Jimmy,' will dispense liquors at the bar. We refer our readers to the advertisement in another column. Visitors to Sandy Bar cannot do better than give 'Jimmy' a call." Among the local items occurred the following: "H. J. York, Esq., of Sandy Bar, has offered a reward of $100 for the detection of the parties who hauled away the steps of the new Presbyterian Church, C Street, Sandy Bar, during divine service on Sabbath evening last. Captain Scott adds another hundred for the capture of the miscreants who broke the magnificent plate-glass windows of the new saloon on the following evening. There is some talk of reorganizing the old Vigilance Committee at Sandy Bar."

When, for many months of cloudless weather, the hard, unwinking sun of Sandy Bar had regularly gone down on the unpacified wrath of these men, there was some talk of mediation. In particular, the pastor of the church to which I have just referred — a sincere, fearless, but perhaps not fully enlightened man — seized gladly upon the occasion of York's liberality to attempt to reunite the former partners. He preached an earnest sermon on the abstract sinfulness of discord and rancor. But the excellent sermons of the Rev. Mr. Daws were directed to an ideal congregation that did not exist at Sandy Bar, — a congregation of beings of unmixed vices and virtues, of single impulses, and perfectly logical motives, of preternatural simplicity, of childlike faith, and grown-up responsibilities. As unfortunately the people who actually attended Mr. Daws's church were mainly very human, somewhat artful, more self-excusing than self-accusing, rather good-natured, and decidedly weak, they quietly shed that portion of the sermon which referred to themselves, and accepting York and Scott — who were both in defiant attendance — as curious examples of those ideal beings above referred to, felt a certain satisfaction — which, I fear, was not altogether Christian-like — in their "raking-down." If Mr. Daws expected York and Scott to shake hands after the sermon, he was disappointed. But he did not relax his purpose. With that quiet fearlessness and determination which had won for him the respect of men who were too apt to regard piety as synonymous with effeminacy, he attacked Scott in his own house. What he said has not been recorded, but it is to be feared that it was part of his sermon. When he had concluded, Scott looked at him, not unkindly, over the glasses of his bar, and said, less irreverently than the words might convey, "Young man, I rather like your style; but when you know York and me as well as you do God Almighty, it'll be time to talk."

And so the feud progressed; and so, as in more illustrious examples, the private and personal enmity of two representative men led gradually to the evolution of some crude, half-expressed principle or belief. It was not long before it was made evident that those beliefs were identical with certain broad principles laid down by the founders of the American Constitution, as expounded by the statesmanlike A., or were the fatal quicksands on which the ship of state might be wrecked, warningly pointed out by the eloquent

B. The practical result of all which was the nomination of York and Scott to represent the opposite factions of Sandy Bar in legislative councils.

For some weeks past the voters of Sandy Bar and the adjacent camps had been called upon, in large type, to "RALLY!" In vain the great pines at the cross-roads — whose trunks were compelled to bear this and other legends — moaned and protested from their windy watch-towers. But one day, with fife and drum and flaming transparency, a procession filed into the triangular grove at the head of the gulch. The meeting was called to order by Colonel Starbottle, who, having once enjoyed legislative functions, and being vaguely known as "war-horse," was considered to be a valuable partisan of York. He concluded an appeal for his friend with an enunciation of principles, interspersed with one or two anecdotes so gratuitously coarse that the very pines might have been moved to pelt him with their cast-off cones as he stood there. But he created a laugh, on which his candidate rode into popular notice; and when York rose to speak, he was greeted with cheers. But, to the general astonishment, the new speaker at once launched into bitter denunciation of his rival. He not only dwelt upon Scott's deeds and example as known to Sandy Bar, but spoke of facts connected with his previous career hitherto unknown to his auditors. To great precision of epithet and directness of statement, the speaker added the fascination of revelation and exposure. The crowd cheered, yelled, and were delighted; but when this astounding philippic was concluded, there was a unanimous call for "Scott!" Colonel Starbottle would have resisted this manifest impropriety, but in vain. Partly from a crude sense of justice, partly from a meaner craving for excitement, the assemblage was inflexible; and Scott was dragged, pushed, and pulled upon the platform. As his frowsy head and unkempt beard appeared above the railing, it was evident that he was drunk. But it was also evident, before he opened his lips, that the orator of Sandy Bar — the one man who could touch their vagabond sympathies (perhaps because he was not above appealing to them) — stood before them. A consciousness of this power lent a certain dignity to his figure, and I am not sure but that his very physical condition impressed them as a kind

of regal unbending and large condescension. Howbeit, when this
unexpected Hector rose from this ditch, York's myrmidons trembled. "There's naught, gentlemen," said Scott, leaning forward on
the railing, — "there's naught as that man hez said as isn't true.
I *was* run outer Cairo; I *did* belong to the Regulators; I *did* desert
from the army; I *did* leave a wife in Kansas. But thar's one thing he
didn't charge me with, and maybe he's forgotten. For three years,
gentlemen, I was that man's pardner!" Whether he intended to
say more, I cannot tell; a burst of applause artistically rounded and
enforced the climax, and virtually elected the speaker. That fall
he went to Sacramento, York went abroad, and for the first time in
many years distance and a new atmosphere isolated the old antagonists.

With little of change in the green wood, gray rock, and yellow
river, but with much shifting of human landmarks and new faces
in its habitations, three years passed over Sandy Bar. The two men,
once so identified with its character, seemed to have been quite
forgotten. "You will never return to Sandy Bar," said Miss Folinsbee, the "Lily of Poverty Flat," on meeting York in Paris, "for
Sandy Bar is no more. They call it Riverside now; and the new
town is built higher up on the river bank. By the bye, 'Jo' says
that Scott has won his suit about the 'Amity Claim,' and that he
lives in the old cabin, and is drunk half his time. Oh, I beg your
pardon," added the lively lady, as a flush crossed York's sallow
cheek; "but, bless me, I really thought that old grudge was made
up. I'm sure it ought to be."

It was three months after this conversation, and a pleasant summer evening, that the Poverty Flat coach drew up before the veranda of the Union Hotel at Sandy Bar. Among its passengers was
one, apparently a stranger, in the local distinction of well-fitting
clothes and closely shaven face, who demanded a private room and
retired early to rest. But before sunrise next morning he arose,
and, drawing some clothes from his carpet-bag, proceeded to array
himself in a pair of white duck trousers, a white duck overshirt,
and straw hat. When his toilet was completed, he tied a red bandana handkerchief in a loop and threw it loosely over his shoulders.
The transformation was complete. As he crept softly down the stairs

and stepped into the road, no one would have detected in him the elegant stranger of the previous night, and but few have recognized the face and figure of Henry York, of Sandy Bar.

In the uncertain light of that early hour, and in the change that had come over the settlement, he had to pause for a moment to recall where he stood. The Sandy Bar of his recollection lay below him, nearer the river; the buildings around him were of later date and newer fashion. As he strode towards the river, he noticed here a schoolhouse and there a church. A little farther on, the "Sunny South" came in view, transformed into a restaurant, its gilding faded and its paint rubbed off. He now knew where he was; and running briskly down a declivity, crossed a ditch, and stood upon the lower boundary of the "Amity Claim."

The gray mist was rising slowly from the river, clinging to the tree-tops and drifting up the mountain-side until it was caught among these rocky altars, and held a sacrifice to the ascending sun. At his feet the earth, cruelly gashed and scarred by his forgotten engines, had, since the old days, put on a show of greenness here and there, and now smiled forgivingly up at him, as if things were not so bad after all. A few birds were bathing in the ditch with a pleasant suggestion of its being a new and special provision of Nature, and a hare ran into an inverted sluice-box as he approached, as if it were put there for that purpose.

He had not yet dared to look in a certain direction. But the sun was now high enough to paint the little eminence on which the cabin stood. In spite of his self-control, his heart beat faster as he raised his eyes towards it. Its window and door were closed, no smoke came from its adobe chimney, but it was else unchanged. When within a few yards of it, he picked up a broken shovel, and shouldering it with a smile, he strode towards the door and knocked. There was no sound from within. The smile died upon his lips as he nervously pushed the door open.

A figure started up angrily and came towards him, — a figure whose bloodshot eyes suddenly fixed into a vacant stare, whose arms were at first outstretched and then thrown up in warning gesticulation, — a figure that suddenly gasped, choked, and then fell forward in a fit.

But before he touched the ground, York had him out into the open air and sunshine. In the struggle, both fell and rolled over on the ground. But the next moment York was sitting up, holding the convulsed frame of his former partner on his knee, and wiping the foam from his inarticulate lips. Gradually the tremor became less frequent and then ceased, and the strong man lay unconscious in his arms.

For some moments York held him quietly thus, looking in his face. Afar, the stroke of a woodman's axe — a mere phantom of sound — was all that broke the stillness. High up the mountain, a wheeling hawk hung breathlessly above them. And then came voices, and two men joined them.

"A fight?" No, a fit; and would they help him bring the sick man to the hotel?

And there for a week the stricken partner lay, unconscious of aught but the visions wrought by disease and fear. On the eighth day at sunrise he rallied, and opening his eyes, looked upon York and pressed his hand; and then he spoke: —

"And it's you. I thought it was only whiskey."

York replied by only taking both of his hands, boyishly working them backwards and forwards, as his elbow rested on the bed, with a pleasant smile.

"And you've been abroad. How did you like Paris?"

"So, so! How did *you* like Sacramento?"

"Bully!"

And that was all they could think to say. Presently Scott opened his eyes again.

"I'm mighty weak."

"You'll get better soon."

"Not much."

A long silence followed, in which they could hear the sounds of wood-chopping, and that Sandy Bar was already astir for the coming day. Then Scott slowly and with difficulty turned his face to York and said, —

"I might hev killed you once."

"I wish you had."

They pressed each other's hands again, but Scott's grasp was

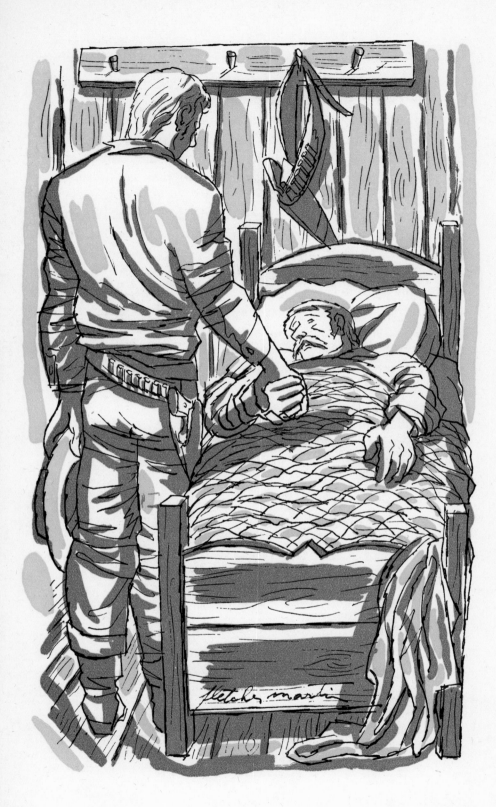

evidently failing. He seemed to summon his energies for a special effort.

"Old man!"

"Old chap."

"Closer!"

York bent his head towards the slowly fading face.

"Do ye mind that morning?"

"Yes."

A gleam of fun slid into the corner of Scott's blue eye as he whispered, —

"Old man, thar *was* too much saleratus in that bread!"

It is said that these were his last words. For when the sun, which had so often gone down upon the idle wrath of these foolish men, looked again upon them reunited, it saw the hand of Scott fall cold and irresponsive from the yearning clasp of his former partner, and it knew that the feud of Sandy Bar was at an end.

THE POET
OF SIERRA FLAT

As the enterprising editor of the "Sierra Flat Record" stood at his case setting type for his next week's paper, he could not help hearing the woodpeckers who were busy on the roof above his head. It occurred to him that possibly the birds had not yet learned to recognize in the rude structure any improvement on Nature, and this idea pleased him so much that he incorporated it in the editorial article which he was then doubly composing. For the editor was also printer of the "Record;" and although that remarkable journal was reputed to exert a power felt through all Calaveras and a great part of Tuolumne County, strict economy was one of the conditions of its beneficent existence.

Thus preoccupied, he was startled by the sudden irruption of a small roll of manuscript, which was thrown through the open door and fell at his feet. He walked quickly to the threshold and looked down the tangled trail which led to the highroad. But there was nothing to suggest the presence of his mysterious contributor. A hare limped slowly away, a green-and-gold lizard paused upon a pine stump, the woodpeckers ceased their work. So complete had been his sylvan seclusion, that he found it difficult to connect any human agency with the act; rather the hare seemed to have an inexpressibly guilty look, the woodpeckers to maintain a significant silence, and the lizard to be conscience-stricken into stone.

An examination of the manuscript, however, corrected this injustice to defenseless Nature. It was evidently of human origin, —

being verse, and of exceeding bad quality. The editor laid it aside. As he did so he thought he saw a face at the window. Sallying out in some indignation, he penetrated the surrounding thicket in every direction, but his search was as fruitless as before. The poet, if it were he, was gone.

A few days after this the editorial seclusion was invaded by voices of alternate expostulation and entreaty. Stepping to the door, the editor was amazed at beholding Mr. Morgan McCorkle, a well-known citizen of Angel's and a subscriber to the "Record," in the act of urging, partly by force and partly by argument, an awkward young man toward the building. When he had finally effected his object, and, as it were, safely landed his prize in a chair, Mr. McCorkle took off his hat, carefully wiped the narrow isthmus of forehead which divided his black brows from his stubby hair, and, with an explanatory wave of his hand toward his reluctant companion, said, "A borned poet, and the cussedest fool you ever seed!"

Accepting the editor's smile as a recognition of the introduction, Mr. McCorkle panted and went on: "Didn't want to come! 'Mister Editor don't want to see me, Morg,' sez he. 'Milt,' sez I, 'he do; a borned poet like you and a gifted genius like he oughter come together sociable!' And I fetched him. Ah, will yer?" The born poet had, after exhibiting signs of great distress, started to run. But Mr. McCorkle was down upon him instantly, seizing him by his long linen coat, and settled him back in his chair. "'Tain't no use stampeding. Yer ye are and yer ye stays. For yer a borned poet, — ef ye are as shy as a jackass rabbit. Look at 'im now!"

He certainly was not an attractive picture. There was hardly a notable feature in his weak face, except his eyes, which were moist and shy, and not unlike the animal to which Mr. McCorkle had compared him. It was the face that the editor had seen at the window.

"Knowed him for fower year, — since he war a boy," continued Mr. McCorkle in a loud whisper. "Allers the same, bless you! Can jerk a rhyme as easy as turnin' jack. Never had any eddication; lived out in Missooray all his life. But he's chock full o' poetry. On'y this mornin' sez I to him, — he camps along o' me, — 'Milt!' sez I, 'are breakfast ready?' and he up and answers back quite peart and chipper, 'The breakfast it is ready, and the birds is singing free, and it's risin' in the dawnin' light is happiness to me!' When a man," said Mr. McCorkle, dropping his voice with deep solemnity, "gets off things like them, without any call to do it, and handlin' flapjacks over a cookstove at the same time, — that man's a borned poet."

There was an awkward pause. Mr. McCorkle beamed patronizingly on his protégé. The born poet looked as if he were meditating another flight, — not a metaphorical one. The editor asked if he could do anything for them.

"In course you can," responded Mr. McCorkle, "that's jest it. Milt, where's that poetry?"

The editor's countenance fell as the poet produced from his pocket a roll of manuscript. He, however, took it mechanically and glanced over it. It was evidently a duplicate of the former mysterious contribution.

The editor then spoke briefly but earnestly. I regret that I cannot recall his exact words, but it appeared that never before, in the history of the "Record," had the pressure been so great upon its columns. Matters of paramount importance, deeply affecting the material progress of Sierra, questions touching the absolute integrity of Calaveras and Tuolumne as social communities, were even now waiting expression. Weeks, nay, months, must elapse before that pressure would be removed, and the "Record" could grapple with any but the sternest of topics. Again, the editor had noticed with pain the absolute decline of poetry in the foothills of the Sierras. Even the works of Byron and Moore attracted no attention in Dutch Flat, and a prejudice seemed to exist against Tennyson in Grass Valley. But the editor was not without hope for the future. In the course of four or five years, when the country was settled —

"What would be the cost to print this yer?" interrupted Mr. McCorkle quietly.

"About fifty dollars, as an advertisement," responded the editor with cheerful alacrity.

Mr. McCorkle placed the sum in the editor's hand. "Yer see thet's what I sez to Milt. 'Milt,' sez I, 'pay as you go, for you are a borned poet. Hevin' no call to write, but doin' it free and spontaneous like, in course you pays. Thet's why Mr. Editor never printed your poetry.'"

"What name shall I put to it?" asked the editor.

"Milton."

It was the first word that the born poet had spoken during the interview, and his voice was so very sweet and musical that the editor looked at him curiously, and wondered if he had a sister.

"Milton! is that all?"

"Thet's his furst name," exclaimed Mr. McCorkle.

The editor here suggested that as there had been another poet of that name —

"Milt might be took for him! Thet's bad," reflected Mr. McCorkle with simple gravity. "Well, put down his full name, — Milton Chubbuck."

The editor made a note of the fact. "I'll set it up now," he said. This was also a hint that the interview was ended. The poet and patron, arm in arm, drew towards the door. "In next week's paper," said the editor smilingly, in answer to the childlike look of inquiry in the eyes of the poet, and in another moment they were gone.

The editor was as good as his word. He straightway betook himself to his case, and, unrolling the manuscript, began his task. The woodpeckers on the roof recommenced theirs, and in a few moments the former sylvan seclusion was restored. There was no sound in the barren, barn-like room but the birds above, and below the click of the composing rule as the editor marshaled the types into lines in his stick, and arrayed them in solid column on the galley. Whatever might have been his opinion of the copy before him, there was no indication of it in his face, which wore the stolid indifference of his craft. Perhaps this was unfortunate, for as the day wore on and the level rays of the sun began to pierce the adjacent thicket, they sought out and discovered an anxious ambush figure drawn up beside the editor's window, — a figure that had sat there motionless for hours. Within, the editor worked on as steadily and impassively as Fate. And without, the born poet of Sierra Flat sat and watched him as waiting its decree.

The effect of the poem on Sierra Flat was remarkable and unprecedented. The absolute vileness of its doggerel, the gratuitous imbecility of its thought, and above all the crowning audacity of the fact that it was the work of a citizen and published in the county paper, brought it instantly into popularity. For many months Calaveras had languished for a sensation; since the last Vigilance Committee nothing had transpired to dispel the listless ennui begotten of stagnant business and growing civilization. In

more prosperous moments the office of the "Record" would have been simply gutted and the editor deported; at present the paper was in such demand that the edition was speedily exhausted. In brief, the poem of Mr. Milton Chubbuck came like a special providence to Sierra Flat. It was read by camp-fires, in lonely cabins, in flaring bar-rooms and noisy saloons, and declaimed from the boxes of stage-coaches. It was sung in Poker Flat with the addition of a local chorus, and danced as an unhallowed rhythmic dance by the Pyrrhic phalanx of One Horse Gulch, known as "The Festive Stags of Calaveras." Some unhappy ambiguities of expression gave rise to many new readings, notes, and commentaries, which, I regret to state, were more often marked by ingenuity than delicacy of thought or expression.

Never before did poet acquire such sudden local reputation.

From the seclusion of McCorkle's cabin and the obscurity of culinary labors he was haled forth into the glowing sunshine of Fame.
The name of Chubbuck was written in letters of chalk on unpainted
walls and carved with a pick on the sides of tunnels. A drink known
variously as "The Chubbuck Tranquilizer" or "The Chubbuck
Exalter" was dispensed at the bars. For some weeks a rude design
for a Chubbuck statue, made up of illustrations from circus and
melodeon posters, representing the genius of Calaveras in brief
skirts on a flying steed in the act of crowning the poet Chubbuck,
was visible at Keeler's Ferry. The poet himself was overborne with
invitations to drink and extravagant congratulations. The meeting
between Colonel Starbottle of Siskiyou and Chubbuck, as previously arranged by our "Boston," late of Roaring Camp, is said to
have been indescribably affecting. The Colonel embraced him unsteadily. "I could not return to my constituents at Siskiyou, sir,
if this hand, which has grasped that of the gifted Prentice and the
lamented Poe, should not have been honored by the touch of the
godlike Chubbuck. Gentlemen, American literature is looking up.
Thank you! I will take sugar in mine." It was "Boston" who indited
letters of congratulations from H. W. Longfellow, Tennyson, and
Browning to Mr. Chubbuck, deposited them in the Sierra Flat post-
office, and obligingly consented to dictate the replies.

The simple faith and unaffected delight with which these mani-
festations were received by the poet and his patron might have
touched the hearts of these grim masters of irony, but for the sudden and equal development in both of the vanity of weak natures.
Mr. McCorkle basked in the popularity of his protégé, and became
alternately supercilious or patronizing towards the dwellers of
Sierra Flat; while the poet, with hair carefully oiled and curled,
and bedecked with cheap jewelry and flaunting neck-handkerchief,
paraded himself before the single hotel. As may be imagined, this
new disclosure of weakness afforded intense satisfaction to Sierra
Flat, gave another lease of popularity to the poet, and suggested
another idea to the facetious "Boston."

At that time a young lady popularly and professionally known
as the "California Pet" was performing to enthusiastic audiences
in the interior. Her specialty lay in the personation of youthful

masculine character; as a *gamin* of the street she was irresistible, as a negro-dancer she carried the honest miner's heart by storm. A saucy, pretty brunette, she had preserved a wonderful moral reputation even under the Jove-like advances of showers of gold that greeted her appearance on the stage at Sierra Flat. A prominent and delighted member of that audience was Milton Chubbuck. He attended every night. Every day he lingered at the door of the Union Hotel for a glimpse of the "California Pet." It was not long before he received a note from her, — in "Boston's" most popular and approved female hand, — acknowledging his admiration. It was not long before "Boston" was called upon to indite a suitable reply. At last, in furtherance of his facetious design, it became necessary for "Boston" to call upon the young actress herself and secure her personal participation. To her he unfolded a plan, the successful carrying out of which he felt would secure his fame to posterity as a practical humorist. The "California Pet's" black eyes sparkled approvingly and mischievously. She only stipulated that she should see the man first, — a concession to her feminine weakness which years of dancing Juba and wearing trousers and boots had not wholly eradicated from her willful breast. By all means, it should be done. And the interview was arranged for the next week.

It must not be supposed that during this interval of popularity Mr. Chubbuck had been unmindful of his poetic qualities. A certain portion of each day he was absent from town, — "a-communin' with natur'," as Mr. McCorkle expressed it, — and actually wandering in the mountain trails, or lying on his back under the trees, or gathering fragrant herbs and the bright-colored berries of the Manzanita. These and his company he generally brought to the editor's office late in the afternoon, often to that enterprising journalist's infinite weariness. Quiet and uncommunicative, he would sit there watching him at his work until the hour for closing the office arrived, when he would as quietly depart. There was something so humble and unobtrusive in these visits, that the editor could not find it in his heart to deny them, and accepting them, like the woodpeckers, as a part of his sylvan surroundings, often forgot even his presence. Once or twice, moved by some beauty of expression in the moist, shy eyes, he felt like seriously admonishing his visitor of his idle folly; but his glance falling upon the oiled hair and the gorgeous necktie he invariably thought better of it. The case was evidently hopeless.

The interview between Mr. Chubbuck and the "California Pet" took place in a private room of the Union Hotel; propriety being respected by the presence of that arch-humorist, "Boston." To this gentleman we are indebted for the only true account of the meeting. However reticent Mr. Chubbuck might have been in the presence of his own sex, towards the fairer portion of humanity he was, like most poets, exceedingly voluble. Accustomed as the "California Pet" had been to excessive compliment, she was fairly embarrassed by the extravagant praises of her visitor. Her personation of boy characters, her dancing of the "champion jig," were particularly dwelt upon with fervid but unmistakable admiration. At last, recovering her audacity and emboldened by the presence of "Boston," the "California Pet" electrified her hearers by demanding, half jestingly, half viciously, if it were as a boy or a girl that she was the subject of his flattering admiration.

"That knocked him out o' time," said the delighted "Boston," in his subsequent account of the interview. "But do you believe the d—d fool actually asked her to take him with her; wanted to engage in the company."

The plan, as briefly unfolded by "Boston," was to prevail upon Mr. Chubbuck to make his appearance in costume (already designed and prepared by the inventor) before a Sierra Flat audience, and recite an original poem at the Hall immediately on the conclusion of the "California Pet's" performance. At a given signal the audience were to rise and deliver a volley of unsavory articles (previously provided by the originator of the scheme); then a select few were to rush on the stage, seize the poet, and, after marching him in triumphal procession through the town, were to deposit him beyond its uttermost limits, with strict injunctions never to enter it again. To the first part of the plan the poet was committed; for the latter portion it was easy enough to find participants.

The eventful night came, and with it an audience that packed the long narrow room with one dense mass of human beings. The

"California Pet" never had been so joyous, so reckless, so fascinating and audacious before. But the applause was tame and weak compared to the ironical outburst that greeted the second rising of the curtain and the entrance of the born poet of Sierra Flat. Then there was a hush of expectancy, and the poet stepped to the footlights and stood with his manuscript in his hand.

His face was deadly pale. Either there was some suggestion of his fate in the faces of his audience, or some mysterious instinct told him of his danger. He attempted to speak, but faltered, tottered, and staggered to the wings.

Fearful of losing his prey, "Boston" gave the signal and leaped upon the stage. But at the same moment a light figure darted from behind the scenes, and delivering a kick that sent the discomfited humorist back among the musicians, cut a pigeon-wing, executed a double-shuffle, and then advancing to the footlights with that inimitable look, that audacious swagger and utter abandon which had so thrilled and fascinated them a moment before, uttered the characteristic speech, "Wot are you goin' to hit a man fur when he's down, s-a-a-y?"

The look, the drawl, the action, the readiness, and above all the downright courage of the little woman, had an effect. A roar of sympathetic applause followed the act. "Cut and run while you can," she whispered hurriedly over her one shoulder, without altering the other's attitude of pert and saucy defiance towards the audience. But even as she spoke, the poet tottered and sank fainting upon the stage. Then she threw a despairing whisper behind the scenes, "Ring down the curtain."

There was a slight movement of opposition in the audience, but among them rose the burly shoulders of Yuba Bill, the tall, erect figure of Henry York, of Sandy Bar, and the colorless, determined face of John Oakhurst. The curtain came down.

Behind it knelt the "California Pet" beside the prostrate poet. "Bring me some water. Run for a doctor. Stop!! CLEAR OUT, ALL OF YOU!"

She had unloosed the gaudy cravat and opened the shirt-collar of the insensible figure before her. Then she burst into an hysterical laugh.

"Manuela!"

Her tiring-woman, a Mexican half-breed, came towards her.

"Help me with him to my dressing-room, quick; then stand outside and wait. If any one questions you, tell them he's gone. Do you hear? HE's gone."

The old woman did as she was bade. In a few moments the audience had departed. Before morning so also had the "California Pet," Manuela, and the poet of Sierra Flat.

But, alas! with them also had departed the fair fame of the "California Pet." Only a few, and these, it is to be feared, of not the best moral character themselves, still had faith in the stainless honor of their favorite actress. "It was a mighty foolish thing to do, but it'll all come out right yet." On the other hand, a majority gave her full credit and approbation for her undoubted pluck and gallantry, but deplored that she should have thrown it away upon a worthless object. To elect for a lover the despised and ridiculed vagrant of Sierra Flat, who had not even the manliness to stand up in his own defense, was not only evidence of inherent moral depravity, but was an insult to the community. Colonel Starbottle saw in it only another instance of extreme frailty of the sex; he had known similar cases; and remembered distinctly, sir, how a well known Philadelphia heiress, one of the finest women that ever rode in her kerridge, that, gad, sir! had thrown over a Southern member of Congress to consort with a d—d nigger. The Colonel had also noticed a singular look in the dog's eye which he did not entirely fancy. He would not say anything against the lady, sir, but he had noticed — And here, haply, the Colonel became so mysterious and darkly confidential as to be unintelligible and inaudible to the bystanders.

A few days after the disappearance of Mr. Chubbuck a singular report reached Sierra Flat, and it was noticed that "Boston," who since the failure of his elaborate joke had been even more depressed in spirits than is habitual with great humorists, suddenly found that his presence was required in San Francisco. But as yet nothing but the vaguest surmises were afloat, and nothing definite was known.

It was a pleasant afternoon when the editor of the "Sierra Flat

Record" looked up from his case and beheld the figure of Mr. Morgan McCorkle standing in the doorway. There was a distressed look on the face of that worthy gentleman that at once enlisted the editor's sympathizing attention. He held an open letter in his hand as he advanced towards the middle of the room.

"As a man as has allers borne a fair reputation," began Mr. McCorkle slowly, "I should like, if so be as I could, Mister Editor, to make a correction in the columns of your valooable paper."

Mr. Editor begged him to proceed.

"Ye may not disremember that about a month ago I fetched here what so be as we'll call a young man whose name might be as it were Milton — Milton Chubbuck."

Mr. Editor remembered perfectly.

"Thet same party I'd knowed better for fower year, two on 'em campin' out together. Not that I'd known him all the time, fur he war shy and strange at spells, and had odd ways that I took war nat'ral to a borned poet. Ye may remember that I said he was a borned poet?"

The editor distinctly did.

"I picked this same party up in St. Jo., taking a fancy to his face, and kinder calklating he'd runned away from home; for I'm a married man, Mr. Editor, and hev children of my own, — and thinkin' belike he was a borned poet."

"Well," said the editor.

"And as I said before, I should like now to make a correction in the columns of your valooable paper."

"What correction?" asked the editor.

"I said, ef you remember my words, as how he was a borned poet."

"Yes."

"From statements in this yer letter it seems as how I war wrong."

"Well?"

"She war a woman."

HOW SANTA CLAUS
CAME TO SIMPSON'S BAR

I T HAD BEEN raining in the valley of the Sacramento. The North
Fork had overflowed its banks, and Rattlesnake Creek was im-
passable. The few boulders that had marked the summer ford at
Simpson's Crossing were obliterated by a vast sheet of water stretch-
ing to the foothills. The up-stage was stopped at Granger's; the last
mail had been abandoned in the *tules*, the rider swimming for his
life. "An area," remarked the "Sierra Avalanche," with pensive
local pride, "as large as the State of Massachusetts is now under
water."

Nor was the weather any better in the foothills. The mud lay
deep on the mountain road; wagons that neither physical force nor
moral objurgation could move from the evil ways into which they
had fallen encumbered the track, and the way to Simpson's Bar
was indicated by broken-down teams and hard swearing. And
further on, cut off and inaccessible, rained upon and bedraggled,
smitten by high winds and threatened by high water, Simpson's
Bar, on the eve of Christmas Day, 1862, clung like a swallow's
nest to the rocky entablature and splintered capitals of Table Mountain, and shook in the blast.

As night shut down on the settlement, a few lights gleamed
through the mist from the windows of cabins on either side of the
highway, now crossed and gullied by lawless streams and swept
by marauding winds. Happily most of the population were gathered at Thompson's store, clustered around a redhot stove, at which

107

they silently spat in some accepted sense of social communion that perhaps rendered conversation unnecessary. Indeed, most methods of diversion had long since been exhausted on Simpson's Bar; high water had suspended the regular occupations on gulch and on river, and a consequent lack of money and whiskey had taken the zest from most illegitimate recreation. Even Mr. Hamlin was fain to leave the Bar with fifty dollars in his pocket—the only amount actually realized of the large sums won by him in the successful exercise of his arduous profession. "Ef I was asked," he remarked somewhat later,—"ef I was asked to pint out a purty little village where a retired sport as didn't care for money could exercise hisself, frequent and lively, I'd say Simpson's Bar; but for a young man with a large family depending on his exertions, it don't pay." As Mr. Hamlin's family consisted mainly of female adults, this remark is quoted rather to show the breadth of his humor than the exact extent of his responsibilities.

Howbeit, the unconscious objects of this satire sat that evening in the listless apathy begotten of idleness and lack of excitement. Even the sudden splashing of hoofs before the door did not arouse them. Dick Bullen alone paused in the act of scraping out his pipe, and lifted his head, but no other one of the group indicated any interest in, or recognition of, the man who entered.

It was a figure familiar enough to the company, and known in Simpson's Bar as "The Old Man." A man of perhaps fifty years; grizzled and scant of hair, but still fresh and youthful of complexion. A face full of ready but not very powerful sympathy, with a chameleon-like aptitude for taking on the shade and color of contiguous moods and feelings. He had evidently just left some hilarious companions, and did not at first notice the gravity of the group, but clapped the shoulder of the nearest man jocularly, and threw himself into a vacant chair.

"Jest heard the best thing out, boys! Ye know Smiley, over yar—Jim Smiley—funniest man in the Bar? Well, Jim was jest telling the richest yarn about"—

"Smiley's a—— fool," interrupted a gloomy voice.

"A particular—— skunk," added another in sepulchral accents.

A silence followed these positive statements. The Old Man

glanced quickly around the group. Then his face slowly changed. "That's so," he said reflectively, after a pause, "certainly a sort of a skunk and suthin' of a fool. In course." He was silent for a moment, as in painful contemplation of the unsavoriness and folly of the unpopular Smiley. "Dismal weather, ain't it?" he added, now fully embarked on the current of prevailing sentiment. "Mighty rough papers on the boys, and no show for money this season. And to-morrow's Christmas."

There was a movement among the men at this announcement, but whether of satisfaction or disgust was not plain. "Yes," continued the Old Man in the lugubrious tone he had, within the last few moments, unconsciously adopted, — "yes, Christmas, and to-night's Christmas Eve. Ye see, boys, I kinder thought — that is, I sorter had an idee, jest passin' like, you know — that maybe ye'd all like to come over to my house to-night and have a sort of tear round. But I suppose, now, you wouldn't? Don't feel like it, maybe?" he added with anxious sympathy, peering into the faces of his companions.

"Well, I don't know," responded Tom Flynn with some cheerfulness. "P'r'aps we may. But how about your wife, Old Man? What does *she* say to it?"

The Old Man hesitated. His conjugal experience had not been a happy one, and the fact was known to Simpson's Bar. His first wife, a delicate, pretty little woman, had suffered keenly and secretly from the jealous suspicions of her husband, until one day he invited the whole Bar to his house to expose her infidelity. On arriving, the party found the shy, petite creature quietly engaged in her household duties, and retired abashed and discomfited. But the sensitive woman did not easily recover from the shock of this extraordinary outrage. It was with difficulty she regained her equanimity sufficiently to release her lover from the closet in which he was concealed, and escape with him. She left a boy of three years to comfort her bereaved husband. The Old Man's present wife had been his cook. She was large, loyal, and aggressive.

Before he could reply, Joe Dimmick suggested with great directness that it was the "Old Man's house," and that, invoking the Divine Power, if the case were his own, he would invite whom he pleased, even if in so doing he imperiled his salvation. The Powers of Evil, he further remarked, should contend against him vainly. All this delivered with a terseness and vigor lost in this necessary translation.

"In course. Certainly. Thet's it," said the Old Man with a sympathetic frown. "Thar's no trouble about thet. It's my own house,

built every stick on it myself. Don't you be afeard o' her, boys. She *may* cut up a trifle rough — ez wimmin do — but she'll come round." Secretly the Old Man trusted to the exaltation of liquor and the power of courageous example to sustain him in such an emergency.

As yet, Dick Bullen, the oracle and leader of Simpson's Bar, had not spoken. He now took his pipe from his lips. "Old Man, how's that yer Johnny gettin' on? Seems to me he didn't look so peart last time I seed him on the bluff heavin' rocks at Chinamen. Didn't seem to take much interest in it. Thar was a gang of 'em by yar yesterday — drownded out up the river — and I kinder thought o' Johnny, and how he'd miss 'em! Maybe now, we'd be in the way ef he wus sick?"

The father, evidently touched not only by this pathetic picture of Johnny's deprivation, but by the considerate delicacy of the speaker, hastened to assure him that Johnny was better, and that a "little fun might 'liven him up." Whereupon Dick arose, shook himself, and saying, "I'm ready. Lead the way, Old Man: here goes," himself led the way with a leap, a characteristic howl, and darted out into the night. As he passed through the outer room he caught up a blazing brand from the hearth. The action was repeated by the rest of the party, closely following and elbowing each other, and before the astonished proprietor of Thompson's grocery was aware of the intention of his guests, the room was deserted.

The night was pitchy dark. In the first gust of wind their temporary torches were extinguished, and only the red brands dancing and flitting in the gloom like drunken will-o'-the-wisps indicated their whereabouts. Their way led up Pine-Tree Cañon, at the head of which a broad, low, bark-thatched cabin burrowed in the mountain side. It was the home of the Old Man, and the entrance to the tunnel in which he worked when he worked at all. Here the crowd paused for a moment, out of delicate deference to their host, who came up panting in the rear.

"P'r'aps ye'd better hold on a second out yer, whilst I go in and see that things is all right," said the Old Man, with an indifference he was far from feeling. The suggestion was graciously accepted, the door opened and closed on the host, and the crowd, leaning their backs against the wall and cowering under the eaves, waited and listened.

For a few moments there was no sound but the dripping of water from the eaves, and the stir and rustle of wrestling boughs above them. Then the men became uneasy, and whispered suggestion and suspicion passed from the one to the other. "Reckon she's caved in his head the first lick!" "Decoyed him inter the tunnel and barred him up, likely." "Got him down and sittin' on him." "Prob'ly bilin suthin' to heave on us: stand clear the door, boys!" For just then the latch clicked, the door slowly opened, and a voice said, "Come in out o' the wet."

The voice was neither that of the Old Man nor of his wife. It was the voice of a small boy, its weak treble broken by that preternatural hoarseness which only vagabondage and the habit of premature self-assertion can give. It was the face of a small boy that looked up at theirs, — a face that might have been pretty, and even refined, but that it was darkened by evil knowledge from within, and dirt and hard experience from without. He had a blanket around his shoulders, and had evidently just risen from his bed. "Come in," he repeated, "and don't make no noise. The Old Man's in there talking to mar," he continued, pointing to an adjacent room which seemed to be a kitchen, from which the Old Man's voice came in deprecating accents. "Let me be," he added queru-lously, to Dick Bullen, who had caught him up, blanket and all, and was affecting to toss him into the fire, "let go o' me, you d—d old fool, d' ye hear?"

Thus adjured, Dick Bullen lowered Johnny to the ground with a smothered laugh, while the men, entering quietly, ranged them-selves around a long table of rough boards which occupied the centre of the room. Johnny then gravely proceeded to a cupboard and brought out several articles, which he deposited on the table. "Thar's whiskey. And crackers. And red herons. And cheese." He took a bite of the latter on his way to the table. "And sugar." He scooped up a mouthful *en route* with a small and very dirty hand. "And terbacker. Thar's dried appils too on the shelf, but I don't admire 'em. Appils is swellin'. Thar," he concluded, "now wade in, and don't be afeard. *I* don't mind the old woman. She don't b'long to *me*. S'long."

He had stepped to the threshold of a small room, scarcely larger than a closet, partitioned off from the main apartment, and hold-ing in its dim recess a small bed. He stood there a moment looking at the company, his bare feet peeping from the blanket, and nodded.

"Hello, Johnny! You ain't goin' to turn in agin, are ye?" said Dick. "Yes, I are," responded Johnny decidedly.

"Why, wot's up, old fellow?"

"I'm sick."

"How sick?"

"I've got a fevier. And childblains. And roomatiz," returned Johnny, and vanished within. After a moment's pause, he added in the dark, apparently from under the bedclothes, — "And biles!"

There was an embarrassing silence. The men looked at each

other and at the fire. Even with the appetizing banquet before them, it seemed as if they might again fall into the despondency of Thompson's grocery, when the voice of the Old Man, incautiously lifted, came deprecatingly from the kitchen.

"Certainly! Thet's so. In course they is. A gang o' lazy, drunken loafers, and that ar Dick Bullen's the ornariest of all. Didn't hev no more *sabe* than to come round yar with sickness in the house and no provision. Thet's what I said: 'Bullen,' sez I, 'it's crazy drunk you are, or a fool,' sez I, 'to think o' such a thing.' 'Staples,' I sez, 'be you a man, Staples, and 'spect to raise h—ll under my roof and invalids lyin' round?' But they would come,—they would. Thet's wot you must 'spect o' such trash as lays round the Bar."

A burst of laughter from the men followed this unfortunate exposure. Whether it was overheard in the kitchen, or whether the Old Man's irate companion had just then exhausted all other modes of expressing her contemptuous indignation, I cannot say, but a back door was suddenly slammed with great violence. A moment later and the Old Man reappeared, haply unconscious of the cause of the late hilarious outburst, and smiled blandly.

"The old woman thought she'd jest run over to Mrs. MacFadden's for a sociable call," he explained with jaunty indifference, as he took a seat at the board.

Oddly enough it needed this untoward incident to relieve the embarrassment that was beginning to be felt by the party, and their natural audacity returned with their host. I do not propose to record the convivialities of that evening. The inquisitive reader will accept the statement that the conversation was characterized by the same intellectual exaltation, the same cautious reverence, the same fastidious delicacy, the same rhetorical precision, and the same logical and coherent discourse somewhat later in the evening, which distinguish similar gatherings of the masculine sex in more civilized localities and under more favorable auspices. No glasses were broken in the absence of any; no liquor was uselessly spilt on the floor or table in the scarcity of that article.

It was nearly midnight when the festivities were interrupted. "Hush," said Dick Bullen, holding up his hand. It was the querulous voice of Johnny from his adjacent closet: "O dad!"

The Old Man arose hurriedly and disappeared in the closet. Presently he reappeared. "His rheumatiz is coming on agin bad," he explained, "and he wants rubbin'." He lifted the demijohn of whiskey from the table and shook it. It was empty. Dick Bullen put down his tin cup with an embarrassed laugh. So did the others. The Old Man examined their contents and said hopefully, "I reckon that's enough; he don't need much. You hold on all o' you for a spell, and I'll be back;" and vanished in the closet with an old flannel shirt and the whiskey. The door closed but imperfectly, and the following dialogue was distinctly audible:

"Now, sonny, whar does she ache worst?"

"Sometimes over yar and sometimes under yer; but it's most powerful from yer to yer. Rub yer, dad."

A silence seemed to indicate a brisk rubbing. Then Johnny:

"Hevin' a good time out yer, dad?"

"Yes, sonny."

"To-morrer's Chrismiss, — aint' it?"

"Yes, sonny. How does she feel now?"

"Better. Rub a little furder down. Wot's Chrismiss, anyway? Wot's it all about?"

"Oh, it's a day."

This exhaustive definition was apparently satisfactory, for there was a silent interval of rubbing. Presently Johnny again:

"Mar sez that everywhere else but yer everybody gives things to everybody Chrismiss, and she jist waded inter you. She sez thar's a man they call Sandy Claws, not a white man, you know, but a kind o' Chinemin, comes down the chimbley night afore Chrismiss and gives things to chillern, — boys like me. Puts 'em in their butes! Thet's what she tried to play upon me. Easy now, pop, whar are you rubbin' to, — thet's a mile from the place. She jest made that up, didn't she, jest to aggrewate me and you? Don't rub thar. . . . Why, dad!"

In the great quiet that seemed to have fallen upon the house the sigh of the near pines and the drip of leaves without was very distinct. Johnny's voice, too, was lowered as he went on, "Don't you take on now, for I'm gettin' all right fast. Wot's the boys doin' out thar?"

The Old Man partly opened the door and peered through. His guests were sitting there sociably enough, and there were a few silver coins and a lean buckskin purse on the table. "Bettin' on suthin' — some little game or 'nother. They're all right," he replied to Johnny, and recommenced his rubbing.

"I'd like to take a hand and win some money," said Johnny reflectively after a pause.

The Old Man glibly repeated what was evidently a familiar formula, that if Johnny would wait until he struck it rich in the tunnel he'd have lots of money, etc., etc.

"Yes," said Johnny, "but you don't. And whether you strike it or I win it, it's about the same. It's all luck. But it's mighty cur'o's about Chrismiss — ain't it? Why do they call it Chrismiss?"

Perhaps from some instinctive deference to the overhearing of his guests, or from some vague sense of incongruity, the Old Man's reply was so low as to be inaudible beyond the room.

"Yes," said Johnny, with some slight abatement of interest, "I've heard o' *him* before. Thar, that'll do, dad. I don't ache near so bad as I did. Now wrap me tight in this yer blanket. So. Now," he added in a muffled whisper, "sit down yer by me till I go asleep." To assure himself of obedience, he disengaged one hand from the blanket, and, grasping his father's sleeve, again composed himself to rest.

For some moments the Old Man waited patiently. Then the unwonted stillness of the house excited his curiosity, and without moving from the bed he cautiously opened the door with his disengaged hand, and looked into the main room. To his infinite surprise it was dark and deserted. But even then a smouldering log on the hearth broke, and by the upspringing blaze he saw the figure of Dick Bullen sitting by the dying embers.

"Hello!"

Dick started, rose, and came somewhat unsteadily towards him.

"Whar's the boys?" said the Old Man.

"Gone up the cañon on a little *pasear*. They're coming back for me in a minit. I'm waiting' round for 'em. What are you starin' at, Old Man?" he added, with a forced laugh; "do you think I'm drunk?"

The Old Man might have been pardoned the supposition, for Dick's eyes were humid and his face flushed. He loitered and lounged back to the chimney, yawned, shook himself, buttoned up his coat and laughed. "Liquor ain't so plenty as that, Old Man. Now don't you get up," he continued, as the Old Man made a movement to release his sleeve from Johnny's hand. "Don't you mind manners. Sit jest whar you be; I'm goin' in a jiffy. Thar, that's them now."

There was a low tap at the door. Dick Bullen opened it quickly, nodded "Good-night" to his host, and disappeared. The Old Man would have followed him but for the hand that still unconsciously grasped his sleeve. He could have easily disengaged it: it was small, weak, and emaciated. But perhaps because it *was* small, weak, and emaciated he changed his mind, and, drawing his chair closer to the bed, rested his head upon it. In this defenseless attitude the potency of his earlier potations surprised him. The room flickered and faded before his eyes, reappeared, faded again, went out, and left him — asleep. Meantime Dick Bullen, closing the door, confronted his companions. "Are you ready?" said Staples. "Ready," said Dick; "what's the time?" "Past twelve," was the reply; "can you make it? — it's nigh on fifty miles, the round trip hither and yon." "I reckon," returned Dick shortly. "Whar's the mare?" "Bill and Jack's holdin' her at the crossin'." "Let 'em hold on a minit longer," said Dick.

He turned and reëntered the house softly. By the light of the guttering candle and dying fire he saw that the door of the little room was open. He stepped towards it on tip-toe and looked in. The Old Man had fallen back in his chair, snoring, his helpless feet thrust out in a line with his collapsed shoulders, and his hat pulled over his eyes. Beside him, on a narrow wooden bedstead, lay Johnny, muffled tightly in a blanket that hid all save a strip of forehead and a few curls damp with perspiration. Dick Bullen made a step forwards, hesitated, and glanced over his shoulder into the deserted room. Everything was quiet. With a sudden resolution he parted his huge mustaches with both hands and stooped over the sleeping boy. But even as he did so a mischievous blast, lying in wait, swooped down the chimney, rekindled the hearth, and lit up the room with a shameless glow from which Dick fled in bashful terror.

His companions were already waiting for him at the crossing. Two of them were struggling in the darkness with some strange misshapen bulk, which as Dick came nearer took the semblance of a great yellow horse.

It was the mare. She was not a pretty picture. From her Roman nose to her rising haunches, from her arched spine hidden by the stiff *machillas* of a Mexican saddle, to her thick, straight bony legs, there was not a line of equine grace. In her half-blind but wholly vicious white eyes, in her protruding under-lip, in her monstrous color, there was nothing but ugliness and vice.

"Now then," said Staples, "stand cl'ar of her heels, boys, and up with you. Don't miss your first holt of her mane, and mind ye get your off stirrup *quick*. Ready!"

There was a leap, a scrambling struggle, a bound, a wild retreat of the crowd, a circle of flying hoofs, two springless leaps that jarred the earth, a rapid play and jingle of spurs, a plunge, and then the voice of Dick somewhere in the darkness. "All right!"

"Don't take the lower road back onless you're hard pushed for time! Don't hold her in down hill. We'll be at the ford at five. G'lang! Hoopa! Mula! GO!"

A splash, a spark struck from the ledge in the road, a clatter in the rocky cut beyond, and Dick was gone.

.   .   .   .

Sing, O Muse, the ride of Richard Bullen! Sing, O Muse, of chivalrous men! the sacred quest, the doughty deeds, the battery of low churls, the fearsome ride and gruesome perils of the Flower of Simpson's Bar! Alack! she is dainty, this Muse! She will have none of this bucking brute and swaggering, ragged rider, and I must fain follow him in prose, afoot!

It was one o'clock, and yet he had only gained Rattlesnake Hill. For in that time Jovita had rehearsed to him all her imperfections and practiced all her vices. Thrice had she stumbled. Twice had she thrown up her Roman nose in a straight line with the reins, and, resisting bit and spur, struck out madly across country. Twice had she reared, and, rearing, fallen backwards; and twice had the agile Dick, unharmed, regained his seat before she found her vicious legs again. And a mile beyond them, at the foot of a long hill, was Rattlesnake Creek. Dick knew that here was the crucial test of his ability to perform his enterprise, set his teeth grimly, put his knees well into her flanks, and changed his defensive tactics to brisk aggression. Bullied and maddened, Jovita began the descent of the hill. Here the artful Richard pretended to hold her in with ostentatious objurgation and well-feigned cries of alarm. It is unnecessary to add that Jovita instantly ran away. Nor need I state the time in the descent; it is written in the chronicles of Simpson's Bar. Enough that in another moment, as it seemed to Dick, she was splashing on the overflowed banks of Rattlesnake Creek. As Dick expected, the momentum she had acquired carried her beyond the point of balking, and, holding her well together for a mighty leap, they dashed into the middle of the swiftly flowing current. A few moments of kicking, wading, and swimming, and Dick drew a long breath on the opposite bank.

The road from Rattlesnake Creek to Red Mountain was tolerably level. Either the plunge in Rattlesnake Creek had dampened her baleful fire, or the art which led to it had shown her the superior wickedness of her rider, for Jovita no longer wasted her surplus energy in wanton conceits. Once she bucked, but it was from force of habit; once she shied, but it was from a new, freshly painted meeting-house at the crossing of the country road. Hollows, ditches, gravelly deposits, patches of freshly springing grasses, flew from beneath her rattling hoofs. She began to smell unpleasantly, once or twice she coughed slightly, but there was no abatement of her strength or speed. By two o'clock he had passed Red Mountain and begun the descent to the plain. Ten minutes later the driver of the fast Pioneer coach was overtaken and passed by a "man on a Pinto hoss," — an event sufficiently notable for remark. At half past two Dick rose in his stirrups with a great shout. Stars were glittering through the rifted clouds, and beyond him, out of the plain, rose two spires, a flagstaff, and a straggling line of black objects. Dick jingled his spurs and swung his *riata*, Jovita bounded forwards, and in another moment they swept into Tuttleville, and drew up before the wooden piazza of "The Hotel of All Nations."

What transpired that night at Tuttleville is not strictly a part of

this record. Briefly I may state, however, that after Jovita had been handed over to a sleepy ostler, whom she at once kicked into unpleasant consciousness, Dick sallied out with the barkeeper for a tour of the sleeping town. Lights still gleamed from a few saloons and gambling-houses; but, avoiding these, they stopped before several closed shops, and by persistent tapping and judicious outcry roused the proprietors from their beds, and made them unbar the doors of their magazines and expose their wares. Sometimes they were met by curses, but oftener by interest and some concern in their needs, and the interview was invariably concluded by a drink. It was three o'clock before this pleasantry was given over, and with a small waterproof bag of India-rubber strapped on his shoulders, Dick returned to the hotel. But here he was waylaid by Beauty, — Beauty opulent in charms, affluent in dress, persuasive in speech, and Spanish in accent! In vain she repeated the invitation in "Excelsior," happily scorned by all Alpine-climbing youth, and rejected by this child of the Sierras, — a rejection softened in this instance by a laugh and his last gold coin. And then he sprang to the saddle and dashed down the lonely street and out into the lonelier plain, where presently the lights, the black line of houses, the spires, and the flagstaff sank into the earth behind him again and were lost in the distance. The storm had cleared away, the air was brisk and cold, the outlines of adjacent landmarks were distinct, but it was half-past four before Dick reached the meeting-house and the crossing of the country road. To avoid the rising grade he had taken a longer and more circuitous road, in whose viscid mud Jovita sank fetlock deep at every bound. It was a poor preparation for a steady ascent of five miles more; but Jovita, gathering her legs under her, took it with her usual blind, unreasoning fury, and a half-hour later reached the long level that led to Rattlesnake Creek. Another half-hour would bring him to the creek. He threw the reins lightly upon the neck of the mare, chirruped to her, and began to sing.

Suddenly Jovita shied with a bound that would have unseated a less practiced rider. Hanging to her rein was a figure that had leaped from the bank, and at the same time from the road before her arose a shadowy horse and rider. "Throw up your hands," commanded the second apparition, with an oath.

Dick felt the mare tremble, quiver, and apparently sink under him. He knew what it meant and was prepared.

"Stand aside, Jack Simpson. I know you, you d—d thief! Let me pass, or" —

He did not finish the sentence. Jovita rose straight in the air with a terrific bound, throwing the figure from her bit with a single shake of her vicious head, and charged with deadly malevolence down on the impediment before her. An oath, a pistol-shot, horse and highwayman rolled over in the road, and the next moment Jovita was a hundred yards away. But the good right arm of her rider, shattered by a bullet, dropped helplessly at his side.

Without slacking his speed he shifted the reins to his left hand. But a few moments later he was obliged to halt and tighten the saddle-girths that had slipped in the onset. This in his crippled condition took some time. He had no fear of pursuit, but looking up he saw that the eastern stars were already paling, and that the distant peaks had lost their ghostly whiteness, and now stood out blackly against a lighter sky. Day was upon him. Then completely absorbed in a single idea, he forgot the pain of his wound, and mounting again dashed on towards Rattlesnake Creek. But now Jovita's breath came broken by gasps, Dick reeled in his saddle, and brighter and brighter grew the sky.

Ride, Richard; run, Jovita; linger, O day!

For the last few rods there was a roaring in his ears. Was it exhaustion from loss of blood, or what? He was dazed and giddy as he swept down the hill, and did not recognize his surroundings. Had he taken the wrong road, or was this Rattlesnake Creek?

It was. But the brawling creek he had swam a few hours before had risen, more than doubled its volume, and now rolled a swift and resistless river between him and Rattlesnake Hill. For the first time that night Richard's heart sank within him. The river, the mountain, the quickening east, swam before his eyes. He shut them to recover his self-control. In that brief interval, by some fantastic mental process, the little room at Simpson's Bar and the figures of the sleeping father and son rose upon him. He opened his eyes wildly, cast off his coat, pistol, boots, and saddle, bound his precious pack tightly to his shoulders, grasped the bare flanks of Jovita with his bared knees, and with a shout dashed into the yellow water. A cry rose from the opposite bank as the head of a man and horse struggled for a few moments against the battling current, and then were swept away amidst uprooted trees and whirling driftwood.

.   .   .   .

The Old Man started and woke. The fire on the hearth was dead, the candle in the outer room flickering in its socket, and somebody was rapping at the door. He opened it but fell back with a cry before the dripping, half-naked figure that reeled against the door-post. "Dick?"

"Hush! Is he awake yet?"

"No; but, Dick" —

"Dry up, you old fool! Get me some whiskey, *quick!*" The Old Man flew and returned with — an empty bottle! Dick would have sworn, but his strength was not equal to the occasion. He staggered, caught at the handle of the door, and motioned to the Old Man.

"Thar's suthin' in my pack yer for Johnny. Take it off. I can't."

The Old Man unstrapped the pack, and laid it before the exhausted man. "Open it, quick." He did so with trembling fingers. It contained only a few poor toys, — cheap and barbaric enough, goodness knows, but bright with paint and tinsel. One of them was broken; another, I fear, was irretrievably ruined by water, and on the third — ah me! there was a cruel spot.

"It don't look like much, that's a fact," said Dick ruefully. . . . "But it's the best we could do. . . . Take 'em, Old Man, and put 'em in his stocking, and tell him — tell him, you know — hold me, Old Man" — The Old Man caught at his sinking figure. "Tell him," said Dick, with a weak little laugh, — "tell him Sandy Claus has come."

And even so, bedraggled, ragged, unshaven and unshorn, with one arm hanging helplessly at his side, Santa Claus came to Simpson's Bar and fell fainting on the first threshold. The Christmas dawn came slowly after, touching the remoter peaks with the rosy warmth of ineffable love. And it looked so tenderly on Simpson's Bar that the whole mountain, as if caught in a generous action, blushed to the skies.

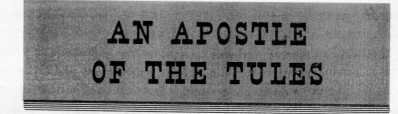

AN APOSTLE
OF THE TULES

I

ON OCTOBER 10, 1856, about four hundred people were camped in Tasajara Valley, California. It could not have been for the prospect, since a more barren, dreary, monotonous, and uninviting landscape never stretched before human eye; it could not have been for convenience or contiguity, as the nearest settlement was thirty miles away; it could not have been for health or salubrity, as the breath of the ague-haunted tules in the outlying Stockton marshes swept through the valley; it could not have been for space or comfort, for, encamped on an unlimited plain, men and women were huddled together as closely as in an urban tenement-house, without the freedom or decency of rural isolation; it could not have been for pleasant companionship, as dejection, mental anxiety, tears, and lamentation were the dominant expression; it was not a hurried flight from present or impending calamity, for the camp had been deliberately planned, and for a week pioneer wagons had been slowly arriving; it was not an irrevocable exodus, for some had already returned to their homes that others might take their places. It was simply a religious revival of one or two denominational sects, known as a "camp-meeting."

A large central tent served for the assembling of the principal congregation; smaller tents served for prayer-meetings and class-rooms, known to the few unbelievers as "side-shows;" while the actual dwellings of the worshipers were rudely extemporized shanties of boards and canvas, sometimes mere corrals or inclosures open to the cloudless sky, or more often the unhitched covered wagon which had brought them there. The singular resemblance to a circus, already profanely suggested, was carried out by a straggling fringe of boys and half-grown men on the outskirts of the encampment, acrimonious with disappointed curiosity, lazy without the careless ease of vagrancy, and vicious without the excitement of dissipation. For the coarse poverty and brutal economy of the larger arrangements, the dreary panorama of unlovely and unwholesome domestic details always before the eyes, were hardly exciting to the senses. The circus might have been more dangerous, but scarcely more brutalizing. The actors themselves, hard and aggressive through practical struggles, often warped and twisted with chronic forms of smaller diseases, or malformed and crippled through carelessness and neglect, and restless and uneasy through some vague mental distress and inquietude that they had added to their burdens, were scarcely amusing performers. The rheumatic Parkinsons, from Green Springs; the ophthalmic Filgees, from Alder Creek; the ague-stricken Harneys, from Martinez Bend; and the feeble-limbed Steptons, from Sugar Mill, might, in their combined families, have suggested a hospital, rather than any other social assemblage. Even their companionship, which had little of cheerful fellowship in it, would have been grotesque but for the pathetic instinct of some mutual vague appeal from the hardness of their lives and the helplessness of their conditions that had brought them together. Nor was this appeal to a Higher Power any the less pathetic that it bore no reference whatever to their respective needs or deficiencies, but was always an invocation for a light which, when they believed they had found it, to unregenerate eyes scarcely seemed to illumine the rugged path in which their feet were continually stumbling. One might have smiled at the idea of the vendetta-following Ferguses praying for "justification by Faith," but the actual spectacle of old Simon Fergus, whose shotgun was still in his wagon, offering up that appeal with streaming eyes and agonized features, was painful beyond a doubt. To seek and obtain an exaltation of feeling vaguely known as "It," or less vaguely veiling a sacred name, was the burden of the general appeal.

The large tent had been filled, and between the exhortations a certain gloomy enthusiasm had been kept up by singing, which had the effect of continuing in an easy, rhythmical, impersonal, and irresponsible way the sympathies of the meeting. This was interrupted by a young man who rose suddenly with that spontaneity of impulse which characterized the speakers; but unlike his predecessors, he remained for a moment mute, trembling, and irresolute. The fatal hesitation seemed to check the unreasoning, monotonous flow of emotion and to recall to some extent the reason and even the criticism of the worshipers. He stammered a prayer whose earnestness was undoubted, whose humility was but too apparent, but his words fell on faculties already benumbed by repetition and rhythm. A slight movement of curiosity in the rear benches, and a whisper that it was the maiden effort of a new preacher, helped to prolong the interruption. A heavy man of strong physical expression sprang to the rescue with a hysterical cry of "Glory!" and a tumultuous fluency of epithet and sacred adjuration. Still the meeting wavered. With one final paroxysmal cry, the powerful man threw his arms around his nearest neighbor and burst into silent tears. An anxious hush followed; the speaker still continued to sob on his neighbor's shoulder. Almost before the fact could be commented upon, it was noticed that the entire rank of worshipers on the bench beside him were crying also; the second and third rows were speedily dissolved in tears, until even the very youthful scoffers in the last benches suddenly found their half-hysterical laughter turned to sobs. The danger was averted, the reaction was complete; the singing commenced, and in a few moments the hapless cause of the interruption and the man who had retrieved the disaster stood together outside the tent. A horse was picketed near them.

The victor was still panting from his late exertions, and was more or less diluvial in eye and nostril, but neither eye nor nostril bore the slightest tremor of other expression. His face was stolid and perfectly in keeping with his physique, — heavy, animal, and unintelligent.

"Ye oughter trusted in the Lord," he said to the young preacher.

"But I did," responded the young man earnestly.

"That's it. Justifyin' yourself by works instead o' leanin' onto Him! Find Him, sez you! Git Him, sez you! Works is vain. Glory! glory!" he continued, with fluent vacuity and wandering, dull, observant eyes.

"But if I had a little more practice in class, Brother Silas, more education?"

"The letter killeth," interrupted Brother Silas. Here his wandering eyes took dull cognizance of two female faces peering through the opening of the tent. "No, yer mishun, Brother Gideon, is to seek Him in the byways, in the wilderness, — where the foxes hev holes and the ravens hev their young, — but not in the Temples of the people. Wot sez Sister Parsons?"

One of the female faces detached itself from the tent flaps, which it nearly resembled in color, and brought forward an angular figure clothed in faded fustian that had taken the various shades and odors of household service.

"Brother Silas speaks well," said Sister Parsons, with stridulous fluency. "It's foreordained. Fore-ordinashun is better nor ordinashun, saith the Lord. He shall go forth, turnin' neither to the right hand nor the left hand, and seek Him among the lost tribes and the ungodly. He shall put aside the temptashun of Mammon and the flesh." Her eyes and those of Brother Silas here both sought the other female face, which was that of a young girl of seventeen.

"Wot sez little Sister Meely, — wot sez Meely Parsons?" continued Brother Silas, as if repeating an unctuous formula.

The young girl came hesitatingly forward, and with a nervous cry of "Oh, Gideon!" threw herself on the breast of the young man.

For a moment they remained locked in each other's arms. In the promiscuous and fraternal embracings which were a part of the devotional exercises of the hour, the act passed without significance. The young man gently raised her face. She was young and comely, albeit marked with a half-frightened, half-vacant sorrow. "Amen!" said Brother Gideon gravely.

He mounted his horse and turned to go. Brother Silas had clasped his powerful arms around both women, and was holding them in a ponderous embrace.

"Go forth, young man, into the wilderness."

The young man bowed his head, and urged his horse forward in the bleak and barren plain. In half an hour every vestige of the camp and its unwholesome surroundings was lost in the distance. It was as if the strong desiccating wind, which seemed to spring up at his horse's feet, had cleanly erased the flimsy structures from the face of the plain, swept away the lighter breath of praise and plaint, and dried up the easy flowing tears. The air was harsh but pure; the grim economy of form and shade and color in the level plain was coarse but not vulgar; the sky above him was cold and distant but not repellent, the moisture that had been denied his eyes at the prayer-meeting overflowed them here; the words that had choked his utterance an hour ago now rose to his lips. He threw himself from his horse, and kneeling in the withered grass, — a mere atom in the boundless plain, — lifted his pale face against the irresponsive blue and prayed.

He prayed that the unselfish dream of his bitter boyhood, his disappointed youth, might come to pass. He prayed that he might in higher hands become the humble instrument of good to his fellow man. He prayed that the deficiencies of his scant education, his self-taught learning, his helpless isolation, and his inexperience might be overlooked or reinforced by grace. He prayed that the Infinite Compassion might enlighten his ignorance and solitude with a manifestation of the Spirit; in his very weakness he prayed for some special revelation, some sign or token, some visitation or gracious unbending from that coldly lifting sky. The low sun burned the black edge of the distant tules with dull eating fire as he prayed, lit the dwarfed hills with a brief but ineffectual radiance, and then died out. The lingering trade winds fired a few volleys over its grave, and then lapsed into a chilly silence. The young man staggered to his feet; it was quite dark now, but the coming night had advanced a few starry vedettes so near the plain they looked like human watchfires. For an instant he could not remember where he was. Then a light trembled far down at the entrance of the valley. Brother Gideon recognized it. It was in the lonely farmhouse of the widow of the last Circuit preacher.

II

The abode of the late Reverend Marvin Hiler remained in the disorganized condition he had left it when removed from his sphere of earthly uselessness and continuous accident. The straggling fence that only half inclosed the house and barn had stopped at that point where the two deacons who had each volunteered to do a day's work on it had completed their allotted time. The building of the barn had been arrested when the half load of timber contributed by Sugar Mill brethren was exhausted, and three windows given by "Christian Seekers" at Martinez painfully accented the boarded spaces for the other three that "Unknown Friends" in Tasajara had promised but not yet supplied. In the clearing some trees that had been felled but not taken away added to the general incompleteness.

Something of this unfinished character clung to the Widow Hiler and asserted itself in her three children, one of whom was consistently posthumous. Prematurely old and prematurely disappointed, she had all the inexperience of girlhood with the cares of maternity, and kept in her family circle the freshness of an old maid's misogynistic antipathies with a certain guilty and remorse-

ful consciousness of widowhood. She supported the meagre household to which her husband had contributed only the extra mouths
to feed with reproachful astonishment and weary incapacity. She
had long since grown tired of trying to make both ends meet of
which she declared "the Lord had taken one." During her two
years' widowhood she had waited on Providence, who by a pleasing local fiction had been made responsible for the disused and
cast-off furniture and clothing which, accompanied with scriptural
texts, found their way mysteriously into her few habitable rooms.
The providential manna was not always fresh; the ravens who fed
her and her little ones with flour from the Sugar Mills did not
always select the best quality. Small wonder that, sitting by her
lonely hearthstone, — a borrowed stove that supplemented the unfinished fireplace, — surrounded by her mismatched furniture and
clad in misfitting garments, she had contracted a habit of sniffling
during her dreary watches. In her weaker moments she attributed
it to grief; in her stronger intervals she knew that it sprang from
damp and draught.

In her apathy the sound of horses' hoofs at her unprotected door
even at that hour neither surprised nor alarmed her. She lifted
her head as the door opened, and the pale face of Gideon Deane
looked into the room. She moved aside the cradle she was rocking,
and taking a saucepan and teacup from a chair beside her, absently
dusted it with her apron, and pointing to the vacant seat, said,
"Take a chair" as quietly as if he had stepped from the next room
instead of the outer darkness.

"I'll put up my horse first," said Gideon gently.

"So do," responded the widow briefly.

Gideon led his horse across the inclosure, stumbling over the
heaps of rubbish, dried chips, and weather-beaten shavings with
which it was strewn, until he reached the unfinished barn, where
he temporarily bestowed his beast. Then taking a rusty axe, by the
faint light of the stars, he attacked one of the fallen trees with such
energy that at the end of ten minutes he reappeared at the door
with an armful of cut boughs and chips, which he quietly deposited
behind the stove. Observing that he was still standing as if looking
for something, the widow lifted her eyes and said, "Ef it's the

bucket, I reckon ye'll find it at the spring, where one of them foolish Filgee boys left it. I've been that tuckered out sens sundown, I ain't had the ambition to go and tote it back." Without a word Gideon repaired to the spring, filled the missing bucket, replaced the hoop on the loosened staves of another he found lying useless beside it, and again returned to the house. The widow once more pointed to the chair, and Gideon sat down. "It's quite a spell sens you wos here," said the Widow Hiler, returning her foot to the cradle-rocker; "not sens yer was ordained. Be'n practicin', I reckon, at the meetin'."

A slight color came into his cheek. "My place is not there, Sister Hiler," he said gently; "it's for those with the gift o' tongues. I go forth only a common laborer in the vineyard." He stopped and hesitated; he might have said more, but the widow, who was familiar with that kind of humility as the ordinary perfunctory expression of her class, suggested no sympathetic interest in his mission.

"Thar's a deal o' talk over there," she said dryly, "and thar's folks ez thinks thar's a deal o' money spent in picnicking the Gospel that might be given to them ez wish to spread it, or to their widows and children. But that don't consarn you, Brother Gideon. Sister Parsons hez money enough to settle her darter Meely comfortably on her own land; and I've heard tell that you and Meely was only waitin' till you was ordained to be jined together. You'll hev an easier time of it, Brother Gideon, than poor Marvin Hiler had," she continued, suppressing her tears with a certain astringency that took the place of her lost pride; "but the Lord wills that some should be tried and some not."

"But I am not going to marry Meely Parsons, said Gideon quietly.

The widow took her foot from the rocker. "Not marry Meely!" she repeated vaguely. But relapsing into her despondent mood, she continued: "Then I reckon it's true what other folks sez of Brother Silas Braggley makin' up to her and his powerful exhortin' influence over her ma. Folks sez ez Sister Parsons hez just resigned her soul inter his keepin'."

"Brother Silas hez a heavenly gift," said the young man, with gentle enthusiasm; "and perhaps it may be so. If it is, it is the Lord's will. But I do not marry Meely because my life and my ways hence-forth must lie far beyond her sphere of strength. I oughtn't to drag a young, inexperienced soul with me to battle and struggle in the thorny paths that I must tread."

"I reckon you know your own mind," said Sister Hiler grimly. "But thar's folks ez might allow that Meely Parsons ain't any better than others, that she shouldn't have her share o' trials and keers and crosses. Riches and bringin' up don't exempt folks from the shadder. *I* married Marvin Hiler outer a house ez good ez Sister Parsons', and at a time when old Cyrus Parsons hadn't a roof to his head but the cover of the emigrant wagon he kem across the plains in. I might say ez Marvin knowed pretty well wot it was to have a helpmeet in his ministration, if it wasn't vanity of sperit to say it now. But the flesh is weak, Brother Gideon."

Her influenza here resolved itself unto unmistakable tears, which she wiped away with the first article that was accessible in the work-bag before her. As it chanced to be a black silk neckerchief of the deceased Hiler, the result was funereal, suggestive, but prac-tically ineffective.

"You were a good wife to Brother Hiler," said the young man gently. "Everybody knows that."

"It's suthin' to think of since he's gone," continued the widow, bringing her work nearer to her eyes to adjust it to their tear-dimmed focus. "It's suthin' to lay to heart in the lonely days and nights when thar's no man round to fetch water and wood and lend a hand to doin' chores; it's suthin' to remember, with his three children to feed, and little Selby, the eldest, that vain and useless that he can't even tote the baby round while I do the work of a hired man."

"It's a hard trial, Sister Hiler," said Gideon, "but the Lord has His appointed time."

Familiar as consolation by vague quotation was to Sister Hiler, there was an occult sympathy in the tone in which this was offered that lifted her for an instant out of her narrower self. She raised her eyes to his. The personal abstraction of the devotee had no place in the deep dark eyes that were lifted from the cradle to hers with a sad, discriminating, and almost womanly sympathy. Surprised out of her selfish preoccupation, she was reminded of her apparent callousness to what might be his present disappointment. Perhaps it seemed strange to her, too, that those tender eyes should go a-begging.

"Yer takin' a Christian view of yer own disappointment, Brother Gideon," she said, with less astringency of manner; "but every heart knoweth its own sorrer. I'll be gettin' supper now that the baby's sleepin' sound, and ye'll sit by and eat."

"If you let me help you, Sister Hiler," said the young man with a cheerfulness that belied any overwhelming heart affection, and awakened in the widow a feminine curiosity as to his real feelings to Meely. But her further questioning was met with a frank, amiable, and simple brevity that was as puzzling as the most artful periphrase of tact. Accustomed as she was to the loquacity of grief and the confiding prolixity of disappointed lovers, she could not understand her guest's quiescent attitude. Her curiosity, however, soon gave way to the habitual contemplation of her own sorrows, and she could not forego the opportune presence of a sympathizing auditor to whom she could relieve her feelings. The preparations for the evening meal were therefore accompanied by a dreary monotone of lamentation. She bewailed her lost youth, her brief courtship, the struggles of her early married life, her premature widowhood, her penurious and helpless existence, the disruption of all her present ties, the hopelessness of the future. She rehearsed the unending plaint of those long evenings, set to the music of the restless wind around her bleak dwelling, with something of its stridulous reiteration. The young man listened, and replied with softly assenting eyes, but without pausing in the material aid that he was quietly giving her. He had removed the cradle of the sleeping child to the bedroom, quieted the sudden wakefulness of "Pinkey," rearranged the straggling furniture of the sitting-room with much order and tidiness, repaired the hinges of a rebellious shutter and the lock of an unyielding door, and yet had apparently retained an unabated interest in her spoken woes. Surprised once more into recognizing this devotion, Sister Hiler abruptly arrested her monologue.

"Well, if you ain't the handiest man I ever seed about a house!"

"Am I?" said Gideon, with suddenly sparkling eyes. "Do you really think so?"

"I do."

"Then you don't know how glad I am." His frank face so unmistakably showed his simple gratification that the widow, after gazing at him for a moment, was suddenly seized with a bewildering fancy. The first effect of it was the abrupt withdrawal of her eyes, then a sudden effusion of blood to her forehead that finally extended to her cheek-bones, and then an interval of forgetfulness where she remained with a plate held vaguely in her hand. When she succeeded at last in putting it on the table instead of the young man's lap, she said in a voice quite unlike her own: — "Sho!"

"I mean it," said Gideon cheerfully. After a pause, in which he unostentatiously rearranged the table which the widow was abstractedly disorganizing, he said gently, "After tea, when you're not so much flustered with work and worry, and more composed in spirit, we'll have a little talk, Sister Hiler. I'm in no hurry to-night, and if you don't mind I'll make myself comfortable in the barn with my blanket until sunup to-morrow. I can get up early enough to do some odd chores round the lot before I go."

"You know best, Brother Gideon," said the widow faintly, "and if you think it's the Lord's will, and no speshal trouble to you, so do. But sakes alive! it's time I tidied myself a little," she continued, lifting one hand to her hair, while with the other she endeavored to fasten a buttonless collar; "leavin' alone the vanities o' dress, it's ez much as one can do to keep a clean rag on with the children climbin' over ye. Sit by, and I'll be back in a minit." She retired to the back room, and in a few moments returned with smoothed hair and a palm-leaf broché shawl thrown over her shoulders, which not only concealed the ravages made by time and maternity on the gown beneath, but to some extent gave her the suggestion of being a casual visitor in her own household. It must be confessed that for the rest of the evening Sister Hiler rather lent herself to this idea, possibly from the fact that it temporarily obliterated the children, and quite removed her from any responsibility in the unpicturesque household. This effect was only marred by the absence of any impression upon Gideon, who scarcely appeared to notice the change, and whose soft eyes seemed rather to identify the miserable woman under her forced disguise. He prefaced the meal with a fervent grace, to which the widow listened with something of the conscious attitude she had adopted at church during her late husband's ministration, and during the meal she ate with a like consciousness of "company manners."

Later that evening Selby Hiler woke up in his little truckle bed, listening to the rising midnight wind, which in his childish fancy he confounded with the sound of voices that came through the open door of the living-room. He recognized the deep voice of the young minister, Gideon, and the occasional tearful responses of his mother, and he was fancying himself again at church when he heard a step, and the young preacher seemed to enter the room, and going to the bed leaned over it and kissed him on the forehead, and then bent over his little brother and sister and kissed them too. Then he slowly reëntered the living-room. Lifting himself softly on his elbow, Selby saw him go up towards his mother, who was crying, with her head on the table, and kiss her also on the forehead. Then he said "Good-night," and the front door closed, and Selby heard his footsteps crossing the lot towards the barn. His mother was still sitting with her face buried in her hands when he fell asleep.

She sat by the dying embers of the fire until the house was still again; then she rose and wiped her eyes. "Et's a good thing," she said, going to the bedroom door, and looking in upon her sleeping children; "et's a mercy and a blessing for them and — for — me. But — but — he might — hev — said — he — loved me!"

III

Although Gideon Deane contrived to find a nest for his blanket in the mouldy straw of the unfinished barn loft, he could not sleep. He restlessly watched the stars through the cracks of the boarded roof, and listened to the wind that made the half-open structure as vocal as a sea-shell, until past midnight. Once or twice he had fancied he heard the tramp of horse-hoofs on the far-off trail, and now it seemed to approach nearer, mingled with the sound of voices. Gideon raised his head and looked through the doorway of the loft. He was not mistaken; two men had halted in the road before the house, and were examining it as if uncertain if it were the dwelling they were seeking, and were hesitating if they should rouse the inmates. Thinking he might spare the widow the disturbance to her slumbers, and possibly some alarm, he rose quickly, and descending to the inclosure walked towards the house. As he approached the men advanced to meet him, and by accident or design ranged themselves on either side. A glance showed him they were strangers to the locality.

"We're lookin' fer the preacher that lives here," said one, who seemed to be the elder. "A man by the name o' Hiler, I reckon!"

"Brother Hiler has been dead two years," responded Gideon. "His widow and children live here."

The two men looked at each other. The younger one laughed; the elder mumbled something about its being "three years ago," and then turning suddenly on Gideon, said: —

"P'r'aps *you're* a preacher?"

"I am."

"Can you come to a dying man?"

"I will."

The two men again looked at each other. "But," continued Gideon softly, "you'll please keep quiet so as not to disturb the widow and her children while I get my horse." He turned away; the younger man made a movement as if to stop him, but the elder quickly restrained his hand. "He isn't goin' to run away," he whispered. "Look," he added, as Gideon a moment later reappeared mounted and equipped.

"Do you think we'll be in time?" asked the young preacher as they rode quickly away in the direction of the tules.

The younger repressed a laugh; the other answered grimly, "I reckon."

"And is he conscious of his danger?"

"I reckon."

Gideon did not speak again. But as the onus of that silence seemed to rest upon the other two, the last speaker, after a few moments' silent and rapid riding, continued abruptly, "You don't seem curious?"

"Of what?" said Gideon, lifting his soft eyes to the speaker. "You tell me of a brother at the point of death, who seeks the Lord through an humble vessel like myself. *He* will tell me the rest."

A silence still more constrained on the part of the two strangers followed, which they endeavored to escape from by furious riding; so that in half an hour the party had reached a point where the tules began to sap the arid plain, while beyond them broadened the lagoons of the distant river. In the foreground, near a clump of dwarfed willows, a camp-fire was burning, round which fifteen or twenty armed men were collected, their horses picketed in an outer circle guarded by two mounted sentries. A blasted cottonwood with a single black arm extended over the tules stood ominously against the dark sky.

The circle opened to receive them and closed again. The elder man dismounted, and leading Gideon to the blasted cottonwood, pointed to a pinioned man seated at its foot with an armed guard over him. He looked up at Gideon with an amused smile.

"You said it was a dying man," said Gideon, recoiling.

"He will be a dead man in half an hour," returned the stranger.

"And you?"

"We are the Vigilantes from Alamo. This man," pointing to the prisoner, "is a gambler who killed a man yesterday. We hunted him here, tried him an hour ago, and found him guilty. The last man we hung here, three years ago, asked for a parson. We brought him the man who used to live where we found you. So we thought we'd give this man the same show, and brought you."

"And if I refuse?" said Gideon.

The leader shrugged his shoulders.

"That's *his* lookout, not ours. We've given him the chance. Drive ahead, boys," he added, turning to the others; "the parson allows he won't take a hand."

"One moment," said Gideon, in desperation, "one moment, for the sake of that God you have brought me here to invoke in behalf of this wretched man. One moment, for the sake of Him in whose presence you must stand one day as he does now." With passionate earnestness he pointed out the vindictive impulse they were mistaking for Divine justice; with pathetic fervency he fell upon his knees and implored their mercy for the culprit. But in vain. As at the camp-meeting of the day before, he was chilled to find his words seemed to fall on unheeding and unsympathetic ears. He looked around on their abstracted faces; in their gloomy savage enthusiasm for expiatory sacrifice, he was horrified to find the same unreasoning exaltation that had checked his exhortations then. Only one face looked upon his, half mischievously, half compassionately. It was the prisoner's.

"Yer wastin' time on us," said the leader dryly; "wastin' *his* time. Hadn't you better talk to him?"

Gideon rose to his feet, pale and cold. "He may have something to confess. May I speak with him alone?" he said gently.

The leader motioned to the sentry to fall back. Gideon placed himself before the prisoner so that in the faint light of the camp-fire the man's figure was partly hidden by his own. "You meant well with your little bluff, pardner," said the prisoner, not unkindly, "but they've got the cards to win."

"Kneel down with your back to me," said Gideon in a low voice. The prisoner fell on his knees. At the same time he felt Gideon's hand and the gliding of steel behind his back, and the severed cords hung loosely on his arms and legs.

"When I lift my voice to God, brother," said Gideon softly, "drop on your face and crawl as far as you can in a straight line in my shadow, then break for the tules. I will stand between you and their first fire."

"Are you mad?" said the prisoner. "Do you think they won't fire lest they should hurt you? Man! they'll kill *you*, the first thing."

"So be it — if your chance is better."

Still on his knees, the man grasped Gideon's two hands in his own and devoured him with his eyes.

"You mean it?"

"I do."

"Then," said the prisoner quietly, "I reckon I'll stop and hear what you've got to say about God until they're ready."

"You refuse to fly?"

"I reckon I was never better fitted to die than now," said the prisoner, still grasping his hand. After a pause he added in a lower

tone, "I can't pray — but — I think," he hesitated — "I think I
could manage to ring in in a hymn."

"Will you try, brother?"

"Yes."

With their hands tightly clasped together, Gideon lifted his
gentle voice. The air was a common one, familiar in the local
religious gatherings, and after the first verse one or two of the
sullen lookers-on joined not unkindly in the refrain. But as he
went on the air and words seemed to offer a vague expression to
the dull, lowering animal emotion of the savage concourse; and at
the end of the second verse the refrain, augmented in volume and
swelled by every voice in the camp, swept out over the hollow plain.

It was met in the distance by a far-off cry. With an oath taking
the place of his supplication, the leader sprang to his feet. But too
late! The cry was repeated as a nearer slogan of defiance — the
plain shook — there was the tempestuous onset of furious hoofs —
a dozen shots — the scattering of the embers of the camp-fire into
a thousand vanishing sparks even as the lurid gathering of savage
humanity was dispersed and dissipated over the plain, and Gideon
and the prisoner stood alone. But as the sheriff of Contra Costa with
his rescuing posse swept by, the man they had come to save fell
forward in Gideon's arms with a bullet in his breast — the Parthian
shot of the flying Vigilante leader.

The eager crowd that surged around him with outstretched,
helping hands would have hustled Gideon aside. But the wounded
man roused himself, and throwing an arm around the preacher's
neck, warned them back with the other. "Stand back!" he gasped.
"He risked his life for mine! Look at him, boys! Wanted ter stand
up 'twixt them hounds and me and draw their fire on himself!
Ain't he just hell?" he stopped; an apologetic smile crossed his lips.
"I clean forgot, pardner; but it's all right. I said I was ready to go;
and I am." His arm slipped from Gideon's neck; he slid to the
ground; he had fainted.

A dark, military-looking man pushed his way through the crowd
— the surgeon, one of the posse, accompanied by a younger man
fastidiously dressed. The former bent over the unconscious prisoner, and tore open his shirt; the latter followed his movements

with a flush of anxious inquiry in his handsome, careless face. After a moment's pause the surgeon, without looking up, answered the young man's mute questioning. "Better send the sheriff here at once, Jack."

"He is here," responded the official, joining the group.

The surgeon looked up at him. "I am afraid they've put the case out of your jurisdiction, sheriff," he said grimly. "It's only a matter of a day or two at best — perhaps only a few hours. But he won't live to be taken back to jail."

"Will he live to go as far as Martinez?" asked the young man addressed as Jack.

"With care, perhaps."

"Will you be responsible for him, Jack Hamlin?" said the sheriff suddenly.

"I will."

"Then take him. Stay, he's coming to."

The wounded man slowly opened his eyes. They fell upon Jack Hamlin with a pleased look of recognition, but almost instantly and anxiously glanced around as if seeking another. Leaning over him, Jack said gayly, "They've passed you over to me, old man; are you willing?"

The wounded man's eyes assented, but still moved restlessly from side to side.

"Is there any one you want to go with you?"

"Yes," said the eyes.

"The doctor, of course?"

The eyes did not answer. Gideon dropped on his knees beside him. A ray of light flashed in the helpless man's eyes and transfigured his whole face.

"You want *him?*" said Jack incredulously.

"Yes," said the eyes.

"What — the preacher?"

The lips struggled to speak. Everybody bent down to hear his reply.

"You bet," he said faintly.

IV

It was early morning when the wagon containing the wounded man, Gideon, Jack Hamlin, and the surgeon crept slowly through the streets of Martinez and stopped before the door of the "Palmetto Shades." The upper floor of this saloon and hostelry was occupied by Mr. Hamlin as his private lodgings, and was fitted up with the usual luxury and more than the usual fastidiousness of his extravagant class. As the dusty and travel-worn party trod the soft carpets and brushed aside the silken hangings in their slow progress with their helpless burden to the lace-canopied and snowy couch of the young gambler, it seemed almost a profanation of some feminine seclusion. Gideon, to whom such luxury was unknown, was profoundly troubled. The voluptuous ease and sensuousness, the refinements of a life of irresponsible indulgence, affected him with a physical terror to which in his late moment of real peril he had been a stranger; the gilding and mirrors blinded his eyes; even the faint perfume seemed to him an unhallowed incense, and turned him sick and giddy. Accustomed as he had been to disease and misery in their humblest places and meanest surroundings, the wounded desperado lying in laces and fine linen seemed to him monstrous and unnatural. It required all his self-abnegation, all his sense of duty, all his deep pity, and all the instinctive tact which was born of his gentle thoughtfulness for others, to repress a shrinking. But when the miserable cause of all again opened his eyes and sought Gideon's hand, he forgot it all. Happily, Hamlin, who had been watching him with wondering but critical eyes, mistook his concern. "Don't you worry about that gin-mill and hash-gymnasium downstairs," he said. "I've given the proprietor a thousand dollars to shut up shop as long as this thing lasts." That this was done from some delicate sense of respect to the preacher's domiciliary presence, and not entirely to secure complete quiet and seclusion for the invalid, was evident from the fact that Mr. Hamlin's drawing and dining rooms, and even the hall, were filled with eager friends and inquirers. It was discomposing to Gideon to find himself almost an equal subject of interest and curiosity to the visitors. The story of his simple devotion had lost nothing by report; hats were doffed in his presence that might have grown to their wearers' heads; the boldest eyes dropped as he passed by; he had only to put his pale face out of the bedroom door and the loudest discussion, heated by drink or affection, fell to a whisper. The surgeon, who had recognized the one dominant wish of the hopelessly sinking man, gravely retired, leaving Gideon a few simple instructions and directions for their use. "He'll last as long as he has need of you," he said respectfully. "My art is only second here. God help you both! When he wakes, make the most of your time."

In a few moments he did waken, and as before turned his fading look almost instinctively on the faithful, gentle eyes that were watching him. How Gideon made the most of his time did not transpire, but at the end of an hour, when the dying man had again lapsed into unconsciousness, he softly opened the door of the sitting-room.

Hamlin started hastily to his feet. He had cleared the room of his visitors, and was alone. He turned a moment towards the window before he faced Gideon with inquiring but curiously shining eyes.

"Well?" he said hesitatingly.

"Do you know Kate Somers?" asked Gideon.

Hamlin opened his brown eyes. "Yes."

"Can you send for her?"

"What, *here?*"

"Yes, here."

"What for?"

"To marry him," said Gideon gently. "There's no time to lose."

"To *marry* him?"

"He wishes it."

"But say — oh, come, now," said Hamlin confidentially, leaning back with his hands on the top of a chair. "Ain't this playing it a little — just a *little* — too low down? Of course you mean well, and all that; but come, now, say — couldn't you just let up on him there? Why, she" — Hamlin softly closed the door — "she's got no character."

"The more reason he should give her one."

A cynical knowledge of matrimony imparted to him by the

wives of others evidently colored Mr. Hamlin's views. "Well, perhaps it's all the same if he's going to die. But isn't it rather rough
on *her?* I don't know," he added reflectively; "she was sniveling
round here a little while ago, until I sent her away."

"You sent her away!" echoed Gideon.

"I did."

"Why?"

"Because *you* were here."

Nevertheless Mr. Hamlin departed, and in half an hour reappeared with two brilliantly dressed women. One, hysterical, tearful, frightened, and pallid, was the destined bride; the other, highly
colored, excited, and pleasantly observant, was her friend. Two men
hastily summoned from the anteroom as witnesses completed the
group that moved into the bedroom and gathered round the bed.

The ceremony was simple and brief. It was well, for of all who
took part in it none was more shaken by emotion than the officiating
priest. The brilliant dresses of the women, the contrast of their
painted faces with the waxen pallor of the dying man; the terrible incongruity of their voices, inflections, expressions, and familiarity; the mingled perfume of cosmetics and the faint odor of
wine; the eyes of the younger woman following his movements
with strange absorption, so affected him that he was glad when
he could fall on his knees at last and bury his face in the pillow
of the sufferer. The hand that had been placed in the bride's cold
fingers slipped from them and mechanically sought Gideon's again.
The significance of the unconscious act brought the first spontaneous tears into the woman's eyes. It was his last act, for when
Gideon's voice was again lifted in prayer, the spirit for whom it
was offered had risen with it, as it were, still lovingly hand in hand,
from the earth forever.

The funeral was arranged for two days later, and Gideon found
that his services had been so seriously yet so humbly counted upon
by the friends of the dead man that he could scarce find it in his
heart to tell them that it was the function of the local preacher —
an older and more experienced man than himself. "If it is," said
Jack Hamlin coolly, "I'm afraid he won't get a yaller dog to come
to his church; but if you say you'll preach at the grave, there ain't

a man, woman, or child that will be kept away. Don't you go back on your luck, now; it's something awful and nigger-like. You've got this crowd where the hair is short; excuse me, but it's so. Talk of revivals! You could give that one-horse show in Tasajara a hundred points, and skunk them easily." Indeed had Gideon been accessible to vanity, the spontaneous homage he met with everywhere would have touched him more sympathetically and kindly than it did; but in the utter unconsciousness of his own power and the quality they worshiped in him, he felt alarmed and impatient of what he believed to be their weak sympathy with his own human weakness. In the depth of his unselfish heart, it must be confessed, only by the scant, inefficient lamp of his youthful experience, he really believed he had failed in his apostolic mission because he had been unable to touch the heart of the Vigilantes by oral appeal and argument. Feeling thus, the reverence of these irreligious people that surrounded him, the facile yielding of their habits and prejudices to his half-uttered wish, appeared to him only a temptation of the flesh. No one had sought him after the manner of the camp-meeting; he had converted the wounded man through a common weakness of their humanity. More than that, he was conscious of a growing fascination for the truthfulness and sincerity of that class; particularly of Mr. Jack Hamlin, whose conversion he felt he could never attempt, yet whose strange friendship alternately thrilled and frightened him.

It was the evening before the funeral. The coffin, half smothered in wreaths and flowers, stood upon trestles in the anteroom, a large silver plate bearing an inscription on which for the second time Gideon read the name of the man he had converted. It was a name associated on the frontier so often with reckless hardihood, dissipation, and blood, that even now Gideon trembled at his presumption, and was chilled by a momentary doubt of the efficiency of his labor. Drawing unconsciously nearer to the mute subject of his thoughts, he threw his arms across the coffin and buried his face between them.

A stream of soft music, the echo of some forgotten song, seemed to Gideon to suddenly fill and possess the darkened room, and then to slowly die away like the opening and shutting of a door upon a flood of golden radiance. He listened with hushed breath and a beating heart. He had never heard anything like it before. Again the strain arose, the chords swelled round him, until from their midst a tenor voice broke high and steadfast, like a star in troubled skies. Gideon scarcely breathed. It was a hymn — but such a hymn. He had never conceived there could be such beautiful words, joined to such exquisite melody, and sung with a grace so tender and true. What were all other hymns to this ineffable yearning for light, for love, and for infinite rest? Thrilled and exalted, Gideon felt his doubts pierced and scattered by that illuminating cry. Suddenly he rose, and with a troubled thought pushed open the door to the sitting-room. It was Mr. Jack Hamlin sitting before a parlor organ. The music ceased.

"It was *you*," stammered Gideon.

Jack nodded, struck a few chords by way of finish, and then wheeled round on the music-stool towards Gideon. His face was slightly flushed. "Yes. I used to be the organist and tenor in our church in the States. I used to snatch the sinners bald-headed with that. Do you know I reckon I'll sing that to-morrow, if you like, and maybe afterwards we'll — but" — he stopped — "we'll talk of that after the funeral. It's business." Seeing Gideon still glancing with a troubled air from the organ to himself, he said: "Would you like to try that hymn with me? Come on!"

He again struck the chords. As the whole room seemed to throb with the music, Gideon felt himself again carried away. Glancing over Jack's shoulders, he could read the words but not the notes; yet, having a quick ear for rhythm, he presently joined in with a deep but uncultivated baritone. Together they forgot everything else, and at the end of an hour were only recalled by the presence of a silently admiring concourse of votive-offering friends who had gathered round them.

The funeral took place the next day at the grave dug in the public cemetery — a green area fenced in by the palisading tules. The words of Gideon were brief but humble; the strongest partisan of the dead man could find no fault in a confession of human frailty in which the speaker humbly confessed his share; and when the hymn was started by Hamlin and taken up by Gideon, the vast multitude, drawn by interest and curiosity, joined as in a solemn Amen.

Later, when those two strangely assorted friends had returned to Mr. Hamlin's rooms previous to Gideon's departure, the former, in a manner more serious than his habitual cynical good humor, began: "I said I had to talk business with you. The boys about here want to build a church for you, and are ready to plank the money down if you'll say it's a go. You understand they aren't asking you to run in opposition to that Gospel sharp — excuse me — that's here now, nor do they want you to run a side show in connection with it. They want you to be independent. They don't pin you down to any kind of religion, you know; whatever you care to give them — Methodist, Roman Catholic, Presbyterian — is mighty good enough for them, if you'll expound it. You might give a little of each, or one on one day and one another — they'll never know the difference if you only mix the drinks yourself. They'll give you a house and guarantee you fifteen hundred dollars the first year."

He stopped and walked towards the window. The sunlight that fell upon his handsome face seemed to call back the careless smile to his lips and the reckless fire to his brown eyes. "I don't suppose there's a man among them that wouldn't tell you all this in a great deal better way than I do. But the darned fools — excuse me — would have *me* break it to you. Why, I don't know. I needn't tell you I like you — not only for what you did for George — but I like you for your style — for yourself. And I want you to accept. You could keep these rooms till they got a house ready for you. Together — you and me — we'd make that organ howl. But because I like it — because it's everything to us — and nothing to you, it don't seem square for me to ask it. Does it?"

Gideon replied by taking Hamlin's hand. His face was perfectly pale, but his look collected. He had not expected this offer, and yet when it was made he felt as if he had known it before — as if he had been warned of it — as if it was the great temptation of his life. Watching him with an earnestness only slightly overlaid by his usual manner, Hamlin went on: —

"I know it would be lonely here, and a man like you ought to have a wife for" — he slightly lifted his eyebrows — "for example's

sake. I heard there was a young lady in the case over there in
Tasajara — but the old people didn't see it on account of your position. They'd jump at it now. Eh? No? Well," continued Jack, with
a decent attempt to conceal his cynical relief, "perhaps those boys
have been so eager to find out all they could do for you that they've
been sold. Perhaps we're making equal fools of ourselves now in
asking you to stay. But don't say no just yet — take a day or a week
to think of it."

Gideon still pale but calm, cast his eyes around the elegant room,
at the magic organ, then upon the slight handsome figure before
him. "I *will* think of it," he said in a low voice, as he pressed Jack's
hand. "And if I accept you will find me here to-morrow afternoon
at this time; if I do not you will know that I keep with me where-
ever I go the kindness, the brotherly love, and the grace of God
that prompts your offer, even though He withholds from me His
blessed light, which alone can make me know His wish." He
stopped and hesitated. "If you love me, Jack, don't ask me to stay,
but pray for that light which alone can guide my feet back to you,
or take me hence forever."

He once more tightly pressed the hand of the embarrassed man
before him and was gone.

Passers-by on the Martinez road that night remembered a mute
and ghostly rider who, heedless of hail or greeting, moved by them
as in a trance or vision. But the Widow Hiler the next morning,
coming from the spring, found no abstraction or preoccupation in
the soft eyes of Gideon Deane as he suddenly appeared before her,
and gently relieved her of the bucket she was carrying. A quick flush
of color over her brow and cheek-bones, as if a hot iron had passed
there, and a certain astringent coyness, would have embarrassed
any other man than him.

"Sho, it's *you*. I reck'ned I'd seen the last of you."

"You don't mean that, Sister Hiler?" said Gideon, with a gentle
smile.

"Well, what with the report of your goin's on at Martinez and
improvin' the occasion of that sinner's death, and leadin' a revival,
I reckoned you'd have forgotten low folks at Tasajara. And if you're
goin' to be settled there in a new church, with new hearers, I reckon

you'll want new surroundings too. Things change and young folks change with 'em."

They had reached the house. Her breath was quick and short as if she and not Gideon had borne the burden. He placed the bucket in its accustomed place and then gently took her hand in his. The act precipitated the last drop of feeble coquetry she had retained, and the old tears took its place. Let us hope for the last time. For as Gideon stooped and lifted her ailing babe in his strong arms, he said softly, "Whatever God has wrought for me since we parted, I know now He has called me to but one work."

"And that work?" she asked tremulously.

"To watch over the widow and fatherless. And with God's blessing, sister, and His holy ordinance, I am here to stay."

AN INGENUE
OF THE SIERRAS

I

WE ALL HELD our breath as the coach rushed through the semi-darkness of Galloper's Ridge. The vehicle itself was only a huge lumbering shadow; its side-lights were carefully extinguished, and Yuba Bill had just politely removed from the lips of an outside passenger even the cigar with which he had been ostentatiously exhibiting his coolness. For it had been rumored that the Ramon Martinez gang of "road agents" were "laying" for us on the second grade, and would time the passage of our lights across Galloper's in order to intercept us in the "brush" beyond. If we could cross the ridge without being seen, and so get through the brush before they reached it, we were safe. If they followed, it would only be a stern chase with the odds in our favor.

The huge vehicle swayed from side to side, rolled, dipped, and plunged, but Bill kept the track, as if, in the whispered words of the Expressman, he could "feel and smell" the road he could no longer see. We knew that at times we hung perilously over the edge of slopes that eventually dropped a thousand feet sheer to the tops of the sugar-pines below, but we knew that Bill knew it also. The half visible heads of the horses, drawn wedge-wise together by the tightened reins, appeared to cleave the darkness like a plough-share, held between his rigid hands. Even the hoof-beats of the six horses had fallen into a vague, monotonous, distant roll. Then the ridge was crossed, and we plunged into the still blacker obscurity of the brush. Rather we no longer seemed to move — it was only

151

the phantom night that rushed by us. The horses might have been submerged in some swift Lethean stream; nothing but the top of the coach and the rigid bulk of Yuba Bill arose above them. Yet even in that awful moment our speed was unslackened; it was as if Bill cared no longer to *guide* but only to drive, or as if the direction of this huge machine was determined by other hands than his. An incautious whisperer hazarded the paralyzing suggestion of our "meeting another team." To our great astonishment Bill overheard it; to our greater astonishment he replied. "It 'ud be only a neck and neck race which would get to h—ll first," he said quietly. But we were relieved — for he had *spoken!* Almost simultaneously the wider turnpike began to glimmer faintly as a visible track before us; the wayside trees fell out of line, opened up, and dropped off one after another; we were on the broader tableland, out of danger, and apparently unperceived and unpursued.

Nevertheless in the conversation that broke out again with the relighting of the lamps, and the comments, congratulations, and reminiscences that were freely exchanged, Yuba Bill preserved a dissatisfied and even resentful silence. The most generous praise of his skill and courage awoke no response. "I reckon the old man waz just spilin' for a fight, and is feelin' disappointed," said a passenger. But those who knew that Bill had the true fighter's scorn for any purely purposeless conflict were more or less concerned and watchful of him. He would drive steadily for four or five minutes with thoughtfully knitted brows, but eyes still keenly observant under his slouched hat, and then, relaxing his strained attitude, would give way to a movement of impatience. "You ain't uneasy about anything, Bill, are you?" asked the Expressman confidentially. Bill lifted his eyes with a slightly contemptuous surprise. "Not about anything ter *come*. It's what *hez* happened that I don't exackly *sabe*. I don't see no signs of Ramon's gang ever havin' been out at all, and ef they were out I don't see why they didn't go for us."

"The simple fact is that our ruse was successful," said an outside passenger. "They waited to see our lights on the ridge, and, not seeing them, missed us until we had passed. That's my opinion."

"You ain't puttin' any price on that opinion, air ye?" inquired Bill politely.

"No."

"'Cos thar's a comic paper in 'Frisco pays for them things, and I've seen worse things in it."

"Come off, Bill," retorted the passenger, slightly nettled by the tittering of his companions. "Then what did you put out the lights for?"

"Well," returned Bill grimly, "it mout have been because I didn't keer to hev you chaps blazin' away at the first bush you *thought* you saw move in your skeer, and bringin' down their fire on us."

The explanation, though unsatisfactory, was by no means an improbable one, and we thought it better to accept it with a laugh. Bill, however, resumed his abstracted manner.

"Who got in at the Summit?" he at last asked abruptly of the Expressman.

"Derrick and Simpson of Cold Spring, and one of the 'Excelsior' boys," responded the Expressman.

"And that Pike County girl from Dow's Flat, with her bundles. Don't forget her," added the outside passenger ironically.

"Does anybody here know her?" continued Bill, ignoring the irony.

"You'd better ask Judge Thompson; he was mighty attentive to her; gettin' her a seat by the off window, and lookin' after her bundles and things."

"Gettin' her a seat by the *window?*" repeated Bill.

"Yes, she wanted to see everything, and wasn't afraid of the shooting."

"Yes," broke in a third passenger, "and he was so d——d civil that when she dropped her ring in the straw, he struck a match agin all your rules, you know, and held it for her to find it. And it was just as we were crossin' through the brush, too. I saw the hull thing through the window, for I was hanging over the wheels with my gun ready for action. And it wasn't no fault of Judge Thompson if his d——d foolishness hadn't shown us up, and got us a shot from the gang."

Bill gave a short grunt, but drove steadily on without further comment or even turning his eyes to the speaker.

We were now not more than a mile from the station at the cross-roads where we were to change horses. The lights already glimmered in the distance, and there was a faint suggestion of the coming dawn on the summits of the ridge to the west. We had plunged into a belt of timber, when suddenly a horseman emerged at a sharp canter from a trail that seemed to be parallel with our own. We

were all slightly startled; Yuba Bill alone preserving his moody calm.

"Hullo!" he said.

The stranger wheeled to our side as Bill slackened his speed. He seemed to be a "packer" or freight muleteer.

"Ye didn't get 'held up' on the Divide?" continued Bill cheerfully.

"No," returned the packer, with a laugh; "*I* don't carry treasure. But I see you're all right, too. I saw you crossin' over Galloper's."

"*Saw* us?" said Bill sharply. "We had our lights out."

"Yes, but there was suthin' white—a handkerchief or woman's veil, I reckon—hangin' from the window. It was only a movin' spot agin the hillside, but ez I was lookin' out for ye I knew it was you by that. Good-night!"

He cantered away. We tried to look at each other's faces, and at Bill's expression in the darkness, but he neither spoke nor stirred until he threw down the reins when we stopped before the station. The passengers quickly descended from the roof; the Expressman was about to follow, but Bill plucked his sleeve.

"I'm goin' to take a look over this yer stage and these yer passengers with ye, afore we start."

"Why, what's up?"

"Well," said Bill, slowly disengaging himself from one of his enormous gloves, "when we waltzed down into the brush up there I saw a man, ez plain ez I see you, rise up from it. I thought our time had come and the band was goin' to play, when he sorter drew back, made a sign, and we just scooted past him."

"Well?"

"Well," said Bill, "it means that this yer coach was *passed through free* to-night."

"You don't object to *that*—surely? I think we were deucedly lucky."

Bill slowly drew off his other glove. "I've been riskin' my everlastin' life on this d—d line three times a week," he said with mock humility, "and I'm allus thankful for small mercies. *But,*" he added grimly, "when it comes down to being passed free by some pal of a hoss thief, and thet called a speshal Providence, *I ain't in it!* No, sir, I ain't in it!"

II

It was with mixed emotions that the passengers heard that a delay of fifteen minutes to tighten certain screwbolts had been ordered by the autocratic Bill. Some were anxious to get their breakfast at Sugar Pine, but others were not averse to linger for the daylight that promised greater safety on the road. The Expressman, knowing the real cause of Bill's delay, was nevertheless at a loss to understand the object of it. The passengers were all well known; any idea of complicity with the road agents was wild and impossible, and, even if there was a confederate of the gang among them, he would have been more likely to precipitate a robbery than to check it. Again, the discovery of such a confederate—to whom they clearly owed their safety—and his arrest would have been quite against the Californian sense of justice, if not actually il-legal. It seemed evident that Bill's quixotic sense of honor was lead-ing him astray.

The station consisted of a stable, a wagon shed, and a building containing three rooms. The first was fitted up with "bunks" or sleeping berths for the employees; the second was the kitchen; and the third and larger apartment was dining-room or sitting-room, and was used as general waiting-room for the passengers. It was not a refreshment station, and there was no "bar." But a mysterious command from the omnipotent Bill produced a demijohn of whis-key, with which he hospitably treated the company. The seductive influence of the liquor loosened the tongue of the gallant Judge Thompson. He admitted to having struck a match to enable the fair Pike Countian to find her ring, which, however, proved to have fallen in her lap. She was "a fine, healthy young woman — a type of the Far West, sir; in fact, quite a prairie blossom! yet simple and guile-less as a child." She was on her way to Marysville, he believed, "al-though she expected to meet friends — a friend, in fact — later on." It was her first visit to a large town — in fact, any civilized centre — since she crossed the plains three years ago. Her girlish curiosity was quite touching, and her innocence irresistible. In fact, in a country whose tendency was to produce "frivolity and forwardness in young girls, he found her a most interesting young person." She was even then out in the stable-yard watching the horses being harnessed, "preferring to indulge a pardonable healthy young curiosity than to listen to the empty compliments of the younger passengers."

The figure which Bill saw thus engaged, without being otherwise distinguished, certainly seemed to justify the Judge's opinion. She appeared to be a well-matured country girl, whose frank gray eyes and large laughing mouth expressed a wholesome and abiding grati-fication in her life and surroundings. She was watching the replac-ing of luggage in the boot. A little feminine start, as one of her own parcels was thrown somewhat roughly on the roof, gave Bill his opportunity. "Now there," he growled to the helper, "ye ain't cart-ing stone! Look out, will yer! Some of your things, miss?" he added, with gruff courtesy, turning to her. "These yer trunks, for in-stance?"

She smiled a pleasant assent, and Bill, pushing aside the helper, seized a large square trunk in his arms. But from excess of zeal, or some other mischance, his foot slipped, and he came down heavily, striking the corner of the trunk on the ground and loosening its hinges and fastenings. It was a cheap, common-looking affair, but the accident discovered in its yawning lid a quantity of white, lace-edged feminine apparel of an apparently superior quality.

The young lady uttered another cry and came quickly forward, but Bill was profuse in his apologies, himself girded the broken box with a strap, and declared his intention of having the company "make it good" to her with a new one. Then he casually accompanied her to the door of the waiting-room, entered, made a place for her before the fire by simply lifting the nearest and most youthful passenger by the coat collar from the stool that he was occupying, and, having installed the lady in it, displaced another man who was standing before the chimney, and, drawing himself up to his full six feet of height in front of her, glanced down upon his fair passenger as he took his waybill from his pocket.

"Your name is down here as Miss Mullins?" he said.

She looked up, became suddenly aware that she and her questioner were the centre of interest to the whole circle of passengers, and, with a slight rise of color, returned, "Yes."

"Well, Miss Mullins, I've got a question or two to ask ye. I ask it straight out afore this crowd. It's in my rights to take ye aside and ask it— but that ain't my style; I'm no detective. I needn't ask it at all, but act as ef I knowed the answer, or I might leave it to be asked by others. Ye needn't answer it ef ye don't like; ye've got a friend over ther— Judge Thompson— who is a friend to ye, right or wrong, jest as any other man here is— as though ye'd packed your own jury. Well, the simple question I've got to ask ye is *this:* Did you signal to anybody from the coach when we passed Galloper's an hour ago?"

We all thought that Bill's courage and audacity had reached its climax here. To openly and publicly accuse a "lady" before a group of chivalrous Californians, and that lady possessing the further attractions of youth, good looks, and innocence, was little short of desperation. There was an evident movement of adhesion towards the fair stranger, a slight muttering broke out on the right, but the very boldness of the act held them in stupefied surprise. Judge Thompson, with a bland propitiatory smile began: "Really, Bill, I must protest on behalf of this young lady" — when the fair accused, raising her eyes to her accuser, to the consternation of everybody answered with the slight but convincing hesitation of conscientious truthfulness: —

"*I did.*"

"Ahem!" interposed the Judge hastily, "er — that is — er — you allowed your handkerchief to flutter from the window, — I noticed it myself, — casually — one might say even playfully — but without any particular significance."

The girl, regarding her apologist with a singular mingling of pride and impatience, returned briefly: —

"I signaled."

"Who did you signal to?" asked Bill gravely.

"The young gentleman I'm going to marry."

A start, followed by a slight titter from the younger passengers, was instantly suppressed by a savage glance from Bill.

"What did you signal to him for?" he continued.

"To tell him I was here, and that it was all right," returned the young girl, with a steadily rising pride and color.

"Wot was all right?" demanded Bill.

"That I wasn't followed, and that he could meet me on the road beyond Cass's Ridge Station." She hesitated a moment, and then, with a still greater pride, in which a youthful defiance was still mingled, said: "I've run away from home to marry him. And I mean to! No one can stop me. Dad didn't like him just because he was poor, and dad's got money. Dad wanted me to marry a man I hate, and got a lot of dresses and things to bribe me."

"And you're taking them in your trunk to the other feller?" said Bill grimly.

"Yes, he's poor," returned the girl defiantly.

"Then your father's name is Mullins?" asked Bill.

"It's not Mullins. I — I — took that name," she hesitated, with her first exhibition of self-consciousness.

"Wot *is* his name?"

"Eli Hemmings."

A smile of relief and significance went around the circle. The fame of Eli or "Skinner" Hemmings, as a notorious miser and usurer, had passed even beyond Galloper's Ridge.

"The step that you're taking, Miss Mullins, I need not tell you, is one of great gravity," said Judge Thompson, with a certain paternal seriousness of manner, in which, however, we were glad to detect a glaring affectation; "and I trust that you and your affianced have fully weighed it. Far be it from me to interfere with or question the natural affections of two young people, but may I ask you what you know of the — er — young gentleman for whom you are sacrificing so much, and, perhaps, imperiling your whole future? For instance, have you known him long?"

The slightly troubled air of trying to understand, — not unlike the vague wonderment of childhood, — with which Miss Mullins had received the beginning of this exordium, changed to a relieved smile of comprehension as she said quickly, "Oh yes, nearly a whole year."

"And," said the Judge, smiling, "has he a vocation — is he in business?"

"Oh yes," she returned; "he's a collector."

"A collector?"

"Yes; he collects bills, you know, — money," she went on, with childish eagerness, "not for himself, — *he* never has any money, poor Charley, — but for his firm. It's dreadful hard work, too; keeps him out for days and nights, over bad roads and baddest weather. Sometimes, when he's stole over to the ranch just to see me, he's been so bad he could scarcely keep his seat in the saddle, much less stand. And he's got to take mighty big risks, too. Times the folks are cross with him and won't pay; once they shot him in the arm, and he came to me, and I helped do it up for him. But he don't mind. He's real brave, — jest as brave as he's good." There was such a wholesome ring of truth in this pretty praise that we were touched in sympathy with the speaker.

"What firm does he collect for?" asked the Judge gently.

"I don't know exactly — he won't tell me; but I think it's a Spanish firm. You see"—she took us all into her confidence with a sweeping smile of innocent yet half-mischievous artfulness—"I only know because I peeped over a letter he once got from his firm, telling him he must hustle up and be ready for the road the next day; but I think the name was Martinez—yes, Ramon Martinez."

In the dead silence that ensued—a silence so profound that we could hear the horses in the distant stable-yard rattling their harness—one of the younger "Excelsior" boys burst into a hysteric laugh, but the fierce eye of Yuba Bill was down upon him, and seemed to instantly stiffen him into a silent, grinning mask. The young girl, however, took no note of it. Following out, with lover-like diffusiveness, the reminiscences thus awakened, she went on:—

"Yes, it's mighty hard work, but he says it's all for me, and as soon as we're married he'll quit it. He might have quit it before, but he won't take no money of me, nor what I told him I could get out of dad! That ain't his style. He's mighty proud—if he is poor—is Charley. Why, thar's all ma's money which she left me in the Savin's Bank that I wanted to draw out—for I had the right—and give it to him, but he wouldn't hear of it! Why, he wouldn't take one of the things I've got with me, if he knew it. And so he goes on ridin' and ridin', here and there and everywhere, and gettin' more and more played out and sad, and thin and pale as a spirit, and always so uneasy about his business, and startin' up at times when we're meetin' out in the South Woods or in the far clearin', and sayin': 'I must be goin' now, Polly,' and yet always tryin' to be chiffle and chipper afore me. Why, he must have rid miles and miles to have watched for me thar in the brush at the foot of Galloper's to-night, jest to see if all was safe; and Lordy! I'd have given him the signal and showed a light if I'd died for it the next minit. There! That's what I know of Charley—that's what I'm running away from home for—that's what I'm running to him for, and I don't care who knows it! And I only wish I'd done it afore—and I would—if—if—if—he'd only *asked me!* There now!" She stopped, panted, and choked. Then one of the sudden transitions of youthful emotion overtook the eager, laughing face; it clouded up with the swift change of childhood, a lightning quiver of expression broke over it, and—then came the rain!

I think this simple act completed our utter demoralization! We smiled feebly at each other with that assumption of masculine superiority which is miserably conscious of its own helplessness at such moments. We looked out of the window, blew our noses, said: "Eh — what?" and "I say," vaguely to each other, and were greatly relieved, and yet apparently astonished, when Yuba Bill, who had turned his back upon the fair speaker, and was kicking the logs in the fireplace, suddenly swept down upon us and bundled us all into the road, leaving Miss Mullins alone. Then he walked aside with Judge Thompson for a few moments; returned to us, autocratically demanded of the party a complete reticence towards Miss Mullins on the subject-matter under discussion, reëntered the station, reappeared with the young lady, suppressed a faint idiotic cheer which broke from us at the spectacle of her innocent face once more cleared and rosy, climbed the box, and in another moment we were under way.

"Then she don't know what her lover is yet?" asked the Expressman eagerly.

"No."

"Are *you* certain it's one of the gang?"

"Can't say *for sure*. It mout be a young chap from Yolo who bucked agin the tiger at Sacramento, got regularly cleaned out and busted, and joined the gang for a flier. They say thar was a new hand in that job over at Keeley's, — and a mighty game one, too; and ez there was some buckshot onloaded that trip, he might hev got his share, and that would tally with what the girl said about his arm. See! Ef that's the man, I've heered he was the son of some big preacher in the States, and a college sharp to boot, who ran wild in 'Frisco, and played himself for all he was worth. They're the wust kind to kick when they once get a foot over the traces. For stiddy, comf'ble kempany," added Bill reflectively, "give *me* the son of a man that was *hanged!*"

"But what are you going to do about this?"

"That depends upon the feller who comes to meet her."

"But you ain't going to try to take him? That would be playing it pretty low down on them both."

"Keep your hair on, Jimmy! The Judge and me are only going to rastle with the sperrit of that gay young galoot, when he drops down for his girl — and exhort him pow'ful! Ef he allows he's convicted of sin and will find the Lord, we'll marry him and the gal offhand at the next station, and the Judge will officiate himself for nothin'. We're going' to have this yer elopement done on the square — and our waybill clean — you bet!"

"But you don't suppose he'll trust himself in your hands?"

"Polly will signal to him that it's all square."

"Ah!" said the Expressman. Nevertheless in those few moments the men seemed to have exchanged dispositions. The Expressman looked doubtfully, critically, and even cynically before him. Bill's face had relaxed, and something like a bland smile beamed across it, as he drove confidently and unhesitatingly forward.

Day, meantime, although full blown and radiant on the mountain summits around us, was yet nebulous and uncertain in the valleys into which we were plunging. Lights still glimmered in the cabins and few ranch buildings which began to indicate the thicker settlements. And the shadows were heaviest in a little copse, where a note from Judge Thompson in the coach was handed up to Yuba Bill, who at once slowly began to draw up his horses. The coach stopped finally near the junction of a small crossroad. At the same moment Miss Mullins slipped down from the vehicle, and, with a parting wave of her hand to the Judge, who had assisted her from the steps, tripped down the crossroad, and disappeared in its semi-obscurity. To our surprise the stage waited, Bill holding the reins listlessly in his hands. Five minutes passed — an eternity of expectation, and, as there was that in Yuba Bill's face which forbade idle questioning, an aching void of silence also! This was at last broken by a strange voice from the road: —

"Go on — we'll follow."

The coach started forward. Presently we heard the sound of other wheels behind us. We all craned our necks backward to get a view of the unknown, but by the growing light we could only see that we were followed at a distance by a buggy with two figures in it. Evidently Polly Mullins and her lover! We hoped that they would pass us. But the vehicle, although drawn by a fast horse, preserved its distance always, and it was plain that its driver had no desire to satisfy our curiosity. The Expressman had recourse to Bill.

"Is it the man you thought of?" he asked eagerly.

"I reckon," said Bill briefly.

"But," continued the Expressman, returning to his former skepticism, "what's to keep them both from levanting together now?"

Bill jerked his hand towards the boot with a grim smile.

"Their baggage."

"Oh!" said the Expressman.

"Yes," continued Bill. "We'll hang on to that gal's little frills and fixin's until this yer job's settled, and the ceremony's over, jest as ef we waz her own father. And, what's more, young man," he added, suddenly turning to the Expressman, *"you'll* express them trunks of hers *through to Sacramento* with your kempany's labels, and hand her the receipt and checks for them, so she *can get 'em there.* That'll keep *him* outer temptation and the reach o' the gang, until they get away among white men and civilization again. When your hoary-headed ole grandfather, or, to speak plainer, that partikler old whiskey-soaker known as Yuba Bill, wot sits on this box," he continued, with a diabolical wink at the Expressman, "waltzes in to pervide for a young couple jest startin' in life, thar's nothin' mean about his style, you bet. He fills the bill every time! Speshul Providences takes a back seat when he's around."

When the station hotel and straggling settlement of Sugar Pine, now distinct and clear in the growing light, at last rose within rifleshot on the plateau, the buggy suddenly darted swiftly by us, so swiftly that the faces of the two occupants were barely distinguishable as they passed, and keeping the lead by a dozen lengths, reached the door of the hotel. The young girl and her companion leaped down and vanished within as we drew up. They had evidently determined to elude our curiosity, and were successful.

But the material appetites of the passengers, sharpened by the keen mountain air, were more potent than their curiosity, and, as the breakfast-bell rang out at the moment the stage stopped, a majority of them rushed into the dining-room and scrambled for places without giving much heed to the vanished couple or to the

Judge and Yuba Bill, who had disappeared also. The through coach to Marysville and Sacramento was likewise waiting, for Sugar Pine was the limit of Bill's ministration, and the coach which we had just left went no farther. In the course of twenty minutes, however, there was a slight and somewhat ceremonious bustling in the hall and on the veranda, and Yuba Bill and the Judge reappeared. The latter was leading, with some elaboration of manner and detail, the shapely figure of Miss Mullins, and Yuba Bill was accompanying her companion to the buggy. We all rushed to the windows to get a good view of the mysterious stranger and probable ex-brigand whose life was now linked with our fair fellow-passenger. I am afraid, however, that we all participated in a certain impression of disappointment and doubt. Handsome and even cultivated-looking, he assuredly was — young and vigorous in appearance. But there was a certain half-shamed, half-defiant suggestion in his expression, yet coupled with a watchful lurking uneasiness which was not pleasant and hardly becoming in a bridegroom — and the possessor of such a bride. But the frank, joyous, innocent face of Polly Mullins, resplendent with a simple, happy confidence, melted our hearts again, and condoned the fellow's shortcomings. We waved our hands; I think we would have given three rousing cheers as they drove away if the omnipotent eye of Yuba Bill had not been upon us. It was well, for the next moment we were summoned to the presence of that soft-hearted autocrat.

We found him alone with the Judge in a private sitting-room, standing before a table on which there were a decanter and glasses. As we filed expectantly into the room and the door closed behind us, he cast a glance of hesitating tolerance over the group.

"Gentlemen," he said slowly, "you was all present at the beginnin' of a little game this mornin', and the Judge thar thinks that you oughter be let in at the finish. *I* don't see that it's any of *your* d—d business — so to speak; but ez the Judge here allows you're all in the secret, I've called you in to take a partin' drink to the health of Mr. and Mrs. Charley Byng — ez is now comf'ably off on their bridal tower. What *you* know or what *you* suspects of the young galoot that's married the gal ain't worth shucks to anybody, and I wouldn't give it to a yaller pup to play with, but the Judge thinks you ought all to promise right here that you'll keep it dark. That's his opinion. Ez far as my opinion goes, gen'l'men," continued Bill, with greater blandness and apparent cordiality, "I wanter simply remark, in a keerless, offhand, gin'ral way, that ef I ketch any God-forsaken, lop-eared, chuckle-headed blatherin' idjet airin' *his* opinion"—

"One moment, Bill," interposed Judge Thompson with a grave smile; "let me explain. You understand, gentlemen," he said, turning to us, "the singular, and I may say affecting, situation which our good-hearted friend here has done so much to bring to what we hope will be a happy termination. I want to give here, as my professional opinion, that there is nothing in his request which, in your capacity as good citizens and law-abiding men, you may not grant. I want to tell you, also, that you are condoning no offense against the statutes; that there is not a particle of legal evidence before us of the criminal antecedents of Mr. Charles Byng, except that which has been told you by the innocent lips of his betrothed, which the law of the land has now sealed forever in the mouth of his wife, and that our own actual experience of his acts has been in the main exculpatory of any previous irregularity—if not incompatible with it. Briefly, no judge would charge, no jury convict, on such evidence. When I add that the young girl is of legal age, that there is no evidence of any previous undue influence, but rather of the reverse, on the part of the bridegroom, and that I was content, as a magistrate, to perform the ceremony, I think you will be satisfied to give your promise, for the sake of the bride, and drink a happy life to them both."

I need not say that we did this cheerfully, and even extorted from Bill a grunt of satisfaction. The majority of the company, however, who were going with the through coach to Sacramento, then took their leave, and, as we accompanied them to the veranda, we could see that Miss Polly Mullins's trunks were already transferred to the other vehicle under the protecting seals and labels of the all-potent Express Company. Then the whip cracked, the coach rolled away, and the last traces of the adventurous young couple disappeared in the hanging red dust of its wheels.

But Yuba Bill's grim satisfaction at the happy issue of the episode

seemed to suffer no abatement. He even exceeded his usual deliberately regulated potations, and, standing comfortably with his back
to the centre of the now deserted bar-room, was more than usually
loquacious with the Expressman. "You see," he said, in bland
reminiscence, "when your old Uncle Bill takes hold of a job like
this, he puts it straight through without changin' hosses. Yet thar
was a moment, young feller, when I thought I was stompt! It was
when we'd made up our mind to make that chap tell the gal fust
all what he was! Ef she'd rared or kicked in the traces, or hung
back only ez much ez that, we'd hev given him jest five minits'
law to get up and get and leave her, and we'd hev toted that gal
and her fixin's back to her dad again! But she just gave a little
scream and start, and then went off inter hysterics, right on his
buzzum, laughin' and cryin' and sayin' that nothin' should part
'em. Gosh! if I didn't think *he* woz more cut up than she about it;
a minit it looked as ef *he* didn't allow to marry her arter all, but
that passed, and they was married hard and fast—you bet! I
reckon he's had enough of stayin' out o' nights to last him, and
ef the valley settlements hevn't got hold of a very shinin' member,
at least the foothills hev got shut of one more of the Ramon Martinez gang."

"What's that about the Ramon Martinez gang?" said a quiet
potential voice.

Bill turned quickly. It was the voice of the Divisional Superintendent of the Express Company, — a man of eccentric determination of character, and one of the few whom the autocratic Bill recognized as an equal, — who had just entered the bar-room. His dusty
pongee cloak and soft hat indicated that he had that morning arrived on a round of inspection.

"Don't care if I do, Bill," he continued, in response to Bill's
invitatory gesture, walking to the bar. "It's a little raw out on the
road. Well, what were you saying about the Ramon Martinez gang?
You haven't come across one of 'em, have you?"

"No," said Bill, with a slight blinking of his eye, as he ostentatiously lifted his glass to the light.

"And you *won't*," added the Superintendent, leisurely sipping
his liquor. "For the fact is, the gang is about played out. Not from

want of a job now and then, but from the difficulty of disposing of the results of their work. Since the new instructions to the agents to identify and trace all dust and bullion offered to them went into force, you see, they can't get rid of their swag. All the gang are spotted at the offices, and it costs too much for them to pay a fence or a middleman of any standing. Why, all that flaky river gold they took from the Excelsior Company can be identified as easy as if it was stamped with the company's mark. They can't melt it down themselves; they can't get others to do it for them; they can't ship it to the Mint or Assay Offices in Marysville and 'Frisco, for they won't take it without our certificate and seals; and *we* don't take any undeclared freight *within* the lines that we've drawn around their beat, except from people and agents known. Why, *you* know that well enough, Jim," he said, suddenly appealing to the Expressman, "don't you?"

Possibly the suddenness of the appeal caused the Expressman to swallow his liquor the wrong way, for he was overtaken with a fit of coughing, and stammered hastily as he laid down his glass, "Yes — of course — certainly."

"No, sir," resumed the Superintendent cheerfully, "they're pretty well played out. And the best proof of it is that they've lately been robbing ordinary passengers' trunks. There was a freight wagon 'held up' near Dow's Flat the other day, and a lot of baggage gone through. I had to go down there to look into it. Darned if they hadn't lifted a lot o' woman's wedding things from that rich couple who got married the other day out at Marysville. Looks as if they were playing it rather low down, don't it? Coming down to hardpan and the bed rock — eh?"

The Expressman's face was turned anxiously towards Bill, who, after a hurried gulp of his remaining liquor, still stood staring at the window. Then he slowly drew on one of his large gloves. "Ye didn't," he said, with a slow, drawling, but perfectly distinct, articulation, "happen to know old 'Skinner' Hemmings when you were over there?"

"Yes."

"And his daughter?"

"He hasn't got any."

"A sort o' mild, innocent, guileless child of nature?" persisted Bill, with a yellow face, a deadly calm, and Satanic deliberation.

"No. I tell you he *hasn't* any daughter. Old man Hemmings is a confirmed old bachelor. He's too mean to support more than one."

"And you didn't happen to know any o' that gang, did ye?" continued Bill, with infinite protraction.

"Yes. Knew 'em all. There was French Pete, Cherokee Bob, Kanaka Joe, One-eyed Stillson, Softy Brown, Spanish Jack, and two or three Greasers."

"And ye didn't know a man by the name of Charley Byng?"

"No," returned the Superintendent, with a slight suggestion of weariness and a distraught glance towards the door.

"A dark, stylish chap, with shifty black eyes and a curled-up merstache?" continued Bill, with dry, colorless persistence.

"No. Look here, Bill, I'm in a little bit of a hurry — but I suppose you must have your little joke before we part. Now, what *is* your little game?"

"Wot you mean?" demanded Bill, with sudden brusqueness.

"Mean? Well, old man, you know as well as I do. You're giving me the very description of Ramon Martinez himself, ha! ha! No —Bill! you didn't play me this time. You're mighty spry and clever, but you didn't catch on just then."

He nodded and moved away with a light laugh. Bill turned a stony face to the Expressman. Suddenly a gleam of mirth came into his gloomy eyes. He bent over the young man, and said in a hoarse, chuckling whisper: —

"But I got even after all!"

"How?"

"He's tied up to that lying little she-devil, hard and fast!"

A PROTEGEE
OF JACK HAMLIN'S

I

THE STEAMER SILVEROPOLIS was sharply and steadily cleaving the broad, placid shallows of the Sacramento River. A large wave like an eagre, diverging from its bow, was extending to either bank, swamping the tules and threatening to submerge the lower levees. The great boat itself — a vast but delicate structure of airy stories, hanging galleries, fragile colonnades, gilded cornices, and resplendent frescoes — was throbbing throughout its whole perilous length with the pulse of high pressure and the strong monotonous beat of a powerful piston. Floods of foam pouring from the high paddle-boxes on either side and reuniting in the wake of the boat left behind a track of dazzling whiteness, over which trailed two dense black banners flung from its lofty smokestacks.

Mr. Jack Hamlin had quietly emerged from his stateroom on deck and was looking over the guards. His hands were resting lightly on his hips over the delicate curves of his white waistcoat, and he was whistling softly, possibly some air to which he had made certain card-playing passengers dance the night before. He was in comfortable case, and his soft brown eyes under their long lashes were veiled with gentle tolerance of all things. He glanced lazily along the empty hurricane deck forward; he glanced lazily down to the saloon deck below him. Far out against the guards below him leaned a young girl. Mr. Hamlin knitted his brows slightly.

He remembered her at once. She had come on board that morn-

171

ing with one Ned Stratton, a brother gambler, but neither a favorite nor intimate of Jack's. From certain indications in the pair, Jack had inferred that she was some foolish or reckless creature whom "Ed" had "got on a string," and was spiriting away from her friends and family. With the abstract morality of this situation Jack was not in the least concerned. For himself he did not indulge in that sort of game; the inexperience and vacillations of innocence were apt to be bothersome, and besides, a certain modest doubt of his own competency to make an original selection had always made him prefer to confine his gallantries to the wives of men of greater judgment than himself who had. But it suddenly occurred to him that he had seen Stratton quickly slip off the boat at the last landing stage. Ah! that was it; he had cast away and deserted her. It was an old story. Jack smiled. But he was not greatly amused with Stratton.

She was very pale, and seemed to be clinging to the network railing, as if to support herself, although she was gazing fixedly at the yellow glancing current below, which seemed to be sucked down and swallowed in the paddle-box as the boat swept on. It certainly was a fascinating sight — this sloping rapid, hurrying on to bury itself under the crushing wheels. For a brief moment Jack saw how they would seize anything floating on that ghastly incline, whirl it round in one awful revolution of the beating paddles, and then bury it, broken and shattered out of all recognition, deep in the muddy undercurrent of the stream behind them.

She moved away presently with an odd, stiff step, chafing her gloved hands together as if they had become stiffened, too, in her rigid grasp of the railing. Jack leisurely watched her as she moved along the narrow strip of deck. She was not at all to his taste, — a rather plump girl with a rustic manner and a great deal of brown hair under her straw hat. She might have looked better had she not been so haggard. When she reached the door of the saloon she paused, and then, turning suddenly, began to walk quickly back again. As she neared the spot where she had been standing her pace slackened, and when she reached the railing she seemed to relapse against it in her former helpless fashion. Jack became lazily interested. Suddenly she lifted her head and cast a quick glance around

and above her. In that momentary lifting of her face Jack saw her
expression. Whatever it was, his own changed instantly; the next
moment there was a crash on the lower deck. It was Jack who had
swung himself over the rail and dropped ten feet, to her side. But
not before she had placed one foot in the meshes of the netting and
had gripped the railing for a spring.

The noise of Jack's fall might have seemed to her bewildered
fancy as a part of her frantic act, for she fell forward vacantly on
the railing. But by this time Jack had grasped her arm as if to
help himself to his feet.

"I might have killed myself by that foolin', mightn't I?" he said
cheerfully.

The sound of a voice so near her seemed to recall to her dazed
sense the uncompleted action his fall had arrested. She made a
convulsive bound towards the railing, but Jack held her fast.

"Don't," he said in a low voice, — "don't, it won't pay. It's the
sickest game that ever was played by man or woman. Come here!"

He drew her towards an empty stateroom whose door was swing-
ing on its hinges a few feet from them. She was trembling violently;
he half led, half pushed her into the room, closed the door, and

stood with his back against it as she dropped into a chair. She looked at him vacantly; the agitation she was undergoing inwardly had left her no sense of outward perception.

"You know Stratton would be awfully riled," continued Jack easily. "He's just stepped out to see a friend and got left by the fool boat. He'll be along by the next steamer, and you're bound to meet him in Sacramento."

Her staring eyes seemed suddenly to grasp his meaning. But to his surprise she burst out with a certain hysterical desperation, "No! no! Never! *never* again! Let me pass! I must go," and struggled to regain the door. Jack, albeit singularly relieved to know that she shared his private sentiments regarding Stratton, nevertheless resisted her. Whereat she suddenly turned white, reeled back, and sank in a dead faint in the chair.

The gambler turned, drew the key from the inside of the door, passed out, locking it behind him, and walked leisurely into the main saloon.

"Mrs. Johnson," he said gravely, addressing the stewardess, a tall mulatto, with his usual winsome supremacy over dependents and children, "you'll oblige me if you'll corral a few smelling salts, vinaigrettes, hairpins, and violet powder, and unload them in deck stateroom No. 257. There's a lady" —

"A lady, Marse Hamlin?" interrupted the mulatto, with an archly significant flash of her white teeth.

"A lady," continued Jack with unabashed gravity, "in a sort of conniption fit. A relative of mine; in fact, a niece, my only sister's child. Hadn't seen each other for ten years, and it was too much for her."

The woman glanced at him with a mingling of incredulous belief but delighted obedience, hurriedly gathered a few articles from her cabin, and followed him to No. 257. The young girl was still unconscious. The stewardess applied a few restoratives with the skill of long experience, and the young girl opened her eyes. They turned vacantly from the stewardess to Jack with a look of half recognition and half frightened inquiry.

"Yes," said Jack, addressing the eyes, although ostentatiously speaking to Mrs. Johnson, "she'd only just come by steamer to

'Frisco and wasn't expecting to see me, and we dropped right into each other here on the boat. And I haven't seen her since she was so high. Sister Mary ought to have warned me by letter; but she was always a slouch at letter-writing. There, that'll do, Mrs. Johnson. She's coming round; I reckon I can manage the rest. But you go now and tell the purser I want one of those inside staterooms for my niece, — *my niece*, you hear, — so that you can be near her and look after her."

As the stewardess turned obediently away the young girl attempted to rise, but Jack checked her.

"No," he said, almost brusquely; "you and I have some talking to do before she gets back, and we've no time for foolin'. You heard what I told her just now! Well, it's got to be as I said, you sabe. As long as you're on this boat you're my niece, and my sister Mary's child. As I haven't got any sister Mary, you don't run any risk of falling foul of her, and you ain't taking any one's place. That settles that. Now, do you or do you not want to see that man again? Say yes, and if he's anywhere above ground I'll yank him over to you as soon as we touch shore." He had no idea of interfering with his colleague's amours, but he had determined to make Stratton pay for the bother their slovenly sequence had caused him. Yet he was relieved and astonished by her frantic gesture of indignation and abhorrence. "No?" he repeated grimly. "Well, that settles that. Now, look here; quick, before she comes— do you want to go back home to your friends?"

But here occurred what he had dreaded most and probably thought he had escaped. She had stared at him, at the stewardess, at the walls, with abstracted, vacant, and bewildered, but always undimmed and unmoistened eyes. A sudden convulsion shook her whole frame, her blank expression broke like a shattered mirror, she threw her hands over her eyes and fell forward with her face to the back of her chair in an outburst of tears.

Alas for Jack! with the breaking up of those sealed fountains came her speech also, at first disconnected and incoherent, and then despairing and passionate. No! she had no longer friends or home! She had lost and disgraced them! She had disgraced *herself!* There was no home for her but the grave. Why had Jack snatched her from it? Then bit by bit, she yielded up her story,—a story decidedly commonplace to Jack, uninteresting, and even irritating to his fastidiousness. She was a schoolgirl (not even a convent girl, but the inmate of a Presbyterian female academy at Napa. Jack shuddered as he remembered to have once seen certain of the pupils walking with a teacher), and she lived with her married sister. She had seen Stratton while going to and fro on the San Francisco boat; she had exchanged notes with him, had met him secretly, and finally consented to elope with him to Sacramento, only to discover when the boat had left the wharf the real nature of his intentions. Jack listened with infinite weariness and inward chafing. He had read all this before in cheap novelettes, in the police reports, in the Sunday papers; he had heard a street preacher declaim against it, and warn young women of the serpent-like wiles of tempters of the Stratton variety. But even now Jack failed to recognize Stratton as a serpent, or indeed anything but a blundering cheat and clown, who had left his dirty 'prentice work on his (Jack's) hands. But the girl was helpless and, it seemed, homeless, all through a certain desperation of feeling which, in spite of her tears, he could not but respect. That momentary shadow of death had exalted her. He stroked his mustache, pulled down his white waistcoat, and let her cry, without saying anything. He did not know that this most objectionable phase of her misery was her salvation and his own.

But the stewardess would return in a moment.

"You'd better tell me what to call you," he said quietly. "I ought to know my niece's first name."

The girl caught her breath, and between two sobs said, "Sopho-nisba."

Jack winced. It seemed only to need this last sentimental touch to complete the idiotic situation.

"I'll call you Sophy," he said hurriedly and with an effort. "And now look here! You are going in that cabin with Mrs. Johnson where she can look after you, but I can't. So I'll have to take your word, for I'm not going to give you away before Mrs. Johnson, that you won't try that foolishness — you know what I mean — before I see you again. Can I trust you?"

With her head still bowed over the chair back, she murmured

slowly somewhere from under her disheveled hair: "Yes."

"Honest Injin?" adjured Jack gravely.

"Yes."

The shuffling step of the stewardess was heard slowly approaching.

"Yes," continued Jack abruptly, slightly lifting his voice, as Mrs. Johnson opened the door, — "yes, if you'd only had some of those spearmint drops of your aunt Rachel's that she always gave you when these fits came on you'd have been all right inside of five minutes. Aunty was no slouch of a doctor, was she? Dear me, it only seems yesterday since I saw her. You were just playing round her knee like a kitten on the back porch. How time does fly! But here's Mrs. Johnson coming to take you in. Now rouse up, Sophy, and just hook yourself on to Mrs. Johnson on that side, and we'll toddle along."

The young girl put back her heavy hair, and with her face still averted submitted to be helped to her feet by the kindly stewardess. Perhaps something homely, sympathetic and nurselike in the touch of the mulatto gave her assurance and confidence, for her head lapsed quite naturally against the woman's shoulder, and her face was partly hidden as she moved slowly along the deck. Jack accompanied them to the saloon and the inner stateroom door. A few passengers gathered curiously near, as much attracted by the unusual presence of Jack Hamlin in such a procession as by the girl herself.

"You'll look after her specially, Mrs. Johnson," said Jack, in unusually deliberate terms. "She's been a good deal petted at home, and my sister perhaps has rather spoilt her. She's pretty much of a child still, and you'll have to humor her. Sophy," he continued, with ostentatious playfulness, directing his voice into the dim recesses of the stateroom, "you'll just think Mrs. Johnson's your old nurse, won't you? Think it's old Katy, hey?"

To his great consternation the girl approached tremblingly from the inner shadow. The faintest and saddest of smiles for a moment played around the corners of her drawn mouth and tear-dimmed eyes as she held out her hand and said: —

"God bless you for being so kind."

Jack shuddered and glanced quickly round. But luckily no one heard this crushing sentimentalism, and the next moment the door closed upon her and Mrs. Johnson.

It was past midnight, and the moon was riding high over the narrowing yellow river, when Jack again stepped out on deck. He had just left the captain's cabin, and a small social game with the officers, which had served to some extent to vaguely relieve his irritation and their pockets. He had presumably quite forgotten the incident of the afternoon, as he looked about him, and complacently took in the quiet beauty of the night.

The low banks on either side offered no break to the uninterrupted level of the landscape, through which the river seemed to wind only as a race track for the rushing boat. Every fibre of her vast but fragile bulk quivered under the goad of her powerful engines. There was no other movement but hers, no other sound but this monstrous beat and panting; the whole tranquil landscape seemed to breathe and pulsate with her; dwellers in the tules, miles away, heard and felt her as she passed, and it seemed to Jack, leaning over the railing, as if the whole river swept like a sluice through her paddle-boxes.

Jack had quite unconsciously lounged before that part of the railing where the young girl had leaned a few hours ago. As he looked down upon the streaming yellow millrace below him he noticed — what neither he nor the girl had probably noticed before — that a space of the top bar of the railing was hinged, and could be lifted by withdrawing a small bolt, thus giving easy access to the guards. He was still looking at it, whistling softly, when footsteps approached.

"Jack," said a lazy voice, "how's sister Mary?"

"It's a long time since you've seen her only child, Jack, ain't it?" said a second voice; "and yet it sort o' seems to me somehow that I've seen her before."

Jack recognized the voice of two of his late companions at the card-table. His whistling ceased; so also dropped every trace of color and expression from his handsome face. But he did not turn, and remained quietly gazing at the water.

"Aunt Rachel, too, must be getting on in years, Jack," continued the first speaker, halting behind Jack.

"And Mrs. Johnson does not look so much like Sophy's old nurse as she used to," remarked the second, following his example. Still Jack remained unmoved.

"You don't seem to be interested, Jack," continued the first speaker. "What are you looking at?"

Without turning his head the gambler replied, "Looking at the boat; she's booming along, just chawing up and spitting out the river, ain't she? Look at that sweep of water going under her paddle-wheels," he continued, unbolting the rail and lifting it to allow the two men to peer curiously over the guards as he pointed to the murderous incline beneath them; "a man wouldn't stand much show who got dropped into it. How these paddles would jest snatch him bald-headed, pick him up, and slosh him round and round, and then sling him out down there in such a shape that his own father wouldn't know him."

"Yes," said the first speaker, with an ostentatious little laugh, "but all that ain't telling us how sister Mary is."

"No," said the gambler, slipping into the opening with a white and rigid face in which nothing seemed living but the eyes, — "no; but it's telling you how two d—d fools who didn't know when to shut their mouths might get them shut once and forever. It's telling you what might happen to two men who tried to 'play' a man who didn't care to be 'played,' — a man who didn't care much what he did, when he did it, or how he did it, but would do what he'd set out to do — even if in doing it he went to hell with the men he sent there."

He had stepped out on the guards, beside the two men, closing the rail behind him. He had placed his hands on their shoulders; they had both gripped his arms; yet, viewed from the deck above, they seemed at that moment an amicable, even fraternal group, albeit the faces of the three were dead white in the moonlight.

"I don't think I'm so very much interested in sister Mary," said the first speaker quietly, after a pause.

"And I don't seem to think so much of aunt Rachel as I did," said his companion.

"I thought you wouldn't," said Jack, coolly reopening the rail and stepping back again. "It all depends upon the way you look at those things. Good-night."

"Good-night."

The three men paused, shook each other's hands silently, and separated, Jack sauntering slowly back to his stateroom.

II

The educational establishment of Mrs. Mix and Madame Bance, situated in the best quarter of Sacramento and patronized by the highest state officials and members of the clergy, was a pretty if not an imposing edifice. Although surrounded by a high white picket-fence and entered through a heavily boarded gate, its balconies festooned with jasmine and roses, and its spotlessly draped windows as often graced with fresh, flower-like faces, were still plainly and provokingly visible above the ostentatious spikes of the pickets. Nevertheless, Mr. Jack Hamlin, who had six months before placed his niece, Miss Sophonisba Brown, under its protecting care, felt a degree of uneasiness, even bordering on timidity, which was new to that usually self-confident man. Remembering how his first appearance had fluttered this dovecote and awakened a severe suspicion in the minds of the two principals, he had discarded his usual fashionable attire and elegantly fitting garments for a rough homespun suit, supposed to represent a homely agriculturist, but which had the effect of transforming him into an adorable Strephon, infinitely more dangerous in his rustic shepherd-like simplicity. He had also shaved off his silken mustache for the same prudential reasons, but had only succeeded in uncovering the delicate lines of his handsome mouth, and so absurdly reducing his apparent years that his avuncular pretensions seemed more preposterous than ever; and when he had rung the bell and was admitted by a severe Irish waiting-maid, his momentary hesitation and half-humorous diffidence had such an unexpected effect upon her, that it seemed doubtful if he would be allowed to pass beyond the vestibule.

"Shure, miss," she said in a whisper to an under teacher, "there's wan at the dhure who calls himself 'Mister' Hamlin, but av it is not a young lady maskeradin' in her brother's clothes oim very much mistaken; and av it's a boy, one of the pupil's brothers, shure ye might put a dhress on him when you take the others out for a walk, and he'd pass for the beauty of the whole school."

Meantime the unconscious subject of this criticism was pacing somewhat uneasily up and down the formal reception room into which he had been finally ushered. Its farther end was filled by an enormous parlor organ, a number of music books, and a cheerfully variegated globe. A large presentation Bible, an equally massive illustrated volume on the Holy Land, a few landscapes in cold, bluish milk and water colors, and rigid heads in crayons — the work of pupils — were presumably ornamental. An imposing mahogany sofa and what seemed to be a disproportionate excess of chairs somewhat coldly furnished the room. Jack had reluctantly made up his mind that, if Sophy was accompanied by any one, he would be obliged to kiss her to keep up his assumed relationship. As she entered the room with Miss Mix, Jack advanced and soberly saluted her on the cheek. But so positive and apparent was the gallantry of his presence, and perhaps so suggestive of some pastoral flirtation, that Miss Mix, to Jack's surprise, winced perceptibly and became stony. But he was still more surprised that the young lady herself shrank half uneasily from his lips, and uttered a slight exclamation. It was a new experience to Mr. Hamlin.

But this somewhat mollified Miss Mix, and she slightly relaxed her austerity. She was glad to be able to give the best accounts of Miss Brown, not only as regarded her studies, but as to her conduct and deportment. Really, with the present freedom of manners and laxity of home discipline in California, it was gratifying to meet a young lady who seemed to value the importance of a proper decorum and behavior, especially towards the opposite sex. Mr. Hamlin, although her guardian, was perhaps too young to understand and appreciate this. To this inexperience she must also attribute the indiscretion of his calling during school hours and without preliminary warning. She trusted, however, that this informality could be overlooked after consultation with Madame Bance, but in the mean time, perhaps for half an hour, she must withdraw Miss Brown and return with her to the class. Mr. Hamlin could wait in this public room, reserved especially for visitors, until they returned. Or, if he cared to accompany one of the teachers in a formal inspection of the school, she added doubtfully, with a glance at Jack's distracting attractions, she would submit this also to Madame Bance.

"Thank you, thank you," returned Jack hurriedly, as a depressing vision of the fifty or sixty scholars rose before his eyes, "I'd rather not. I mean, you know, I'd just as lief stay here *alone*. I wouldn't have called anyway, don't you see, only I had a day off, — and — and — I wanted to talk with my niece on family matters."

He did not say that he had received a somewhat distressful letter from her asking him to come; a new instinct made him cautious.

Considerably relieved by Jack's unexpected abstention, which seemed to spare her pupils the distraction of his graces, Miss Mix smiled more amicably and retired with her charge. In the single glance he had exchanged with Sophy he saw that, although resigned and apparently self-controlled, she still appeared thoughtful and melancholy. She had improved in appearance and seemed more refined and less rustic in her school dress, but he was conscious of the same distinct separation of her personality (which was uninteresting to him) from the sentiment that had impelled him to visit her. She was possibly still hankering after that fellow Stratton, in spite of her protestations to the contrary; perhaps she wanted to go back to her sister, although she had declared she would die first, and had always refused to disclose her real name or give any clue by which he could have traced her relations. She would cry, of course; he almost hoped that she would not return alone; he half regretted he had come. She still held him only by a single quality of her nature, — the desperation she had shown on the boat; that was something he understood and respected.

He walked discontentedly to the window and looked out; he walked discontentedly to the end of the room and stopped before the organ. It was a fine instrument; he could see that with an admiring and experienced eye. He was alone in the room; in fact, quite alone in that part of the house which was separated from the classrooms. He would disturb no one by trying it. And if he did, what then? He smiled a little recklessly, slowly pulled off his gloves, and sat down before it.

He played cautiously at first, with the soft pedal down. The instrument had never known a strong masculine hand before, having been fumbled and frivoled over by softly incompetent, feminine fingers. But presently it began to thrill under the passionate hand of its lover, and carried away by his one innocent weakness, Jack was launched upon a sea of musical reminiscences. Scraps of church music, Puritan psalms of his boyhood; dying strains from sad, forgotten operas, fragments of oratorios and symphonies, but chiefly phrases from old masses heard at the missions of San Pedro and Santa Isabel, swelled up from his loving and masterful fingers. He had finished an Agnus Dei; the formal room was pulsating with divine aspiration; the rascal's hands were resting listlessly on the keys, his brown lashes lifted, in an effort of memory, tenderly towards the ceiling.

Suddenly, a subdued murmur of applause and a slight rustle behind him recalled him to himself again. He wheeled his chair quickly round. The two principals of the school and half a dozen teachers were standing gravely behind him, and at the open door a dozen curled and frizzled youthful heads peered in eagerly, but half restrained by their teachers. The relaxed features and apologetic attitude of Madame Bance and Miss Mix showed that Mr. Hamlin had unconsciously achieved a triumph.

He might not have been as pleased to know that his extraordinary performance had solved a difficulty, effaced his other graces, and enabled them to place him on the moral pedestal of a mere musician, to whom these eccentricities were allowable and privileged. He shared the admiration extended by the young ladies to their music teacher, which was always understood to be a sexless enthusiasm and a contagious juvenile disorder. It was also a fine advertisement for the organ. Madame Bance smiled blandly, improved the occasion by thanking Mr. Hamlin for having given the scholars a gratuitous lesson on the capabilities of the instrument, and was glad to be able to give Miss Brown a half-holiday to spend with her accomplished relative. Miss Brown was even now upstairs, putting on her hat and mantle. Jack was relieved. Sophy would not attempt to cry on the street.

Nevertheless, when they reached it and the gate closed behind them, he again became uneasy. The girl's clouded face and melancholy manner were not promising. It also occurred to him that he might meet some one who knew him and thus compromise her. This was to be avoided at all hazards. He began with forced gayety: —

"Well, now, where shall we go?"

She slightly raised her tear-dimmed eyes.

"Where you please — I don't care."

"There isn't any show going on here, is there?"

He had a vague idea of a circus or menagerie — himself behind her in the shadow of the box.

"I don't know of any."

"Or any restaurant — or cake shop?"

"There's a place where the girls go to get candy on Main Street. Some of them are there now."

Jack shuddered; this was not to be thought of.

"But where do you walk?"

"Up and down Main Street."

"Where everybody can see you?" said Jack, scandalized.

The girl nodded.

They walked on in silence for a few moments. Then a bright idea struck Mr. Hamlin. He suddenly remembered that in one of his many fits of impulsive generosity and largess he had given to an old negro retainer — whose wife had nursed him through a dangerous illness — a house and lot on the river bank. He had been told that they had opened a small laundry or wash-house. It occurred to him that a stroll there and a call upon "Uncle Hannibal and Aunt Chloe" combined the propriety and respectability due to the young person he was with, and the requisite secrecy and absence of publicity due to himself. He at once suggested it.

"You see she was a mighty good woman, and you ought to know her, for she was my old nurse" —

The girl glanced at him with a sudden impatience.

"Honest Injin," said Jack solemnly; "she did nurse me through my last cough. I ain't playing old family gags on you now."

"Oh, dear," burst out the girl impulsively, "I do wish you wouldn't ever play them again. I wish you wouldn't pretend to be my uncle; I wish you wouldn't make me pass for your niece. It isn't right. It's all wrong. Oh, don't you know it's all wrong, and can't come right any way? It's just killing me. I can't stand it. I'd rather you'd say what I am and how I came to you and how you pitied me."

They had luckily entered a narrow side street, and the sobs which shook the young girl's frame were unnoticed. For a few moments Jack felt a horrible conviction stealing over him, that in his present attitude towards her he was not unlike that hound Stratton, and that, however innocent his own intent, there was a sickening resemblance to the situation on the boat in the base advantage he had taken of her friendliness.

He had never told her that he was a gambler like Stratton, and that his peculiar infelix reputation among women made it impossible for him to assist her, except by stealth or the deception he had practiced, without compromising her. He who had for years faced the sneers and half-frightened opposition of the world dared not tell the truth to this girl, from whom he expected nothing and who did not interest him. He felt he was almost slinking at her side. At last he said desperately: —

"But I snatched them bald-headed at the organ, Sophy, didn't I?"

"Oh, yes," said the girl, "you played beautifully and grandly. It was so good of you, too. For I think, somehow, Madame Bance had been a little suspicious of you, but that settled it. Everybody thought it was fine, and some thought it was your profession. Perhaps," she added timidly, "it is."

"I play a good deal, I reckon," said Jack, with a grim humor which did not, however, amuse him.

"I wish *I* could, and make money by it," said the girl eagerly. Jack winced, but she did not notice it as she went on hurriedly: "That's what I wanted to talk to you about. I want to leave the school and make my own living. Anywhere where people won't know me and where I can be alone and work. I shall die here among these girls — with all their talk of their friends and their — sisters, — and their questions about you."

"Tell 'em to dry up," said Jack indignantly. "Take 'em to the cake shop and load 'em up with candy and ice cream. That'll stop their mouths. You've got money, — you got my last remittance, didn't you?" he repeated quickly. "If you didn't, here's" — his hand was already in his pocket when she stopped him with a despairing gesture.

"Yes, yes, I got it all. I haven't touched it. I don't want it. For I can't live on you. Don't you understand, — I want to work. Listen, — I can draw and paint. Madame Bance says I do it well; my drawing-master says I might in time take portraits and get paid for it. And even now I can retouch photographs and make colored miniatures from them. And," she stopped and glanced at Jack half timidly, "I've — done some already."

A glow of surprised relief suffused the gambler. Not so much at this astonishing revelation as at the change it seemed to effect in her. Her pale blue eyes, made paler by tears, cleared and brightened under their swollen lids like wiped steel; the lines of her depressed mouth straightened and became firm. Her voice had lost its hopeless monotone.

"There's a shop in the next street, — a photographer's, — where they have one of mine in their windows," she went on, reassured by Jack's unaffected interest. "It's only round the corner, if you care to see."

Jack assented; a few paces farther brought them to the corner of a narrow street, where they presently turned into a broader thoroughfare and stopped before the window of a photographer. Sophy pointed to an oval frame, containing a portrait painted on porcelain. Mr. Hamlin was startled. Inexperienced as he was, a certain artistic inclination told him it was good, although it is to be feared he would have been astonished even if it had been worse. The mere fact that this headstrong country girl, who had run away with a cur like Stratton, should be able to do anything else took him by surprise.

"I got ten dollars for that," she said hesitatingly, "and I could have got more for a larger one, but I had to do that in my room, during recreation hours. If I had more time and a place where I could work" — she stopped timidly and looked tentatively at Jack. But he was already indulging in a characteristically reckless idea of coming back after he had left Sophy, buying the miniature at an extravagant price, and ordering half a dozen more at extraordinary figures. Here, however, two passers-by, stopping ostensibly to look in the window, but really attracted by the picturesque spectacle of the handsome young rustic and his schoolgirl companion, gave Jack such a fright that he hurried Sophy away again into the side street.

"There's nothing mean about that picture business," he said cheerfully; "it looks like a square kind of game," and relapsed into thoughtful silence.

At which Sophy, the ice of restraint broken, again burst into passionate appeal. If she could only go away somewhere — where she saw no one but the people who would buy her work, who knew nothing of her past nor cared to know who were her relations! She would work hard; she knew she could support herself in time. She would keep the name he had given her, — it was not distinctive enough to challenge any inquiry, — but nothing more. She need not assume to be his niece; he would always be her kind friend, to whom she owed everything, even her miserable life. She trusted still to his honor never to seek to know her real name, nor ever to speak to her of that man if he ever met him. It would do no good to her or to them; it might drive her, for she was not quite yet sure of herself, to do that which she had promised him never to do again.

There was no threat, impatience, or acting in her voice, but he recognized the same dull desperation he had once heard in it, and her eyes, which a moment before were quick and mobile, had become fixed and set. He had no idea of trying to penetrate the foolish secret of her name and relations; he had never had the slightest curiosity, but it struck him now that Stratton might at any time force it upon him. The only way that he could prevent it was to let it be known that, for unexpressed reasons, he would shoot Stratton "on sight." This would naturally restrict any verbal communication between them. Jack's ideas of morality were vague, but his convictions on points of honor were singularly direct and positive.

III

Meantime Hamlin and Sophy were passing the outskirts of the town; the open lots and cleared spaces were giving way to grassy stretches, willow copses, and groups of cottonwood and sycamore; and beyond the level of yellowing tules appeared the fringed and raised banks of the river. Half tropical looking cottages with deep verandas — the homes of early Southern pioneers — took the place of incomplete blocks of modern houses, monotonously alike. In these sylvan surroundings Mr. Hamlin's picturesque rusticity looked less incongruous and more Arcadian; the young girl had lost some of her restraint with her confidences, and lounging together side by side, without the least consciousness of any sentiment in their words or actions, they nevertheless contrived to impress the spectator with the idea that they were a charming pair of pastoral lovers. So strong was this impression that, as they approached Aunt Chloe's laundry, a pretty rose-covered cottage with an enormous whitewashed barn-like extension in the rear, the black proprietress herself, standing at the door, called her husband to come and look at them, and flashed her white teeth in such unqualified commendation and patronage that Mr. Hamlin, withdrawing himself from Sophy's side, instantly charged down upon them.

"If you don't slide the lid back over that grinning box of dominoes of yours and take it inside, I'll just carry Hannibal off with me," he said in a quick whisper, with a half-wicked, half-mischievous glitter in his brown eyes. "That young lady's — *a lady* — do you understand? No riffraff friend of mine, but a regular *nun* — a saint — do you hear? So you just stand back and let her take a good look round, and rest herself, until she wants you." "Two black idiots, Miss Brown," he continued cheerfully in a higher voice of explanation, as Sophy approached, "who think because one of 'em used to shave me and the other saved my life they've got a right to stand at their humble cottage door and frighten horses!"

So great was Mr. Hamlin's ascendency over his former servants that even this ingenious pleasantry was received with every sign of affection and appreciation of the humorist, and of profound respect for his companion. Aunt Chloe showed them effusively into her parlor, a small but scrupulously neat and sweet-smelling apartment, inordinately furnished with a huge mahogany centretable and chairs, and the most fragile and meretricious china and glass ornaments on the mantel. But the three jasmine-edged lattice windows opened upon a homely garden of old-fashioned herbs and flowers, and their fragrance filled the room. The cleanest and starchiest of curtains, the most dazzling and whitest of tidies and chair-covers, bespoke the adjacent laundry; indeed, the whole cottage seemed to exhale the odors of lavender soap and freshly ironed linen. Yet the cottage was large for the couple and their assistants.

"Dar was two front rooms on de next flo' dat dey never used," explained Aunt Chloe; "friends allowed dat dey could let 'em to white folks, but dey had always been done kep' for Marse Hamlin, ef he ever wanted to be wid his old niggers again."

Jack looked up quickly with a brightened face, made a sign to Hannibal, and the two left the room together.

When he came through the passage a few moments later, there was a sound of laughter in the parlor. He recognized the full, round, lazy, chuckle of Aunt Chloe, but there was a higher girlish ripple that he did not know. He had never heard Sophy laugh before. Nor, when he entered had he ever seen her so animated. She was helping Chloe set the table, to that lady's intense delight at "Missy's" girlish housewifery. She was picking the berries fresh from the garden, buttering the Sally Lunn, making the tea, and arranging the details of the repast with apparently no trace of her former discontent and unhappiness in either face or manner. He dropped quietly into a chair by the window, and, with the homely scents of the garden mixing with the honest odors of Aunt Chloe's cookery, watched her with an amusement that was as pleasant and grateful as it was strange and unprecedented.

"Now, den," said Aunt Chloe to her husband, as she put the finishing touch to the repast in a plate of doughnuts as exquisitely brown and shining as Jack's eyes were at that moment, "Hannibal, you just come away, and let dem two white quality chillens have dey tea. Dey's done starved, shuah." And with an approving nod to Jack, she bundled her husband from the room.

The door closed; the young girl began to pour out the tea, but Jack remained in his seat by the window. It was a singular sensation which he did not care to disturb. It was no new thing for Mr. Hamlin to find himself at a tête-à-tête repast with the admiring and complaisant fair; there was a cabinet particulier in a certain San Francisco restaurant which had listened to their various vanities and professions of undying faith; he might have recalled certain festal rendezvous with a widow whose piety and impeccable reputation made it a moral duty for her to come to him only in disguise; it was but a few days before that he had been let privately into the palatial mansion of a high official for a midnight supper with a foolish wife. It was not strange, therefore, that he should be alone here, secretly, with a member of that indirect, loving sex. But that he should be sitting there in a cheap negro laundry with absolutely no sentiment of any kind towards the heavy-haired, freckled-faced country schoolgirl opposite him, from whom he sought and expected nothing, and *enjoying* it without scorn of himself or his companion, to use his own expression, "got him." Presently he rose and sauntered to the table with shining eyes.

"Well, what do you think of Aunt Chloe's shebang?" he asked smilingly.

"Oh, it's so sweet and clean and homelike," said the girl quickly.

At any other time he would have winced at the last adjective. It struck him now as exactly the word.

"Would you like to live here, if you could?"

Her face brightened. She put the teapot down and gazed fixedly at Jack.

"Because you can. Look here. I spoke to Hannibal about it. You can have the two front rooms if you want to. One of 'em is big enough for a studio to do your work in. You tell that nigger what you want to put in 'em, and he's got my orders to do it. I told him about your painting; said you were the daughter of an old friend, you know. Hold on, Sophy; d—n it all, I've got to do a little gilt-edged lying; but I let you out of the niece business this time. Yes, from this moment I'm no longer your uncle. I renounce the relationship. It's hard," continued the rascal, "after all these years and considering sister Mary's feelings; but, as you seem to wish it, it must be done."

Sophy's steel-blue eyes softened. She slid her long brown hand across the table and grasped Jack's. He returned the pressure quickly and fraternally, even to that half-shamed half-hurried evasion of emotion peculiar to all brothers. This was also a new sensation; but he liked it.

"You are too — too good, Mr. Hamlin," she said quietly.

"Yes," said Jack cheerfully, "that's what's the matter with me. It isn't natural, and if I keep it up too long it brings on my cough."

Nevertheless, they were happy in a boy and girl fashion, eating heartily, and, I fear, not always decorously; scrambling somewhat for the strawberries, and smacking their lips over the Sally Lunn. Meantime, it was arranged that Mr. Hamlin should inform Miss Mix that Sophy would leave school at the end of the term, only a few days hence, and then transfer herself to lodgings with some old family servants, where she could more easily pursue her studies in her own profession. She need not make her place of abode a secret, neither need she court publicity. She would write to Jack regularly, informing him of her progress, and he would visit her whenever he could. Jack assented gravely to the further proposition that he was to keep a strict account of all the moneys he advanced her, and that she was to repay him out of the proceeds of her first pictures. He had promised also, with a slight mental reservation, not to buy them all himself, but to trust to her success with the public. They were never to talk of what had happened before; she was to begin life anew. Of such were their confidences, spoken often together at the same moment, and with their mouths full. Only one thing troubled Jack: he had not yet told her frankly who he was and what was his reputation. He had hitherto carelessly supposed she would learn it, and in truth had cared little if she did; but it was evident from her conversation that day that by some miracle she was still in ignorance. Unable to tell her himself, he had charged Hannibal to break it to her casually after he was gone.

"You can let me down easy if you like, but you'd better make a square deal of it while you're about it. And," Jack had added cheerfully, "if she thinks after that she'd better drop me entirely, you just say that if she wishes to *stay*, you'll see that I don't ever come here again. And you keep your word about it too, you black nigger, or I'll be the first to thrash you."

Nevertheless, when Hannibal and Aunt Chloe returned to clear away the repast, they were a harmonious party; albeit Mr. Hamlin seemed more content to watch them silently from his chair by the window, a cigar between his lips, and the pleasant distraction of the homely scents and sounds of the garden in his senses. Allusion having been made again to the morning performance of the organ, he was implored by Hannibal to diversify his talent by exercising it on an old guitar which had passed into that retainer's possession with certain clothes of his master's when they separated. Mr. Hamlin accepted it dubiously; it had twanged under his volatile fingers in more pretentious but less innocent halls. But presently he raised his tenor voice and soft brown lashes to the humble ceiling and sang.

"Way down upon the Swanee River,"

discoursed Jack plaintively, —

"Far, far away,
Thar's whar my heart is turning ever,
Thar's whar the old folks stay."

The two dusky scions of an emotional race, that had been wont to sweeten its toils and condone its wrongs with music, sat wrapt and silent, swaying with Jack's voice until they could burst in upon the chorus. The jasmine vines trilled softly with the afternoon breeze; a slender yellow-hammer, perhaps emulous of Jack, swung himself from an outer spray and peered curiously into the room; and a few neighbors, gathering at their doors and windows, remarked that "after all, when it came to real singing, no one could beat those d—d niggers."

The sun was slowly sinking in the rolling gold of the river when Jack and Sophy started leisurely back through the broken shafts of light, and across the far-stretching shadows of the cottonwoods. In the midst of a lazy silence they were presently conscious of a distant monotonous throb, the booming of the up boat on the river. The sound came nearer — passed them, the boat itself hidden by the trees; but a trailing cloud of smoke above cast a momentary shadow upon their path. The girl looked up at Jack with a troubled face. Mr. Hamlin smiled reassuringly; but in that instant he had made up his mind that it was his moral duty to kill Mr. Edward Stratton.

IV

For the next two months Mr. Hamlin was professionally engaged in San Francisco and Marysville, and the transfer of Sophy from the school to her new home was effected without his supervision. From letters received by him during that interval, it seemed that the young girl had entered energetically upon her new career, and that her artistic efforts were crowned with success. There were a few Indian-ink sketches, studies made at school and expanded in her own "studio," which were eagerly bought as soon as exhibited in the photographer's window, — notably by a florid and inartistic bookkeeper, an old negro woman, a slangy stable boy, a gorgeously dressed and painted female, and the bearded second officer of a river steamboat, without hesitation and without comment. This, as Mr. Hamlin intelligently pointed out in a letter to Sophy, showed a general and diversified appreciation on the part of the public. Indeed, it emboldened her, in the retouching of photographs, to offer sittings to the subjects, and to undertake even large crayon copies, which had resulted in her getting so many orders that she was no longer obliged to sell her drawings, but restricted herself solely to profitable portraiture. The studio became known; even its quaint surroundings added to the popular interest, and the originality and independence of the young painter helped her to a genuine success. All this she wrote to Jack. Meantime Hannibal had assured him that he had carried out his instructions by informing "Missy" of his old master's real occupation and reputation, but that the young lady hadn't "took no notice." Certainly there was no allusion to it in her letters, nor any indication in her manner. Mr. Hamlin was greatly, and it seemed to him properly, relieved. And he looked forward with considerable satisfaction to an early visit to old Hannibal's laundry.

It must be confessed, also, that another matter, a simple affair of gallantry, was giving him an equally unusual, unexpected, and absurd annoyance, which he had never before permitted to such trivialities. In a recent visit to a fashionable watering-place he had attracted the attention of what appeared to be a respectable, matter-of-fact woman, the wife of a recently elected rural senator. She was, however, singularly beautiful, and as singularly cold. It was perhaps this quality, and her evident annoyance at some unreasoning prepossession which Jack's fascinations exercised upon her, that heightened that reckless desire for risk and excitement which really made up the greater part of his gallantry. Nevertheless, as was his habit, he had treated her always with a charming unconsciousness of his own attentions, and a frankness that seemed inconsistent with any insidious approach. In fact, Mr. Hamlin seldom made love to anybody, but permitted it to be made to him with good-humored deprecation and cheerful skepticism. He had once, quite accidentally, while riding, come upon her when she had strayed from her own riding party, and had behaved with such unexpected circumspection and propriety, not to mention a certain thoughtful abstraction, — it was the day he had received Sophy's letter, — that she was constrained to make the first advances. This led to a later innocent rendezvous, in which Mrs. Camperly was impelled to confide to Mr. Hamlin the fact that her husband had really never understood her. Jack listened with an understanding and sympathy quickened by long experience of such confessions. If anything had kept him from marriage it was this evident incompatibility of the conjugal relations with a just conception of the feminine soul and its aspirations.

And so eventually this yearning for sympathy dragged Mrs. Camperly's clean skirts and rustic purity after Jack's heels into various places and various situations not so clean, rural, or innocent; made her miserably unhappy in his absence, and still more miserably happy in his presence; impelled her to lie, cheat, and bear false witness; forced her to listen with mingled shame and admiration to narrow criticism of his faults, from natures so palpably inferior to his own that her moral sense was confused and shaken; gave her two distinct lives, but so unreal and feverish that, with a recklessness equal to his own, she was at last ready to merge them both into his. For the first time in his life Mr. Hamlin found himself bored at the beginning of an affair, actually hesitated, and suddenly disappeared from San Francisco.

He turned up a few days later at Aunt Chloe's door, with various packages of presents and quite the air of a returning father of a family, to the intense delight of that lady and to Sophy's proud gratification. For he was lost in a profuse, boyish admiration of her pretty studio, and in wholesome reverence of her art and her astounding progress. They were also amused at his awe and evident

alarm at the portraits of two ladies, her latest sitters, that were still on the easels, and, in consideration of his half-assumed, half-real bashfulness, they turned their faces to the wall. Then his quick, observant eye detected a photograph of himself on the mantel.

"What's that?" he asked suddenly.

Sophy and Aunt Chloe exchanged meaning glances. Sophy had, as a surprise to Jack, just completed a handsome crayon portrait of himself from an old photograph furnished by Hannibal, and the picture was at that moment in the window of her former patron, — the photographer.

"Oh, dat! Miss Sophy jus' put it dar fo' de lady sitters to look at to gib 'em a pleasant 'spresshion," said Aunt Chloe, chuckling.

Mr. Hamlin did not laugh, but quietly slipped the photograph into his pocket. Yet, perhaps, it had not been recognized.

Then Sophy proposed to have luncheon in the studio; it was quite "Bohemian" and fashionable, and many artists did it. But to her surprise Jack gravely objected, preferring the little parlor of Aunt Chloe, the vine-fringed windows, and the heavy respectable furniture. He thought it was profaning the studio, and then — anybody might come in. This unusual circumspection amused them, and was believed to be part of the boyish awe with which Jack regarded the models, the draperies, and the studies on the walls. Certain it was that he was much more at his ease in the parlor, and when he and Sophy were once more alone at their meal, although he ate nothing, he had regained all his old naïveté. Presently he leaned forward and placed his hand fraternally on her arm. Sophy looked up with an equally frank smile.

"You know I promised to let bygones be bygones, eh? Well, I intended it, and more, — I intended to make 'em so. I told you I'd never speak to you again of that man who tried to run you off, and I intended that no one else should. Well, as he was the only one who could talk — that meant him. But the cards are out of my hands; the game's been played without me. For he's dead!"

The girl started. Mr. Hamlin's hand passed caressingly twice or thrice along her sleeve with a peculiar gentleness that seemed to magnetize her.

"Dead," he repeated slowly. "Shot in San Diego by another man, but not by me. I had him tracked as far as that, and had my eyes on him, but it wasn't my deal. But there," he added, giving her magnetized arm a gentle and final tap as if to awaken it, "he's dead, and so is the whole story. And now we'll drop it forever."

The girl's downcast eyes were fixed on the table.

"But there's my sister," she murmured.

"Did she know you went with him?" asked Jack.

"No; but she knows I ran away."

"Well, you ran away from home to study how to be an artist, don't you see? Some day she'll find out you *are one*; that settles the whole thing."

They were both quite cheerful again when Aunt Chloe returned to clear the table, especially Jack, who was in the best spirits, with preternaturally bright eyes and a somewhat rare color on his cheeks. Aunt Chloe, who had noticed that his breathing was hurried at times, watched him narrowly, and when later he slipped from the room, followed him into the passage. He was leaning against the wall. In an instant the negress was at his side.

"De Lawdy Gawd, Marse Jack, not *agin?*"

He took his handkerchief, slightly streaked with blood, from his lips and said faintly, "Yes, it came on — on the boat; but I thought the d—d thing was over. Get me out of this, quick, to some hotel, before she knows it. You can tell her I was called away. Say that" — but his breath failed him, and when Aunt Chloe caught him like a child in her strong arms he could make no resistance.

In another hour he was unconscious, with two doctors at his bedside, in the little room that had been occupied by Sophy. It was a sharp attack, but prompt attendance and skillful nursing availed; he rallied the next day, but it would be weeks, the doctors said, before he could be removed in safety. Sophy was transferred to the parlor, but spent most of her time at Jack's bedside with Aunt Chloe, or in the studio with the door open between it and the bedroom. In spite of his enforced idleness and weakness, it was again a singularly pleasant experience to Jack; it amused him to sometimes see Sophy at her work through the open door, and when sitters came, — for he had insisted on her continuing her duties as before, keeping his invalid presence in the house a secret, — he had all the satisfaction of a mischievous boy in rehearsing to Sophy such of the conversation as could be overheard through the closed door, and speculating on the possible wonder and chagrin of the sitters had they discovered him. Even when he was convalescent and strong enough to be helped into the parlor and garden, he preferred to remain propped up in Sophy's little bedroom. It was evident, however, that this predilection was connected with no suggestion nor reminiscence of Sophy herself. It was true that he had once asked her if it didn't make her "feel like home." The decided negative from Sophy seemed to mildly surprise him. "That's odd," he said; "now all these fixings and things," pointing to the flowers in a vase, the little hanging shelf of books, the knickknacks on the mantel-shelf, and the few feminine ornaments that still remained, "look rather like home to me."

So the days slipped by, and although Mr. Hamlin was soon able to walk short distances, leaning on Sophy's arm, in the evening twilight, along the river bank, he was still missed from the haunts of dissipated men. A good many people wondered, and others, chiefly of the more irrepressible sex, were singularly concerned. Apparently one of these, one sultry afternoon, stopped before the shadowed window of a photographer's; she was a handsome, well-dressed woman, yet bearing a certain country-like simplicity that was unlike the restless smartness of the more urban promenaders who passed her. Nevertheless she had halted before Mr. Hamlin's picture, which Sophy had not yet dared to bring home and present to him, and was gazing at it with rapt and breathless attention. Suddenly she shook down her veil and entered the shop. Could the proprietor kindly tell her if that portrait was the work of a local artist?

The proprietor was both proud and pleased to say that *it was!* It was the work of a Miss Brown, a young girl student; in fact, a mere schoolgirl, one might say. He could show her others of her pictures.

Thanks. But could he tell her if this portrait was from life?

No doubt; the young lady had a studio, and he himself had sent her sitters.

And perhaps this was the portrait of one that he had sent her?

No; but she was very popular and becoming quite the fashion. Very probably this gentleman, who, he understood, was quite a public character, had heard of her, and selected her on that account.

The lady's face flushed slightly. The photographer continued. The picture was not for sale; it was only there on exhibition; in fact it was to be returned to-morrow.

To the sitter?

He couldn't say. It was to go back to the studio. Perhaps the sitter would be there.

And this studio? Could she have its address?

The man wrote a few lines on his card. Perhaps the lady would be kind enough to say that he had sent her. The lady, thanking him, partly lifted her veil to show a charming smile, and gracefully withdrew. The photographer was pleased. Miss Brown had evidently got another sitter, and, from that momentary glimpse of her face, it would be a picture as beautiful and attractive as the man's. But what was the odd idea that struck him? She certainly reminded him of some one! There was the same heavy hair, only this lady's was golden, and she was older and more mature. And he remained for a moment with knitted brows musing over his counter.

Meantime the fair stranger was making her way towards the river suburb. When she reached Aunt Chloe's cottage, she paused, with the unfamiliar curiosity of a new-comer, over its quaint and incongruous exterior. She hesitated a moment also when Aunt Chloe appeared in the doorway, and, with a puzzled survey of her features, went upstairs to announce a visitor. There was the sound of hurried shutting of doors, of the moving of furniture, quick footsteps across the floor, and then a girlish laugh that startled her. She ascended the stairs breathlessly to Aunt Chloe's summons, found the negress on the landing, and knocked at a door which bore a card marked "Studio." The door opened; she entered; there were two sudden outcries that might have come from one voice.

"Sophonisba!"

"Marianne!"

"Hush."

The woman had seized Sophy by the wrist and dragged her to

the window. There was a haggard look of desperation in her face akin to that which Hamlin had once seen in her sister's eyes on the boat, as she said huskily: "I did not know *you* were here. I came to see the woman who had painted Mr. Hamlin's portrait. I did not know it was *you*. Listen! Quick! answer me one question. Tell me — I implore you — for the sake of the mother who bore us both! — tell me — is this the man for whom you left home?"

"No! No! A hundred times no!"

Then there was a silence. Mr. Hamlin from the bedroom heard no more.

An hour later, when the two women opened the studio door, pale but composed, they were met by the anxious and tearful face of Aunt Chloe.

"Lawdy Gawd, Missy, — but dey done gone! — bofe of 'em!"

"Who is gone?" demanded Sophy, as the woman beside her trembled and grew paler still.

"Marse Jack and dat fool nigger, Hannibal."

"Mr. Hamlin gone?" repeated Sophy incredulously. "When? Where?"

"Jess now — on de down boat. Sudden business. Didn't like to disturb yo' and yo' friend. Said he'd write."

"But he was ill — almost helpless," gasped Sophy.

"Dat's why he took dat old nigger. Lawdy, Missy, bress yo' heart. Dey both knows aich udder, shuah! It's all right. Dar now, dar dey are; listen."

She held up her hand. A slow pulsation, that might have been the dull, labored beating of their own hearts, was making itself felt throughout the little cottage. It came nearer, — a deep regular inspiration that seemed slowly to fill and possess the whole tranquil summer twilight. It was nearer still — was abreast of the house — passed — grew fainter — and at last died away like a deep-drawn sigh. It was the down boat, that was now separating Mr. Hamlin and his protégée, even as it had once brought them together.

PROSPER'S "OLD MOTHER"

"IT'S ALL VERY WELL," said Joe Wynbrook, "for us to be sittin' here, slingin' lies easy and comfortable, with the wind whistlin' in the pines outside, and the rain just liftin' the ditches to fill our sluice boxes with gold ez we're smokin' and waitin', but I tell you what, boys — it ain't home! No, sir, it ain't *home!*"

The speaker paused, glanced around the bright, comfortable barroom, the shining array of glasses beyond, and the circle of complacent faces fronting the stove, on which his own boots were cheerfully steaming, lifted a glass of whiskey from the floor under his chair, and in spite of his deprecating remark, took a long draught of the spirits with every symptom of satisfaction.

"If ye mean," returned Cyrus Brewster, "that it ain't the old farmhouse of our boyhood, 'way back in the woods, I'll agree with you; but ye'll just remember that there wasn't any gold placers lying round on the medder on *that* farm. Not much! Ef thar had been, we wouldn't have left it."

" I don't mean that," said Joe Wynbrook, settling himself comfortably back in his chair; "it's the family hearth I'm talkin' of. The soothin' influence, ye know — the tidiness of the women folks."

"Ez to the soothin' influence," remarked the barkeeper, leaning his elbows meditatively on his counter, "afore I struck these diggin's I had a grocery and bar, 'way back in Mizzoori, where there was five old-fashioned farms jined. Blame my skin ef the men folks weren't a darned sight oftener over in my grocery, sittin' on barrils

202

and histin' in their reg'lar corn-juice, than ever any of you be here
—with all these modern improvements."

"Ye don't catch on, any of you," returned Wynbrook impatiently. "Ef it was a mere matter o' buildin' houses and becomin' family men, I reckon that this yer camp is about prosperous enough to do it, and able to get gals enough to marry us, but that would be

only borryin' trouble and lettin' loose a lot of jabberin' women to gossip agin' each other and spile all our friendships. No, gentlemen! What we want here—each of us—is a good old mother! Nothin' new-fangled or fancy, but the reg'lar old-fashioned mother we was used to when we was boys!"

The speaker struck a well-worn chord—rather the worse for wear, and one that had jangled falsely ere now, but which still produced its effect. The men were silent. Thus encouraged, Wynbrook proceeded:—

"Think o' comin' home from the gulch a night like this and findin' yer old mother a-waitin' ye! No fumblin' around for the matches ye'd left in the gulch; no high old cussin' because the wood was wet or you forgot to bring it in; no bustlin' around for your dry things and findin' you forgot to dry 'em that mornin'—

but everything waitin' for ye and ready. And then, mebbe, she brings ye in some doughnuts she's just cooked for ye — cooked ez only *she* kin cook 'em! Take Prossy Riggs — alongside of me here — for instance! *He's* made the biggest strike yet, and is puttin' up a high-toned house on the hill. Well! he'll hev it finished off and furnished slap-up style, you bet! with a Chinese cook, and a Biddy, and a Mexican vaquero to look after his horse — but he won't have no mother to housekeep! That is," he corrected himself perfunctorily, turning to his companion, "you've never spoke o' your mother, so I reckon you're about fixed up like us."

The young man thus addressed flushed slightly, and then nodded his head with a sheepish smile. He had, however, listened to the conversation with an interest almost childish, and a reverent admiration of his comrades — qualities which, combined with an intellect not particularly brilliant, made him alternately the butt and the favorite of the camp. Indeed, he was supposed to possess that proportion of stupidity and inexperience which, in mining superstition, gives "luck" to its possessor. And this had been singularly proven in the fact that he had made the biggest "strike" of the season.

Joe Wynbrook's sentimentalism, albeit only argumentative and half serious, had unwittingly touched a chord of "Prossy's" simple history, and the flush which had risen to his cheek was not entirely bashfulness. The home and relationship of which they spoke so glibly, *he* had never known; he was a foundling! As he lay awake that night he remembered the charitable institution which had protected his infancy, the master to whom he had later been apprenticed; that was all he knew of his childhood. In his simple way he had been greatly impressed by the strange value placed by his companions upon the family influence, and he had received their extravagance with perfect credulity. In his absolute ignorance and his lack of humor he had detected no false quality in their sentiment. And a vague sense of his responsibility, as one who had been the luckiest, and who was building the first "house" in the camp, troubled him. He lay staringly wide awake, hearing the mountain wind, and feeling warm puffs of it on his face through the crevices of the log cabin, as he thought of the new house on the hill that was to be lathed and plastered and clapboarded, and yet void and vacant of that mysterious "mother"! And then, out of the solitude and darkness, a tremendous idea struck him that made him sit up in his bunk!

A day or two later "Prossy" Riggs stood on a sand-blown, wind-swept suburb of San Francisco, before a large building whose forbidding exterior proclaimed that it was an institution of formal charity. It was, in fact, a refuge for the various waifs and strays of ill-advised or hopeless immigration. As Prosper paused before the door, certain old recollections of a similar refuge were creeping over him, and, oddly enough, he felt as embarrassed as if he had been seeking relief for himself. The perspiration stood out on his forehead as he entered the room of the manager.

It chanced, however, that this official, besides being a man of shrewd experience of human weakness, was also kindly hearted, and having, after his first official scrutiny of his visitor and his resplendent watch chain, assured himself that he was not seeking personal relief, courteously assisted him in his stammering request.

"If I understand you, you want some one to act as your house-keeper?"

"That's it! Somebody to kinder look arter things — and me — ginrally," returned Prosper, greatly relieved.

"Of what age?" continued the manager, with a cautious glance at the robust youth and good-looking, simple face of Prosper.

"I ain't nowise partickler — ez long ez she's old — ye know. Ye follow me? Old — ez ef — betwixt you an' me, she might be my own mother."

The manager smiled inwardly. A certain degree of discretion was noticeable in this rustic youth! "You are quite right," he answered gravely, "as yours is a mining camp where there are no other women. Still, you don't want any one *too* old or decrepit. There is an elderly maiden lady" — But a change was transparently visible on Prosper's simple face, and the manager paused.

"She oughter be kinder married, you know — ter be like a mother," stammered Prosper.

"Oh, ay. I see," returned the manager, again illuminated by Prosper's unexpected wisdom.

He mused for a moment. "There is," he began tentatively, "a lady in reduced circumstances — not an inmate of this house, but who has received some relief from us. She was the wife of a whaling captain who died some years ago, and broke up her home. She was not brought up to work, and this, with her delicate health, has prevented her from seeking active employment, As you don't seem to require that of her, but rather want an overseer, and as your purpose, I gather, is somewhat philanthropical, you might induce her to accept a 'home' with you. Having seen better days, she is rather particular," he added, with a shrewd smile.

Simple Prosper's face was radiant. "She'll have a Chinaman and a Biddy to help her," he said quickly. Then recollecting the tastes of his comrades, he added, half apologetically, half cautiously, "Ef she could, now and then, throw herself into a lemming pie or a pot of doughnuts, jest in a motherly kind o' way, it would please the boys."

"Perhaps you can arrange that, too," returned the manager, "but I shall have to broach the whole subject to her, and you had better call again to-morrow, when I will give you her answer."

"Ye kin say," said Prosper, lightly fingering his massive gold chain and somewhat vaguely recalling the language of advertisement, "that she kin have the comforts of a home and no questions asked, and fifty dollars a month."

Rejoiced at the easy progress of his plan, and half inclined to believe himself a miracle of cautious diplomacy, Prosper, two days later, accompanied the manager to the cottage on Telegraph Hill where the relict of the late Captain Pottinger lamented the loss of her spouse, in full view of the sea he had so often tempted. On their way thither the manager imparted to Prosper how, according to hearsay, that lamented seaman had carried into the domestic circle those severe habits of discipline which had earned for him the prefix of "Bully" and "Belaying-pin" Pottinger during his strenuous life. "They say that though she is very quiet and resigned, she once or twice stood up to the captain; but that's not a bad quality to have, in a rough community, as I presume yours is, and would insure her respect."

Ushered at last into a small tank-like sitting room, whose chief

decorations consisted of large *abalone* shells, dried marine algæ, coral, and a swordfish's broken weapon, Prosper's disturbed fancy discovered the widow, sitting, apparently, as if among her husband's remains at the bottom of the sea. She had a dejected yet somewhat ruddy face; her hair was streaked with white, but primly disposed over her ears like lappets, and her garb was cleanly but sombre. There was no doubt but that she was a lugubrious figure, even to Prosper's optimistic and inexperienced mind. He could not imagine her as beaming on his hearth! It was with some alarm that, after the introduction had been completed, he beheld the manager take his leave. As the door closed, the bashful Prosper felt the murky eyes of the widow fixed upon him. A gentle cough, accompanied with the resigned laying of a black mittened hand upon her chest, suggested a genteel prelude to conversation, with possible pulmonary complications.

"I am induced to accept your proposal temporarily," she said, in a voice of querulous precision, "on account of pressing pecuniary circumstances which would not have happened had my claim against the shipowners for my dear husband's loss been properly raised. I hope you fully understand that I am unfitted both by ill health and early education from doing any menial or manual work in your household. I shall simply oversee and direct. I shall expect that the stipend you offer shall be paid monthly in advance. And as my medical man prescribes a certain amount of stimulation for my system, I shall expect to be furnished with such viands — or even" — she coughed slightly — "such beverages as may be necessary. I am far from strong — yet my wants are few."

"Ez far ez I am ketchin' on and followin' ye, ma'am," returned Prosper timidly, "ye'll have everything ye want — jest like it was yer own home. In fact," he went on, suddenly growing desperate as the difficulties of adjusting this unexpectedly fastidious and superior woman to his plan seemed to increase, "ye'll jest consider me ez yer" — But here her murky eyes were fixed on his and he faltered. Yet he had gone too far to retreat. "Ye see," he stammered, with a hysterical grimness that was intended to be playful — "ye see, this is jest a little secret betwixt and between you and me; there'll be only you and me in the house, and it would kinder seem to the boys more homelike — ef — ef — you and me had — you bein' a widder, you know — a kind of — of" — here his smile became ghastly — "close relationship."

The widow of Captain Pottinger here sat up so suddenly that she seemed to slip through her sombre and precise enwrappings with an exposure of the real Mrs. Pottinger that was almost improper. Her high color deepened; the pupils of her black eyes contracted in the light the innocent Prosper had poured into them. Leaning forward, with her fingers clasped on her bosom, she said: "Did you tell this to the manager?"

"Of course not," said Prosper; "ye see, it's only a matter 'twixt you and me."

Mrs. Pottinger looked at Prosper, drew a deep breath, and then gazed at the *abalone* shells for moral support. A smile, half querulous, half superior, crossed her face as she said: "This is very abrupt and unusual. There is, of course, a disparity in our ages! You have never seen me before — at least to my knowledge — although you may have heard of me. The Spraggs of Marblehead are well known — perhaps better than the Pottingers. And yet, Mr. Griggs" —

"Riggs," suggested Prosper hurriedly.

"Riggs. Excuse me! I was thinking of young Lieutenant Griggs of the Navy, whom I knew in the days now past. Mr. Riggs, I should say. Then you want me to" —

"To be my old mother, ma'am," said Prosper tremblingly. "That is, to pretend and look ez if you was! You see, I haven't any, but I thought it would be nice for the boys, and make it more like home in my new house, ef I allowed that *my* old mother would be comin' to live with me. They don't know I never had a mother to speak of. They'll never find it out! Say ye will, Mrs. Pottinger! Do!"

And here the unexpected occurred. Against all conventional rules and all accepted traditions of fiction, I am obliged to state that Mrs. Pottinger did *not* rise up and order the trembling Prosper to leave the house! She only gripped the arm of her chair a little tighter, leaned forward, and disdaining her usual precision and refinement of speech, said quietly: "It's a bargain. If *that's* what you're wanting, my son, you can count upon me as becoming your old mother, Cecilia Jane Pottinger Riggs, every time!"

A few days later the sentimentalist Joe Wynbrook walked into the Wild Cat Saloon, where his comrades were drinking, and laid a letter down on the bar with every expression of astonishment and disgust. "Look," he said, "if that don't beat all! Ye wouldn't believe it, but here's Prossy Riggs writin' that he came across his mother — his *mother*, gentlemen — in 'Frisco; she hevin', unbeknownst to him, joined a party visiting the coast! And what does this blamed fool do? Why, he's goin' to bring her — that old woman — *here!* Here — gentlemen — to take charge of that new house — and spoil our fun. And the God-forsaken idiot thinks that we'll *like* it!"

It was one of those rare mornings in the rainy season when there was a suspicion of spring in the air, and after a night of rainfall the sun broke through fleecy clouds with little islets of blue sky — when Prosper Riggs and his mother drove into Wild Cat camp. An expression of cheerfulness was on the faces of his old comrades. For it had been recognized that, after all, "Prossy" had a perfect right to bring his old mother there — his well-known youth and inexperience preventing this baleful performance from being established as a precedent. For these reasons hats were cheerfully doffed, and some jackets put on, as the buggy swept up the hill to the pretty new cottage, with its green blinds and white veranda, on the crest.

Yet I am afraid that Prosper was not perfectly happy, even in the triumphant consummation of his plans. Mrs. Pottinger's sudden and business-like acquiescence in it, and her singular lapse from her genteel precision, were gratifying but startling to his ingenuousness. And although from the moment she accepted the situation she was fertile in resources and full of precaution against any possibility of detection, he saw, with some uneasiness, that its control had passed out of his hands.

"You say your comrades know nothing of your family history?" she said to him on the journey thither. "What are you going to tell them?"

"Nothin', 'cept your bein' my old mother," said Prosper hopelessly.

"That's not enough, my son." (Another embarrassment to Prosper was her easy grasp of the maternal epithets.) "Now listen! You were born just six months after your father, Captain Riggs (formerly Pottinger) sailed on his first voyage. You remember very little of him, of course, as he was away so much."

"Hadn't I better know suthin about his looks?" said Prosper submissively.

"A tall dark man, that's enough," responded Mrs. Pottinger sharply.

"Hadn't he better favor me?" said Prosper, with his small cunning recognizing the fact that he himself was a decided blond.

"Ain't at all necessary," said the widow firmly. "You were always wild and ungovernable," she continued, "and ran away from school to join some Western emigration. That accounts for the difference of our styles."

"But," continued Prosper, "I oughter remember suthin about our old times — runnin' arrants for you, and bringin' in the wood o' frosty mornin's, and you givin' me hot doughnuts," suggested Prosper dubiously.

"Nothing of the sort," said Mrs. Pottinger promptly. "We lived in the city, with plenty of servants. Just remember, Prosper dear, your mother wasn't *that* low-down country style."

Glad to be relieved from further invention, Prosper was, nevertheless, somewhat concerned at this shattering of the ideal mother in the very camp that had sung her praises. But he could only trust to her recognizing the situation with her usual sagacity, of which he stood in respectful awe.

Joe Wynbrook and Cyrus Brewster had, as old members of the camp, purposely lingered near the new house to offer any assistance to "Prossy and his mother," and had received a brief and passing introduction to the latter. So deep and unexpected was the impression she made upon them that these two oracles of the camp retired down the hill in awkward silence for some time, neither daring to risk his reputation by comment or oversurprise.

But when they approached the curious crowd below awaiting them, Cyrus Brewster ventured to say, "Struck me ez ef that old gal was rather high-toned for Prossy's mother."

Joe Wynbrook instantly seized the fatal admission to show the advantage of superior insight: —

"Struck *you!* Why, it was no more than *I* expected all along! What did we know of Prossy? Nothin'! What did he ever tell us? Nothin'! And why? 'Cos it was his secret. Lord! a blind mule could see that. All this foolishness and simplicity o' his come o' his bein' cuddled and pampered as a baby. Then, like ez not, he was either kidnapped or led away by some feller—and nearly broke his mother's heart. I'll bet my bottom dollar he has been advertised for afore this—only we didn't see the paper. Like as not they had agents out seekin' him, and he jest ran into their hands in 'Frisco! I had a kind o' presentiment o' this when he left, though I never let on anything."

"I reckon, too, that she's kinder afraid he'll bolt agin. Did ye notice how she kept watchin' him all the time, and how she did the bossin' o' everything? And there's *one* thing sure! He's changed —yes! He don't look as keerless and free and foolish ez he uster."

Here there was an unmistakable chorus of assent from the crowd that had joined them. Every one—even those who had not been introduced to the mother—had noticed his strange restraint and reticence. In the impulsive logic of the camp, conduct such as this, in the face of that superior woman—his mother—could only imply that her presence was distasteful to him; that he was either ashamed of their noticing his inferiority to her, or ashamed of *them!* Wild and hasty as was their deduction, it was, nevertheless, voiced by Joe Wynbrook in a tone of impartial and even reluctant conviction. "Well, gentlemen, some of ye may remember that when I heard that Prossy was bringin' his mother here I kicked— kicked because it only stood to reason that, being *his* mother, she'd be that foolish she'd upset the camp. There wasn't room enough for two such chuckle-heads—and one of 'em being a woman, she couldn't be shut up or sat upon ez we did to *him.* But now, gentle- men, ez we see she ain't that kind, but high-toned and level-headed, and that she's got the grip on Prossy—whether he likes it or not —we ain't goin' to let him go back on her! No, sir! we ain't goin' to let him break her heart the second time! He may think we ain't good enough for her, but ez long ez she's civil to us, we'll stand by her."

In this conscientious way were the shackles of that unhallowed

relationship slowly riveted on the unfortunate Prossy. In his inter-
course with his comrades during the next two or three days their
attitude was shown in frequent and ostentatious praise of his
mother, and suggestive advice, such as: "I wouldn't stop at the
saloon, Prossy; your old mother is wantin' ye;" or, "Chuck that 'ere
tarpolin over your shoulders, Pross, and don't take your wet duds
into the house that your old mother's bin makin' tidy." Oddly
enough, much of this advice was quite sincere, and represented —
for at least twenty minutes — the honest sentiments of the speaker.
Prosper was touched at what seemed a revival of the sentiment
under which he had acted, forgot his uneasiness, and became quite
himself again — a fact also noticed by his critics. "Ye've only to
keep him up to his work and he'll be the widder's joy agin," said
Cyrus Brewster. Certainly he was so far encouraged that he had a
long conversation with Mrs. Pottinger that night, with the result
that the next morning Joe Wynbrook, Cyrus Brewster, Hank Mann,
and Kentucky Ike were invited to spend the evening at the new
house. As the men, clean shirted and decently jacketed, filed into
the neat sitting room with its bright carpet, its cheerful fire, its
side table with a snowy cloth on which shining tea and coffee pots
were standing, their hearts thrilled with satisfaction. In a large
stuffed rocking chair, Prossy's old mother, wrapped up in a shawl
and some mysterious ill health which seemed to forbid any exer-
tion, received them with genteel languor and an extended black
mitten.

"I cannot," said Mrs. Pottinger, with sad pensiveness, "offer you
the hospitality of my own home, gentlemen — you remember,
Prosper, dear, the large salon and our staff of servants at Lexing-
ton Avenue! — but since my son has persuaded me to take charge
of his humble cot, I hope you will make all allowances for its deficiencies — even," she added, casting a look of mild reproach on the
astonished Prosper — "even if *he* cannot."

"I'm sure he oughter to be thankful to ye, ma'am," said Joe Wynbrook quickly, "for makin' a break to come here to live, jest ez
we're thankful — speakin' for the rest of this camp — for yer
lightin' us up ez you're doin'! I reckon I'm speakin' for the crowd,"
he added, looking round him.

Murmurs of "That's so" and "You bet" passed through the company, and one or two cast a half-indignant glance at Prosper.

"It's only natural," continued Mrs. Pottinger resignedly, "that having lived so long alone, my dear Prosper may at first be a little impatient of his old mother's control, and perhaps regret his invitation."

"Oh no, ma'am," said the embarrassed Prosper.

But here the mercurial Wynbrook interposed on behalf of amity and the camp's *esprit de corps*. "Why, Lord! ma'am, he's jest bin longin' for ye! Times and times agin he's talked about ye; sayin' how ef he could only get ye out of your Fifth Avenue saloon to share his humble lot with him here, he'd die happy! *You* 've heard him talk, Brewster?"

"Frequent," replied the accommodating Brewster.

"Part of the simple refreshment I have to offer you," continued Mrs. Pottinger, ignoring further comment, "is a viand the exact quality of which I am not familiar with, but which my son informs me is a great favorite with you. It has been prepared by Li Sing, under my direction. Prosper, dear, see that the — er — doughnuts — are brought in with the coffee."

Satisfaction beamed on the faces of the company, with perhaps the sole exception of Prosper. As a dish containing a number of brown glistening spheres of baked dough was brought in, the men's eyes shone in sympathetic appreciation. Yet that epicurean light was for a moment dulled as each man grasped a sphere, and then sat motionless with it in his hand, as if it was a ball and they were waiting the signal for playing.

"I am told," said Mrs. Pottinger, with a glance of Christian tolerance at Prosper, "that lightness is considered desirable by some — perhaps you gentlemen may find them heavy."

"Thar is two kinds," said the diplomatic Joe cheerfully, as he began to nibble his, sideways, like a squirrel, "light and heavy; some likes 'em one way, and some another."

They were hard and heavy, but the men, assisted by the steaming coffee, finished them with heroic politeness. "And now, gentlemen," said Mrs. Pottinger, leaning back in her chair and calmly surveying the party, "you have my permission to light your pipes while you partake of some whiskey and water."

The guests looked up — gratified but astonished. "Are ye sure, ma'am, you don't mind it?" said Joe politely.

"Not at all," responded Mrs. Pottinger briefly. "In fact, as my physician advises the inhalation of tobacco smoke for my asthmatic difficulties, I will join you." After a moment's fumbling in a beaded bag that hung from her waist, she produced a small black clay pipe, filled it from the same receptacle, and lit it.

A thrill of surprise went round the company, and it was noticed that Prosper seemed equally confounded. Nevertheless, this awkwardness was quickly overcome by the privilege and example given them, and with a glass of whiskey and water before them, the men were speedily at their ease. Nor did Mrs. Pottinger disdain to mingle in their desultory talk. Sitting there with her black pipe in her mouth, but still precise and superior, she told a thrilling whaling adventure of Prosper's father (drawn evidently from the experience of the lamented Pottinger), which not only deeply interested her hearers, but momentarily exalted Prosper in their minds as the son of that hero. "Now you speak o' that, ma'am," said the ingenuous Wynbrook, "there's a good deal o' Prossy in that yarn o' his father's; same kind o' keerless grit! You remember, boys, that day the dam broke and he stood thar, the water up to his neck, heavin' logs in the break till he stopped it." Briefly, the evening, in spite of its initial culinary failure and its surprises, was a decided social success, and even the bewildered and doubting Prosper went to bed relieved. It was followed by many and more informal gatherings at the house, and Mrs. Pottinger so far unbent — if that term could be used of one who never altered her primness of manner — as to join in a game of poker — and even permitted herself to win.

But by the end of six weeks another change in their feelings towards Prosper seemed to creep insidiously over the camp. He had been received into his former fellowship, and even the presence of his mother had become familiar, but he began to be an object of secret commiseration. They still frequented the house, but among themselves afterwards they talked in whispers. There was no doubt to them that Prosper's old mother drank not only what her son had provided, but what she surreptitiously obtained from the saloon. There was the testimony of the barkeeper, himself concerned equally with the camp in the integrity of the Riggs household. And there was an even darker suspicion. But this must be given in Joe Wynbrook's own words: —

"I didn't mind the old woman winnin' and winnin' reg'lar — for poker's an unsartin game; — it aint' the money that we're losin' — for it's all in the camp. But when she's developing a habit o' holding' *four* aces when somebody else hez *two*, who don't like to let on because it's Prosper's old mother — it's gettin' rough! And dangerous too, gentlemen, if there happened to be an outsider in, or one of the boys should kick. Why, I saw Bilson grind his teeth — he holdin' a sequence flush — ace high — when the dear old critter laid down her reg'lar four aces and raked in the pile. We had to nearly kick his legs off under the table afore he'd understand — not havin' an old mother himself."

"Some un will hev to tackle her without Prossy knowin' it. For it would jest break his heart, arter all he's gone through to get her here!" said Brewster significantly.

"Onless he *did* know it and it was that what made him so sorrowful when they first came. B'gosh! I never thought o' that," said Wynbrook, with one of his characteristic sudden illuminations.

"Well, gentlemen, whether he did or not," said the barkeeper stoutly, "he must never know that *we* know it. No, not if the old gal cleans out my bar and takes the last scad in the camp."

And to this noble sentiment they responded as one man.

How far they would have been able to carry out that heroic resolve was never known, for an event occurred which eclipsed its importance. One morning at breakfast Mrs. Pottinger fixed a clouded eye upon Prosper.

"Prosper," she said, with fell deliberation, "you ought to know you have a sister."

"Yes, ma'am," returned Prosper, with that meekness with which he usually received these family disclosures.

"A sister," continued the lady, "whom you haven't seen since you were a child; a sister who for family reasons has been living with other relatives; a girl of nineteen."

"Yes, ma'am," said Prosper humbly. "But ef you wouldn't mind writin' all that down on a bit o' paper — ye know my short memory! — I would get it by heart to-day in the gulch. I'd have it all pat enough by night, ef," he added, with a short sigh, "ye was kalkilatin' to make any illusions to it when the boys are here."

"Your sister Augusta," continued Mrs. Pottinger, camly ignoring these details, "will be here to-morrow to make me a visit."

But here the worm Prosper not only turned, but stood up, nearly upsetting the table. "It can't be did, ma'am! it *mustn't* be did!" he said wildly. "It's enough for me to have played this camp with *you* — but now to run in" —

"Can't be did!" repeated Mrs. Pottinger, rising in her turn and fixing upon the unfortunate Prosper a pair of murky piratical eyes that had once quelled the sea-roving Pottinger. "Do you, my adopted son, dare to tell me that I can't have my own flesh and blood beneath my roof?"

"Yes! I'd rather tell the whole story — I'd rather tell the boys I fooled them — than go on again!" burst out the excited Prosper.

But Mrs. Pottinger only set her lips implacably together. "Very well, tell them then," she said rigidly: "tell them how you lured me from my humble dependence in San Francisco with the prospect of a home with you; tell them how you compelled me to deceive their trusting hearts with your wicked falsehoods; tell them how you — a foundling — borrowed me for your mother, my poor dead husband for your father, and made me invent falsehood upon falsehood to tell them while you sat still and listened!"

Prosper gasped.

"Tell them," she went on deliberately, "that when I wanted to bring my helpless child to her only home — *then*, only then — you determined to break your word to me, either because you meanly begrudged her that share of your house, or to keep your misdeeds from her knowledge! Tell them that, Prossy, dear, and see what they'll say!"

Prosper sank back in his chair aghast. In his sudden instinct of revolt he had forgotten the camp! He knew, alas, too well what they would say! He knew that, added to their indignation at having been duped, their chivalry and absurd sentiment would rise in arms against the abandonment of two helpless women!

"P'r'aps ye're right, ma'am," he stammered. "I was only thinkin'," he added feebly, "how *she'd* take it."

"She'll take it as I wish her to take it," said Mrs. Pottinger firmly.

"Supposin', ez the camp don't know her, and I ain't bin talkin' o' havin' any *sister*, you ran her in here as my *cousin?* See? You bein' her aunt?"

Mrs. Pottinger regarded him with compressed lips for some time. Then she said, slowly and half meditatively: "Yes, it might be done! She will probably be willing to sacrifice her nearer relationship to save herself from passing as your sister. It would be less galling to her pride, and she wouldn't have to treat you so familiarly."

"Yes, ma'am," said Prosper, too relieved to notice the uncomplimentary nature of the suggestion. "And ye see I could call her 'Miss Pottinger,' which would come easier to me."

In its high resolve to bear with the weaknesses of Prosper's mother, the camp received the news of the advent of Prosper's cousin solely with reference to its possible effect upon the aunt's habits, and very little other curiosity. Prosper's own reticence, they felt, was probably due to the tender age at which he had separated from his relations. But when it was known that Prosper's mother had driven to the house with a very pretty girl of eighteen, there was a flutter of excitement in that impressionable community. Prosper, with his usual shyness, had evaded an early meeting with her, and was even loitering irresolutely on his way home from work, when, as he approached the house, to his discomfiture the door suddenly opened, the young lady appeared and advanced directly towards him.

She was slim, graceful, and prettily dressed, and at any other moment Prosper might have been impressed by her good looks. But her brows were knit, her dark eyes — in which there was an unmistakable reminiscence of Mrs. Pottinger — were glittering, and although she was apparently anticipating their meeting, it was evidently with no cousinly interest. When within a few feet of him she stopped. Prosper with a feeble smile offered his hand. She sprang back.

"Don't touch me! Don't come a step nearer or I'll scream!"

Prosper, still with smiling inanity, stammered that he was only "goin' to shake hands," and moved sideways towards the house.

"Stop!" she said, with a stamp of her slim foot. "Stay where you are! We must have our talk out *here*. I'm not going to waste words with you in there, before *her*."

Prosper stopped.

"What did you do this for?" she said angrily. "How dared you? How could you? Are you a man, or the fool she takes you for?"

"Wot did I do *wot* for?" said Prosper sullenly.

"This! Making my mother pretend you were her son! Bringing her here among these men to live a lie!"

"She was willin'," said Prosper gloomily. "I told her what she had to do, and she seemed to like it."

"But couldn't you see she was old and weak, and wasn't responsible for her actions? Or were you only thinking of yourself?"

This last taunt stung him. He looked up. He was not facing a helpless, dependent old woman as he had been the day before, but a handsome, clever girl, in every way his superior — and in the right! In his vague sense of honor it seemed more creditable for him to fight it out with *her*. He burst out: "I never thought of myself! I never had an old mother; I never knew what it was to want one — but the men did! And as I couldn't get one for them, I got one for myself — to share and share alike — I thought they'd be happier ef there was one in the camp!"

There was the unmistakable accent of truth in his voice. There came a faint twitching of the young girl's lips and the dawning of a smile. But it only acted as a goad to the unfortunate Prosper. "Ye kin laugh, Miss Pottinger, but it's God's truth! But one thing I didn't do. No! When your mother wanted to bring you in here as my sister, I kicked! I did! And you kin thank me, for all your laughin', that you're standing in this camp in your own name — and ain't nothin' but my cousin."

"I suppose you thought your precious friends didn't want a *sister* too?" said the girl ironically.

"It don't make no matter wot they want now," he said gloomily. "For," he added, with sudden desperation, "it's come to an end!

Yes! You and your mother will stay here a spell so that the boys don't suspicion nothin' of either of ye. Then I'll give it out that you're takin' your aunt away on a visit. Then I'll make over to her a thousand dollars for all the trouble I've given her, and you'll take her away. I've bin a fool, Miss Pottinger, mebbe I am one now, but what I'm doin' is on the square, and it's got to be done!"

He looked so simple and so good — so like an honest schoolboy confessing a fault and abiding by his punishment, for all his six feet of altitude and silky mustache — that Miss Pottinger lowered her eyes. But she recovered herself and said sharply: —

"It's all very well to talk of her going away! But she *won't*. You have made her like you — yes! like you better than me — than any of us! She says you're the only one who ever treated her like a mother — as a mother should be treated. She says she never knew what peace and comfort were until she came to you. There! Don't stare like that! Don't you understand? Don't you see? Must I tell you again that she is strange — that — that she was *always* queer and strange — and queerer on account of her unfortunate habits — surely you knew *them*, Mr. Riggs! she quarreled with us all. I went to live with my aunt, and she took herself off to San Francisco with a silly claim against my father's shipowners. Heaven only knows how she managed to live there; but she always impressed people with her manners, and some one always helped her! At last I begged my aunt to let me seek her, and I tracked her here. There! If you've confessed everything to me, you have made me confess everything to you, and about my own mother, too! Now, what is to be done?"

"Whatever is agreeable to you is the same to me, Miss Pottinger," he said formally.

"But you mustn't call me 'Miss Pottinger' so loud. Somebody might hear you," she returned mischievously.

"All right — 'cousin,' then," he said, with a prodigious blush. "Supposin' we go in."

In spite of the camp's curiosity, for the next few days they delicately withheld their usual evening visits to Prossy's mother. "They'll be wantin' to talk o' old times, and we don't wanter be too previous," suggested Wynbrook. But their verdict, when they at last met the new cousin, was unanimous, and their praises extravagant.

To their inexperienced eyes she seemed to possess all her aunt's gentility and precision of language, with a vivacity and playfulness all her own. In a few days the whole camp was in love with her. Yet she dispensed her favors with such tactful impartiality and with such innocent enjoyment — free from any suspicion of coquetry — that there were no heartburnings, and the unlucky man who nourished a fancied slight would have been laughed at by his fellows. She had a town-bred girl's curiosity and interest in camp life, which she declared was like a "perpetual picnic," and her slim, graceful figure halting beside a ditch where the men were working seemed to them as grateful as the new spring sunshine. The whole camp became tidier; a coat was considered *de rigueur* at "Prossy's mother" evenings; there was less horseplay in the trails, and less shouting. "It's all very well to talk about 'old mothers,'" said the cynical barkeeper, "but that gal, single handed, has done more in a week to make the camp decent than old Ma'am Riggs has in a month o' Sundays."

Since Prosper's brief conversation with Miss Pottinger before the house, the question "What is to be done?" had singularly lapsed, nor had it been referred to again by either. The young lady had apparently thrown herself into the diversions of the camp with the thoughtless gayety of a brief holiday maker, and it was not for him to remind her — even had he wished to — that her important question had never been answered. He had enjoyed her happiness with the relief of a secret shared by her. Three weeks had passed; the last of the winter's rains had gone. Spring was stirring in underbrush and wildwood, in the pulse of the waters, in the sap of the great pines, in the uplifting of flowers. Small wonder if Prosper's boyish heart had stirred a little too.

In fact, he had been possessed by another luminous idea — a wild idea that to him seemed almost as absurd as the one which had brought him all this trouble. It had come to him like that one — out of a starlit night — and he had risen one morning with a feverish intent to put it into action! It brought him later to take an unprecedented walk alone with Miss Pottinger, to linger under green leaves in unfrequented woods, and at last seemed about to desert him as he stood in a little hollow with her hand in his —

their only listener an inquisitive squirrel. Yet this was all the disappointed animal heard him stammer, —

"So you see, dear, it would *then* be no lie — for — don't you see? — she'd be really *my* mother as well as *yours*."

The marriage of Prosper Riggs and Miss Pottinger was quietly celebrated at Sacramento, but Prossy's "old mother" did not return with the happy pair.

Of Mrs. Pottinger's later career some idea may be gathered from a letter which Prosper received a year after his marriage. "Circumstances," wrote Mrs. Pottinger, "which had induced me to accept the offer of a widower to take care of his motherless household, have since developed into a more enduring matrimonial position, so that I can always offer my dear Prosper a home with his mother, should he choose to visit this locality, and a second father in Hiram W. Watergates, Esq., her husband."

OF THIS EDITION OF

TALES OF THE GOLD RUSH

TWELVE HUNDRED COPIES HAVE BEEN MADE

FOR THE MEMBERS OF

THE LIMITED EDITIONS CLUB

FROM THE ILLUSTRATIONS OF

FLETCHER MARTIN

WHO HERE SIGNS

[signature: Fletcher Martin]

THIS COPY,

WHICH IS NUMBER

385

THE EDITION HAS BEEN DESIGNED BY

GEORGE MACY

THE COMPOSITION HAVING BEEN DONE BY CHARLES D.
O'BRIEN, THE ENGRAVINGS MADE BY PIONEER-MOSS, THE
PAPER SUPPLIED BY THE WORTHY PAPER COMPANY, THE
PRINTING DONE BY THE ALDUS PRINTERS, THE BINDING BY
THE RUSSELL-RUTTER COMPANY AND THE BOXES
MADE BY BREWER-CANTELMO